The Literature of Hope
in the Middle Ages and Today

The Literature of Hope in the Middle Ages and Today

Connections in Medieval Romance, Modern Fantasy, and Science Fiction

FLO KEYES

McFarland & Company, Inc., Publishers
Jefferson, North Carolina, and London

Excerpt from William Coyle's "Introduction: The Aspects of Fantasy":
*Aspects of Fantasy: Selected Essays From the Second International
Conference on Fantastic Literature and Film*, William Coyle,
copyright (c) 1986 by the Thomas Burnett Swann Fund. Repro-
duced with permission of Greenwood Publishing Group, Inc.,
Westport, CT.
Excerpt from "The Worldview of Science Fiction" used by permission
of James E. Gunn.
Excerpts from Jung, C.G.: *The Archetypes and the Collective Uncon-
scious.* (c) 1959 Bollingen. Reprinted by permission of Princeton
University Press and the Taylor & Francis Group.
Excerpts from "Year of the Unicorn" by Andre Norton reprinted by
permission of the Estate of Andre Norton.
Excerpt from Kathleen Spencer's essay "Victorian Urban Gothic: The
First Modern Fantastic Literature" from *Intersections: Fantasy and
Science Fiction*, George Slusser and Eric S. Rabkin, editors,
reprinted by permission of Southern Illinois University Press.

LIBRARY OF CONGRESS CATALOGUING-IN-PUBLICATION DATA

Keyes, Flo, 1957–
    The literature of hope in the Middle Ages and today :
connections in medieval romance, modern fantasy, and
science fiction / Flo Keyes.
        p.   cm.
    Includes bibliographical references and index.

    ISBN 0-7864-2596-2 (softcover : 50# alkaline paper)

    1. Fantasy literature — History and criticism.   2. Science
fiction — History and criticism.   3. Romances — History and
criticism.   4. Literature, Medieval — History and criticism.
5. Hope in literature.   I. Title.
PN3435.K49 2006
820.9'15 — dc22   2006003238

British Library cataloguing data are available

On the cover: Knight (Clipart.com); astronaut (Photodisc);
moon (PhotoSpin); all images ©2006

Manufactured in the United States of America

McFarland & Company, Inc., Publishers
  Box 611, Jefferson, North Carolina 28640
   www.mcfarlandpub.com

To Mick,
who nagged, critiqued, complimented,
shredded, and generally helped make this work
move from wish to reality

Contents

Preface

This project evolved out of the realization that even though people who read fantasy and science fiction often talk about the obvious connection between those literatures and medieval romance literature, very little had been written about those connections. I began my research intending to tackle the issue from a variety of angles, but as I delved into the material, I found myself increasingly drawn to the Jungian, archetypal elements of the works. From there, it was only a short leap to the realization that, for me, the most essential element that the works have in common is the expression of a deep-seated sense of hope.

After that initial revelation, the pieces began to fall into place. The histories of the respective time periods provided a clear picture of societies in need of hope, a need which I contend was answered, at least in part, through literature. The subtopics arranged themselves along the lines of the archetypal representations manifested in the books under consideration: the hero, the journey, the wise old man, the great mother, the youth, the transformation. Plot analysis became analysis of the recurring tales of birth, life, death, and return, or spring, summer, fall, winter, and spring once again. Criticism of the literature as "unrealistic" fell away as literal, physical and sociological realism conceded to psychological realism.

This distinction between forms of realism is important because these forms of literature — romance literatures in general and science fiction and fantasy in particular — are often seen as less worthy of serious, scholarly consideration because they do not address the "real" world; that is, they do not tell us the condition of our world or delve into the psyche of a character and let us see one person's interaction with the world. In truth, most romance literature does not do these things. But the genre or mode is still worthy of serious study because it does look at the psychological landscape of humans in general. It holds up a character not as an individual to be scrutinized under a psychological microscope but as an archetypal example of what humans are, and of what humans can be at their best. Most of us are admittedly not Sir Gawain or Hari Seldon or Frodo Baggins, but that does not mean we cannot aspire to their successes. Few of us could have been Moses or Odysseus either, but we like to hear about such figures so we know that someone is providing hope for mankind even when we, ourselves, cannot. This is the value of these forms of romance literature; they make us believe in ourselves and our world rather than throwing up our hands in disgust or giving up in despair.

Additionally, even for those who do not share this perception of the role of medieval romance, science fiction, and fantasy, writing down some of the bases of the argument provides groundwork for others' future scholarship, whether of refutation or collaboration. Instead of just saying there are similarities, scholars can now create a written record of the agreements and disagreements over what these types of literature have in common and what they may have to offer the world of literary studies.

Most of the research for this book consisted of reading and analyzing the texts themselves in light of both Jungian theory and each other. The wonderful side effect of this type of research, and fortuitous confirmation of my original idea, was that each time I picked up a new book I saw more and more proof of what I was arguing. Even when I selected a book, William Gibson's *Neuromancer* for example, that I was sure was going to be the exception to the rule and force me to rethink my position or qualify it in some way, I discovered that book contained examples which dovetailed with my argument.

My research was conducted primarily at Drew University in Madison, N.J., with additional research done through Castleton State College, Middlebury College, the University of Vermont, and other sites in Vermont, where I had moved while in the middle of the writing. Interlibrary loan was invaluable in making this work possible, and I thank all of the librarians who helped me track down books, in particular Josie Cook at Drew University and Franny Czarnecki at Castleton State College. Professor James Hala and Professor Frank Occhiogrosso of Drew University provided feedback, advice, and support through the developmental stages of this project, and two of my Castleton State colleagues, Mike Austin, Ph.D., American history, and John Aberth, Ph.D., medieval history, made valiant attempts to keep me from making any grievous errors in the history chapters. If any such errors remain, the fault is entirely mine. Moral support was provided by my parents, Stuart and Florence Keyes, and my significant other, Stuart Strong, all of whom undoubtedly learned much more about this topic then they ever needed or wanted to know as I worked through my ideas with them as audience. My most profound gratitude, however, goes to my friend Mick Bathgate, who kept copies of all the chapters on his computer, kept my computer running, read multiple drafts of the entire book, critiqued, made useful suggestions, and, in times of frustration, kept me from giving up.

Introduction

All one has to do to see that there is a connection between medieval romance literature and fantasy literature is to pick up a book of each and read. Chances are that the fantasy novel will be set in a world reminiscent of the medieval world or, more accurately, the popular image of said medieval world where knights, dragons/ogres/monsters, magical swords or talismans, wizards/sorcerers/magicians, castles, and damsels in distress abound. The hero—or, in these modern times, heroine—rides off alone or with a small group of companions to right some wrong that has been wrought in the world, to make a name for him or herself, to solve a riddle, to answer a call for help, or to find a lost companion.

Even the names sound familiar; no specialized knowledge is required to make the leap from Egwene, Lan, and al Thor, names of characters in an as-yet unfinished fantasy series by Robert Jordan, to Guinevere, Lancelot, and Arthur of the Matter of Britain. In a way, it is not surprising to find these connections between medieval romance and fantasy since the man at the heart of the fantasy tradition, J. R. R. Tolkien, was a medievalist who consciously incorporated elements of the medieval works he knew and loved into his fantasy trilogy masterpiece, The Lord of the Rings.

A comparative reading of a science fiction novel and a medieval romance would also show a strong connection between those two types of literature. Science fiction does not rely overtly on the trappings of the medieval world, but the way the stories are told and the underlying themes upon which the stories are based can be seen to reflect the medieval world nonetheless. The quester still sets out on a journey of discovery meant to test him and in some way affirm or strengthen his society's values. The difference is that the new world of the science fiction quest is often a new planet, the steed a rocket or spaceship of some sort, and the dragon or evil knight a giant sandworm or an evil scientist.

Superficial similarities, of course, are not enough to support an argument for strong ties between the types of work. Deeper connections need to exist, and they do. In fact, the deeper the reader digs for connections, the stronger he will find them to be; themes are repeated, similar balances between plot development and characterization are revealed, the same archetypes are invoked, the same human needs are fulfilled, and the same ultimate goal is achieved, that of providing their respective time periods with hope. The medieval authors and the modern authors have manipulated their material in such a way as to create literature which is, in the words of Thomas Clareson, author of *Understanding Contemporary American Science Fiction: The Formative Period (1926–1970)*, "shamelessly optimistic" (37). This literature reflects the belief that man can be more than he currently is and that it is within him to achieve that refinement, aided possibly by God or that modern god, science.

The comparison is not just founded on casual reading. Critical assessments of the works support these connections. Particularly telling is a comparison of the descriptions written by Clareson talking about science fiction and W. R. J. Barron talking about medieval romance literature. In *English Medieval Romance*, Barron says of romance:

> It is not satisfied with the trappings of realism but strives for the conviction that the world it projects has existed in some past golden age, or will be in some millennium to come, or might be if men were more faithful to their ideals than experience suggests them capable of being [4].

The idea of man and society as being perfectible is echoed by Clareson in a passage explaining the basic concept upon which science fiction is based: "...the universe itself is governed by a unified and rational nature, and that if (scientific) knowledge is pursued and attained, both humanity and society are perfectible" (26). Given, of course, that medieval science was inseparable from religion and philosophy, these two authors can be seen to be describing the same type of literature.

The affinity between the genres about which they are writing has escaped neither author. Clareson remarks in his discussion of American science fiction, in particular the early magazine stories, that "such stories bring to mind Beowulf and other warrior kings as well as the knights of medieval romance" (26). Barron draws a parallel as well, saying of romance literature:

> From age to age, in order to meet that challenge [the attainment of the ideal], it repeatedly changes the nature and form of the perfection which it seeks to express: selfless chivalry inspired by love in the courtly romance of the Middle Ages, ... the vision of a man-made brave new world in the scientific romances of the early twentieth [century] and, in modern space fiction, flight from the failure of that dream to some perfect planet where man has truly mastered the universe [4].

What then is the need for this assessment of the similarities between these two forms of writing? There are, of course, those who disagree with the above authors and their assumption of a strong bond between these forms of literature, but more important is the fact that the word "assumption" has to be used in referring to Clareson's, Barron's, and others' insights since there is no extensive scholarly work that explores the aforementioned bond.

Not until the last thirty years has much serious scholarship been written concerning science fiction and fantasy. Casey Fredricks assesses the situation in the preface of *The Future of Eternity*: "Science fiction criticism did not have a nineteenth century and it is actually only since the early nineteen seventies that everything seems to have been getting done at once: ...." (x). Fredricks makes a similar statement about fantasy criticism in a subsequent paragraph. Much of the early critical work was directed toward proving that science fiction and fantasy were, in fact, literature and worthy of study, an issue that has been only partially resolved. In 1973, science fiction writer Stanislaw Lem argued in his article "Science Fiction: A Hopeless Case — With Exceptions" that science fiction "belongs to two distinct spheres of culture: the 'Lower Realm,' or Realm of Trivial Literature, and the 'Upper Realm,' or Realm of Mainstream Literature" (47). In Lem's opinion nearly all science fiction falls into the first category (58). As late as 1985, Samuel Delaney, another science fiction writer, was arguing *against* classifying science fiction and fantasy as literature because it would limit and devalue the two genres (*Intersections* 71–2).

In more recent years, critical works have accepted that at least some science fiction and fantasy is literature and have begun to explore a wide range of issues from the mythological foundations of science fiction and fantasy (see Fredricks' *The Future of Eternity*) to surrealism as used in science fiction writing (see Heather MacLean's treatment of Samuel Delaney's works in *Science Fiction and Surrealism: A Reader's Dream*). The general approaches critics have used to assess science fiction and fantasy include: the 19th century roots of the genres—*Anticipations: Essays in Early Science Fiction and Its Precursors*, edited by David Seed and *Romantic Fantasy and Science Fiction* by Karl Kroeber; how the genres developed in the 20th century—*Understanding American Science Fiction: The Formative Period (1926–1970)* by Thomas Clareson; where the writing may be headed in the 21st century—*Storm Warnings: Science Fiction Confronts the Future*, edited by George Slusser et al.; and feminist approaches to the literature—*Feminist Fabulations: Space/Postmodern Fiction* by Marleen Barr and *Where No Man Has Gone Before: Women and Science Fiction*, edited by Lucie Armitt. A quick glance at any bibliography of science fiction or fantasy criticism will reveal that many of the critical works deal with individual pieces of literature or individual authors.

An additional complication to critical understanding is that many of the works that address the similarities between romance literature and fantasy are referring to Romance literature of the Romantic Period, not medieval romance. Two works already mentioned fall into this category, *Anticipations* and *Romantic Fantasy and Science Fiction*. Those works that do make the connection between fantasy and the *medieval* romance usually confine the discussion of influences to a single work. Derek Brewer's article "The Lord of the Rings as Romance," for example, does not extend his study or its applications beyond Tolkien's trilogy.

One work that does make an effort to look at the entire question is Kathryn Hume's "Medieval Romance and Science Fiction: The Anatomy of a Resemblance." She does not delve into the topic in any great depth, however, as the entire article is only eleven pages long. While some of the topics she mentions—hero, plot, and social function — are addressed in this study as well, her interpretation of the meaning and significance of these factors is quite different, as her assessment of the works' social function illustrates: "Both medieval romance and science fiction justify an elite in its possession of power" (23).

The studies of science fiction's and fantasy's pasts have been much more popular subjects for scholarly work. Authors tracing science fiction's roots tend to look no further than the 1800s. Those who do try to explore the deeper past leap from Renaissance times back to antiquity: for example, *The Metamorphoses of Science Fiction* by Darko Suvin and *Anatomy of Wonder: Science Fiction* by Neil Barron. The medieval period is deemed to have little or no work that can be categorized with science fiction and fantasy. This may, in fact, be true because the medieval period had its own unique literary form that filled the same societal function — the medieval romance.

It is worth taking a moment here to note that a sizable percentage of the people writing critical articles and books on science fiction and fantasy are the writers of science fiction and fantasy themselves. This would not seem odd were it not for the fact that the ratio does not seem to be in keeping with the mainstream literary world. There have been famous critics over the years who were also writers of creative works: Dante, Sir Philip Sidney, Ben Jonson, Alexander Pope, William Blake, Samuel Coleridge, Matthew Arnold, T.S. Eliot, Henry James, and Virginia Woolf to name some of the best known. Literary criticism and the writing of literature have become increasingly separate activities over the centuries, however, and a list of the prominent critics of the twentieth century placed next to a list of the prominent writers of the twentieth century would show a low level of overlap.

In science fiction and fantasy, this is not the case. The list of critics spans only a hundred-year period, with the greatest concentration in the last forty years, but it includes many of science fiction and fantasy's well-known writers: Ursula LeGuin, Arthur C. Clarke, Isaac Asimov, Brian Aldiss, Stanislaw Lem, and Robert Heinlein. These writers seem to feel the need to critique their own field. The question is: "Why?" Various answers are possible but two stand out. First, these authors write about their own field because for years other critics did not take science fiction seriously and would not write about it. Second, and more important in the context of this study, they write about science fiction and fantasy themselves because they feel it cannot be judged by the same criteria used to judge mainstream fiction.

As with children's literature or mystery novels, science fiction and fantasy will nearly always fall short when assessed by the rules set up for mainstream fiction. To which my answer, and the answer of one faction of the critics, is "Good." Science fiction and fantasy *should* fail to conform to the rules of such fiction. If they did not, they would *be* mainstream fiction, not a separate genre or mode. It is because the writers of science fiction and fantasy are trying to depart from the norms to which critically sanctioned literature conforms that those two marginal forms of literature are valuable. Science fiction and fantasy, like their romance literature predecessors and counterparts, provide a way of looking at the world that is different from the way mainstream literature looks at it, a way that may help the reader come to grips with his or her own psyche and open him or her up to the possibility of positive change in the future.

The influences of medieval romance on fantasy and science fiction are often taken for granted. In order to explore those connections in more depth, it is essential to spell out the comparisons so that they can be considered and evaluated. More detailed analyses of the medieval influence on modern science fiction and fantasy are needed. This work is a first step in opening the discussion.

1

In Pursuit of the Elusive
Literary Definition

Before any useful analysis of these literatures of hope can ensue, some attempt must be made to define the principal terms involved. Phrases like "medieval romance," "science fiction," and "fantasy" are often bandied about as though they had clear definitions. Unfortunately, literary definitions are neither easy to come by nor easy to maintain. As Ezra Pound points out in *The Spirit of Romance*, "The history of literary criticism is largely the history of a vain struggle to find a terminology which will define something" (13). Does science fiction include fantasy? Or is it the other way around? How do we distinguish fantasy from the fantastic? What constitutes a medieval romance? Does a romance have to be a poem? Are there length requirements? Does it depend on the subject matter? Definitions will be provided, but these terms are difficult to pin down and the critics have reached no consensus. The definitions provided here are only a starting point for such study. If at times this chapter seems confusing and unclear, that is a result of the confusing and unclear subject matter upon which it is founded. Every effort has been made to simplify and clarify the material; the reader will have to judge the success of that effort.

Perhaps the least controversial definition is the definition of medieval romance literature. Though the boundaries are never precise, as is the case with most literary categories, and fade off into the mists the closer one gets to them and the more adamantly one wants to chart them, there has been sufficient debate regarding the boundaries of this type of literature to generate an island of material which is generally agreed to be romance. Surrounding that stable center are the shifting sands of works whose relationship to the center is tenuous and accepted only by some of the critics.

The operative definition that will be used for this study is based on Northrop Frye's definition of romance literature as set forth in *Anatomy of Criticism*. Frye deems romance to be a mode rather than a genre. His definition in turn harks back to Aristotle and the relationship of the hero to his world. In the romantic mode, the hero is "superior in *degree* to other men and to his environment" (33). It is essential that the hero be mortal, for his achievements symbolize achievements for which we can all strive if we have the courage and the strength. Were the romantic hero to be superior to man in essence, were he to be a god for example, his achievements would be beyond us and the story would not serve the same instructional and inspirational purposes. In fact, according to Frye's schema, if the hero were to become a god, the story would then become myth instead of romance.

Frye refines his definition to illustrate that the hero has to draw on extraordinary skills to deal with rather exceptional circumstances:

> The hero of romance moves in a world in which the ordinary laws of nature are slightly suspended: prodigies of courage and endurance, unnatural to us, are natural to him, and enchanted weapons, talking animals, terrifying ogres and witches, and talismans of miraculous power violate no rule of probability once the postulates of romance have been established [33].

W. R. J. Barron, author of *English Medieval Romance*, adds the observation that medieval and all other romances, "represent life as it is *and* as it might be, as imperfect reality *and* imagined ideal in one" (6). Medieval romance literature then can be written about someone as famous as Arthur or as little known as Havelock, be brief or lengthy, and be in either poetry or prose so long as it is literature in which a very human, though superior or gifted, hero provides a bridge between the imperfect world of human reality and the idealized world of human perfection. This hero allows man hope for himself and his society by showing that something better can be attained, maybe not here and now, but somewhere and somewhen.

For modern readers that "somewhen" may be the future and the somewhere may be a place other than Earth, hence definitions of science fiction and fantasy also need to be provided. Nearly all of the scholarly works dealing with science fiction and fantasy devote a chapter or a half a chapter to the usually fruitless attempt to pin down a literary definition of science fiction or fantasy. Definitions are as insubstantial and hard to capture as the unicorns and dragons that frequent fantasy stories. There is general agreement that definitions exist, but no one agrees on exactly what shape they should take, whether they are good or evil, and how to get them to do your bidding. This study concedes the nature of the difficulty and makes no claims to provide final "authoritative" definitions. The definitions that appear here are those that seem to make the most sense in light of the discussion to follow and to provide clarity without unduly restricting the material available.

The first obstacle is the question of whether to consider science fiction and fantasy as a single genre, a somewhat flawed and limited technique, or as two separate genres, more accurate but cumbersome. In the real world, meaning in the publishing houses and on the bookshelves of the world, the two genres are lumped together even as they are noted to be separate entities. Even though a number of academic critics find it irritatingly unprofessional, this blasé treatment is actually the most useful as even though there are works that clearly belong in one or the other category, there are also many works in which, as Clareson notes, "there was no simplistic separation between science fiction and fantasy; the writers mixed elements of the two as they pleased in an individual work, sometimes playing them off against one another, as in the case of Andre Norton" (*Understanding* 187). Since the boundaries between science fiction and fantasy are particularly permeable, even in the eyes of the authors, when one is referred to and the ideas seem to pertain to the other, that connection may be assumed unless specifically excepted. As with medieval romance, there are cores of material that have enough in common to allow the definitions of these two types of literature to be applicable, but there are great quantities of material surrounding each core which fluctuate considerably and resist attempts at categorization.

The core definition of science fiction is rooted in a concept that has become common coin but that is generally attributed to H. G. Wells: science fiction is literature that takes the rules of our existing world and from them extrapolates logical projected futures, parallel presents, or alternate pasts. Around this core various other limitations are often placed. Darko Suvin, one of most prominent modern critics of science fiction, keeps the requirement that the premise of the novel be "perceived as *not impossible* within the cognitive (cosmological and anthropological) norms of the author's epoch," but adds that the work must incorporate a place or persons "*radically or at least significantly different from the empirical times, places, and characters* of 'mimetic' or 'naturalist' fiction" [author's italics] (viii). Suvin sums up science fiction as "a developed oxymoron, a realistic irreality" (viii).

Robert Heinlein, himself a science fiction author, proposes a definition that is at once more limiting and more encompassing: "realistic speculation about possible future events, based solidly on adequate knowledge of the real world, past and present, and on a thorough understanding of the nature and significance of the scientific method" (22). This definition is limiting in that it puts considerable emphasis on the ability of the author to apply to the future the knowledge of the workings and importance of the scientific method and the history of the use of that knowledge, but it opens the door to any novel based on science, including such works as Sinclair Lewis' *Arrowsmith* which few would classify as science fiction. Heinlein's definition does bring up an important element of the definition, however, the use of science or technology — the heart of most of the discussion regarding the difference between science fiction and fantasy. Kroeber, who addresses this issue in *Romantic Fantasy and Science Fiction*, is but one of many voices proclaiming this distinction: science fiction "extrapolates consequences of the scientific-technological progress that destroyed superstition" (1). According to many critics, and science fiction authors, science fiction is about science, about technology, about order, and about logic and rationality.

The individual scholar's attitude toward science fiction's literary status tends to determine which definition he or she selects. Some critics, even those who are science fiction writers themselves, take a rather elitist stand on what is and is not science fiction. Suvin while claiming to be considering "the literature that is really read — as opposed to most literature taught in schools" tosses aside Isaac Asimov's widely read Foundation series as "metaphysical gobbledygook" (vii & 24). In fact, he dismisses over 90 percent of published SF as not being "aesthetically significant"; only to writers like "Lem, Le Guin, Dick, Disch, Delaney, the Strugatsky brothers, Jeury, Aldiss, Ballard" and others of their ilk does he accord that designation (vii).

A survey of "595 dedicated members of the science fiction subculture" conducted by Harvard Sociology professor William Sims Bainbridge at the 1978 world science fiction convention (just one year before the publication of Suvin's book) reveals a significantly different picture of what science fiction and fantasy is "really read" (225). The respondents were instructed to rate the authors on a zero to six scale and to skip any authors with whom they were unfamiliar. Isaac Asimov, Ray Bradbury, Arthur C. Clarke, Robert Heinlein, and H. G. Wells, none of whom Suvin included in his list of "significant" authors, were all recognized and rated by over 90 percent of the readers (Asimov was known to over 97 percent of them). Of the names on Suvin's list, only one came close to that level of recognition, and that was Ursula LeGuin, known by 86 percent of the readers. Samuel Delany, Philip K. Dick, and Brian Aldiss were recognized by 70 to 77 percent of the readers, Stanislaw Lem by only 46 percent, and Ballard, Disch, Jeury, and the Strugatsky brothers did not appear on the questionnaire (Bainbridge 225–29). In light of those survey results, it is fair to wonder who is doing the reading Suvin refers to when he says "literature that is really read."

Science fiction writer Lem would no doubt be thrilled to be included in Suvin's "aesthetically significant" group as he, too, divides science fiction into the "haves" and the "have-nots." In Lem's own terms these are the Realms of Upper, or Mainstream, Literature and Lower, or Trivial, Literature. The determinant of whose work gets placed in the Upper Realm is whether or not the public and the critics (this last is an important distinction) "know him by name, or even as a world celebrity (so that, on hearing the name, they know that they are talking about a writer, not an athlete or actor, so his attempts at science fiction and/or fantasy are regarded as 'excursions' or 'side leaps' even if repeated)" (48–9). This implies that a science fiction author is only significant if he is known primarily as a writer, but not as a writer of science fiction. Such ironies and contradictions abound in the critical definitions of science fiction.

Trying to define fantasy is little better. Because the word is used to define both a characteristic of literature and a genre of literature, confusion reigns. William Coyle, in the introduction to *Aspects of Fantasy*, treats fantasy as an umbrella category that covers a variety of literary types: "It should be stressed that fantasy is not a genre; its literary expression includes science fiction, utopias and dystopias, lampoon and parody, fairy tales, folk legend, allegory, myth, fable, nonsense verse, dream literature, absurdist drama, and numerous other forms" (2). He does, however, include fantasy among the forms of romance literature. Having just attempted to define fantasy, he concedes that this attempt to pinpoint a definition of the term is foredoomed by its intrinsic nature. "[M]ost fantasy, like other products of the romantic imagination, resists formalization, so that attempts like this one to confine it within definitions and categories are generally futile and ironic exercises in self-defeat" (2).

Coyle's definition of fantasy sounds more like others' definition of the fantastic, a category more inclusive than the specific literary genre, fantasy. Tzvetan Todorov in his book, *The Fantastic: A Structural Approach to a Literary Genre*, defines the fantastic as: "that hesitation experienced by a person who knows only the laws of nature, confronting an apparently supernatural event" (25). As he notes, the person faced with a contradiction between "known" facts and a nonconforming experience has only two choices: dismiss the contradiction on the grounds that he or she is "the victim of an illusion of the senses" or accept the new experience and its new terms and proceed from there (25). Fantasy literature, then, would be a sub-division of the fantastic.

The fundamental definition of fantasy, distilled from a variety of sources, appears to be: that literature in which a set of rules unlike the rules of the real world is established or in which the rules of the real world are modified to allow for objects or actions impossible in the world as we know it. Once these alternate rules are in place, however, the writer makes the action in the created world abide by those rules throughout the rest of the novel, or series. This definition echoes the words of Frye's description of the world in which the romance hero acts, a world where fantastic occurrences "violate no rule of probability once the postulates of romance have been established" (*Anatomy* 33).

In his book *The Fantastic in Literature*, Eric Rabkin departs from this generally accepted definition of fantasy, building upon Todorov's ideas and taking them a step further. Rabkin posits the idea that fantasy, or what he calls the fantastic, requires the establishment of rules followed by the subsequent undercutting of that rule system over and over, "The fantastic is a direct reversal of ground rules, and therefore is in part determined by those ground rules" (*Fantastic* 14–15). "[A] true Fantasy such as *Alice* continues to reverse its ground rules time and again" (37). This is a unique and interesting concept of the fantastic and may have been the prevailing notion of what constituted the fantastic thirty years ago, but the general public has created a less restrictive definition of fantasy, as given above, that has superseded Rabkin's. His certainly can be applied to *Alice in Wonderland*, the book he uses to illustrate his point, but it does not apply to the majority of what is called "fantasy."

If Rabkin's definition of fantasy were the widely accepted one, very little on any bookshelf anywhere would qualify as fantasy because few of the works that are so called follow this system of setting up and breaking down ground rules. Even Tad Williams' *Otherland*—which begins in the trenches of World War I, sends the hero up a beanpole where he meets a woman with wings who gives the bewildered man a magical feather, and then drops him down a giant's gullet only to have him land once again in the trenches (still in possession of the feather), all before the first real chapter begins—turns out to be set in a world with fairly consistent rules. Part of the challenge for the characters in the book is to discover those rules so they can begin to take control of what is happening to them. For the reader, the challenge is to figure out the rules so the book makes sense—which it does. Rabkin's version of the fantastic is an intriguing theory, but his is so narrow a definition as to make it virtually untenable.

In a way, fantasy includes science fiction because positing an alternate present or extrapolating a future is just another approach to modifying the rules of the real world. Critics, publishers, and readers, however, make a sharp distinction between fantasy and science fiction and that distinction usually cuts down the line between technology and magic. Kroeber goes so far as to claim that fantasy is anti-technology and focuses "the skeptical intelligence on which scientific, technological thinking is founded against itself, thus deliberately and self-consciously creating a reality it understands to be impossible" (10).

Rabkin delves a bit deeper into what comprises fantasy. For Rabkin:

> Fantasy represents a basic mode of human knowing; its polar opposite is Reality. Reality is that collection of perspectives and expectations that we learn in order to survive in the here and now. But the here and now becomes tomorrow; a child grows, a culture develops, a person dreams. In every area of human thought, civilization has evolved a functioning reality, but the universe has suffered no reality to maintain itself unchanged. The glory of man is that he is not bounded by reality. Man travels in fantastic worlds [227].

Fantasy is what we learn to survive tomorrow—whether that tomorrow includes technological changes or mystical ones. The line between fantasy and science fiction remains blurred. As Arthur C. Clarke points out in his Third Law, which appears in a footnote in his nonfiction book

Profiles of the Future, "Any sufficiently advanced technology is indistinguishable from magic" (36 fn). This brings up some interesting questions about the "distinction" between science fiction and fantasy. If Clarke is right, then fantasy is just an imaginative leap further into the future than science fiction is.

It is necessary to take a moment here and address the question of utopias. Utopian literature cuts across science fiction and fantasy literature as it does across literature in general. There are science fiction utopias such as *The Gate to Women's Country* by Sheri Tepper and *The Female Man* by Joanna Russ, but science fiction and fantasy are not by definition utopian literature. If one accepts that science fiction and fantasy are forms of romance literature, this is easily proven. Romance literature, as the term is being used here, deals with the conjunction of the real "warts and all" world and the ideal "world that could be." The inclusion and acceptance of the world in its imperfect present form distinguishes science fiction and fantasy from the "world as it should be" stance taken by utopian literature.

As science fiction writer and critic Brian Aldiss points out in *Billion Year Spree: The True History of Science Fiction,* the "belief in the perfectibility of man and the triumph of altruism over self-interest" (66) has lessened to the point where a utopia like Sir Thomas More's is difficult, if not impossible, for us to accept or even desire. In Tepper's utopia, there is no belief that the inherent nature of man will suddenly change or mankind will one day wake up and see the error of its ways. Instead, a selective breeding program, coupled with the large scale deception of most of the male portion of the population, is being utilized to breed out undesirable tendencies in people — the needs for violence and warfare — and create a race that will only exhibit the desired tendencies — desire for peace and a refined and cultured society. This is as close as science fiction or fantasy normally comes to utopia — the world can be perfect, but we flawed humans have to make it that way. An admirable notion, as Plato pointed out in *The Republic*:

> Until philosophers are kings, or the kings and princes of this world
> have the spirit and power of philosophy, and political greatness and
> wisdom meet in one, and those commoner natures who pursue either
> to the exclusion of the other are compelled to stand aside, cities will
> never have rest from their evils— no, nor the human race, as I
> believe — and then only will this our State have a possibility of life and
> behold the light of day [369].

One of the features that science fiction and fantasy do share with utopias is that both are placed beyond the pale. This is a result of an inherent necessity in each type of literature that its world be unknown to the reader so the reader can see, and perhaps accept, the difference between the world as he or she knows it and the world as portrayed by the author. Whether criticizing the government by creating a fictitious uncharted island in *Utopia* or tracing mankind's efforts to survive its own worst tendencies over thousands of years and millions of miles of *Foundation*'s uncharted space, the goal remains the same. Place the action where the reader's inability to prove that the site does not exist makes it easier to accept that such a world *could* be, somewhere.

Dystopias, products of our disillusionment, also have a different feel to them when written by science fiction or fantasy authors instead of mainstream authors. While Orwell is respected by many readers of science fiction and fantasy, few of those readers classify his work as science fiction, though some critics do. Part of the reason Orwell has to be "rationalized" into the science fiction category may be the fundamentally dark tone of his work. This runs contrary to the strain of optimism, or at least the unwillingness to give over entirely to pessimism, that runs through most science fiction and fantasy. Kingsley Amis illustrates this with an example from Orwell's *1984*.

> But when O'Brien says to Winston: "If you want a picture of the future, imagine a boot stomping on a human face—forever," thus summing up the book, a conclusion is being reached which, whether plausible or not, or hysterical or not, almost no orthodox science-fiction writer would admit [78].

In science fiction and fantasy there is hope, always hope, sometimes faint, but inevitably there.

Even in *Neuromancer*, the hard-edged novel by William Gibson that is considered by many to be the beginning of cyberpunk, a form of science fiction that endeavors to take the possibilities of computers and virtual reality to their logical conclusions, even here, the end is not despair. The main character, Case, is tempted to give up and die when he is trying to break down the code of the artificial intelligence (AI) he has been sent to crack, but he turns his doubts into an anger that helps him achieve his goal. Once inside the AI he discovers the woman he loved and saw die, and he is offered the opportunity to remain in virtual reality with her and escape the real world. Instead, he chooses to return and complete the job he was hired to do. When the job is complete, Case tries to return to his old haunts, but realizes he has changed too much to go back. He could easily give up and escape from the world in one of a variety of drug or computer induced virtual realities, but he does not. He packs his things, moves on, and keeps on living.

Hope is the result of the fundamental tension that inheres in romance literature, the tension between the real and the ideal that places science fiction and fantasy in the romance genre beside medieval romance. This is true for the hero, for the world, for people's expectations, and for the story outcome. Hope, then, is part of the definition of each of these terms, hope that humankind will somehow find a way to be the best it is capable of being whether on an armed charger in the name of God or an armored spaceship in the name of science. With some sense of what constitutes the types of literature under consideration established, the next step is to look at why the times during which these works were created presented such a strong need for hope sustaining literature and examine that literature in greater depth to see how it met the societal need.

2

What Need of a Candle
Unless It Is Dark

If the world around one is a happy, healthy world, one need not search for ways to heal it or change it. Hope is not needed until the world falls short of our needs, expectations, and desires. Jung explains this reaction in reference to the recurrence of UFO stories in the twentieth century: "an *emotional tension* having its cause in a situation of collective distress or danger, or in a vital psychic need" prompts humans to create a solution that will lessen their distress (*Flying Saucers* 13). Despite the differences in types of distress and danger, the solutions humans create for themselves are similar because they arise from the collective unconscious by way of archetypes.

The events that trigger archetypal responses must be ones that have a profound impact on society. While most such events—war, rebellion, famine, disease—are cataclysmic ones of a negative nature, positive events can result in extreme distress as well if the changes to the world are substantial and rapid. Innovations in technology, medicine, transportation, and knowledge acquisition and dispersal can be seen by society as dangerous and stress-inducing. One response to such an unsettled world is for writers to form archetypal images and incorporate them in works that will help people begin to heal psychologically. Both the medieval period and the twentieth century qualify as times of "collective distress" and times of psychic need; in the former, writers responded with medieval romances, and in the latter, writers introduced science fiction and fantasy.

This chapter and the two that follow make no attempt to recount the entire history of the medieval period or of the twentieth century or even to capture the paramount events of each century. The purpose of these three chapters is to convey a sense of the pervasive unrest and instability inherent in the centuries covered. That there were brief times of calm and tranquility is not denied, nor is the fact that during the Middle Ages not all of the countries in Western Europe were undergoing the same degree of disruption at the same time. What these chapters are designed to convey is a picture of a world ripe for the population to call on archetypal images to help allay the fears and distress aroused by the social conditions.

The Catholic Church, which was then the only Christian church, purported to be a stable foundation upon which medieval society could build, but it proved to be incapable of supporting even itself. Like the "foolish man, which built his house upon the sand" (Matthew 7:26), the Church sought worldly possessions and power rather than emulating the "wise man, which built his house upon a rock" by believing in and following the ways of the Lord (Matthew 7:24). There were attempts to reform the Church and bring it back to a godlier state, but the efforts were inadequate and did not result in any longlasting spiritual reforms in the organized Church of the time. As early as the eleventh century, Europe could aptly be described as turbulent. In his medieval history entitled *The Civilization of the Middle Ages*, Norman F. Cantor says that the eighty years from 1050 to 1130 A.D. stood out as "one of those periods during which vitally important changes in all aspects of life occur simultaneously and with such great rapidity that no contemporary could foresee the far-reaching consequences of many of them" (243). At the heart of these changes, Cantor sets the Gregorian reform that shifted the investiture of the clergy from secular to sacred hands (243). Associated with the investiture controversy were numerous other considerations— the balance of secular and church power, the distinction between lay and ordained religious, the place of the church in the growing commercial sector, and the role of the rising middle class.

By the middle of the eleventh century, the Church had attained a position of considerable power and wealth owing in part to the possessions and land donated by various nobles and royalty and to the presence among the monks and priests of many scions of the royal and noble classes. Some monasteries, such as Cluny, were so wealthy that the monks lived a life more befitting a prince than a religious, a life of aesthetic pleasures rather than ascetic privation (Cantor 239). In response to the ostentatious materialism of some of the religious orders, new monastic orders committed to a life eschewing material possessions and power began to spring up and gain followers. In order for the Mother Church and the regular clergy to maintain the power they held, they had to make an effort to encompass these changes as well, lest they look less moral than their monastic brothers (249).

Humbert, one of the men whose writings influenced Pope Gregory VII, shook the fragile alliance between the Church and the secular world by declaring the election of the pope to be the business of the Church and therefore above the influence of the secular political world (Cantor 254). The division of power this evinced was made even clearer in the *Dictatus Papae* issued by Pope Gregory VII in 1073 which set the pope beyond the judgment of earthly authorities, made disagreeing with the pope tantamount to renouncing one's Catholicism; and, most disturbing of all to the royalty, gave the pope the power to depose secular rulers (258).

Henry IV of Germany tried to defy the papal decree but lost, thereby establishing the dominion of the papacy until the 1300s when Philip IV (the Fair) successfully challenged Pope Boniface VIII by exacting a tax on clerical income. Boniface demanded the taxes be remitted and issued the *Unam Sanctum* which decreed that "for every human creature, to be subject to the Roman pontiff is absolutely necessary for salvation" (Hollister 222); Philip's only response was to take Boniface prisoner. The pope was released after a matter of days, but his authority had been compromised (222), and the populace had seen that neither the church nor the secular power had absolute control over the other. The struggle between church and state left people unsure of where their allegiance should lie and to whom they could turn for aid when it was needed.

The people were also seeing that the pope was not always a sterling example of Christian values. Corrupt popes committed nearly every sin imaginable, without fear of earthly retribution. The decline of the papacy continued apace until it reached its nadir in the Borgia pope Alexander VI, who historian C. Warren Hollister claims "divided his time between ruthless political aggrandizement and sensual pleasures" (331).

At the same time the Church was working to strengthen the powers of the pope, it was trying to draw a clearer line between the priest and the layperson. Priests had hitherto been allowed to marry and raise families, although if a man was elevated to a bishopric, he was expected to set his family aside and turn his devotion entirely to the church (Cantor 251). In practice, most of the higher church officials cohabited with women and raised the offspring of their unions as "nephews and nieces." Pope Gregory VII sought to end priestly marriages at all levels and enforce a policy of celibacy — no sex at all — rather than one of chastity — monogamous sex with one's spouse. The emphasis on celibacy in the priesthood fit in with Gregory's division of the sacred and the secular. If a man had no family ties outside the Church, he would not be tempted to try to secure worldly possessions and positions for his heirs (251).

The Crusades were yet another effort at polishing the Church's tarnished image and reassuring the people of its constancy. Initially, it seemed the idea might work. A war could provide employment for the surplus of trained young men, assert the power of Mother Church, and bring needed unity to Western Christendom (Cantor 290–1). The first Crusade set forth in 1096, and by 1099, the Crusaders had taken Jerusalem. This victory did provide some positive results such as shining reflected glory on the Church and giving younger sons an opportunity to make a name for themselves (Hollister 164–5). Unfortunately, the factors that had weakened and divided the Moslems, allowing for the initial Christian victory, did not last and the Moslems began reclaiming the lands they had lost. Additional Crusades were required to try to retain control of the lands gained in the first one.

The Crusade of 1144, graced by the presence of two kings, Louis VII of France, and Conrad III of Germany, never even made it to the Holy Land. The Christian armies were trounced in Asia Minor. The third Crusade of 1190 fared little better. The "three greatest rulers of western Europe at the time," as Cantor calls them, Richard Coeur de Lion, Philip Augustus of France, and Fredrick Barbarossa of Germany, led this third venture to the Holy Land (298). German commitment waned after Barbarossa drowned, and Philip and Richard ended up signing a treaty with the Moslems after only a few skirmishes because the two kings were not able to leave behind their homeland territorial hostilities and set the Holy War foremost in their concerns. As Cantor notes, "The European kings were too busy pursuing their dynastic and territorial interests to give more than perfunctory support to the Latin Kingdom" (299).

Victorious or not, the Crusades forced the Western Christian world to expand its awareness of the world around it. Crusaders traveled to lands they had previously only heard of and encountered men who held different beliefs and lived in vastly different ways. This exposure caused many of the men to realize that the Moslems were men like themselves not the mythical monsters of tales like *The Song of Roland.*

What did not change, unless it was to strengthen it, was the belief that it was perfectly acceptable to kill those with divergent beliefs if it was done in the name of Christianity (Cantor 301). This was brought home clearly in the fourth Crusade of 1204, which set aside fighting Moslems and focused on the Latin Church's efforts to regain control of the Byzantine Christian Church (299). The compulsion to have but *one* Church overrode the foundations of Catholicism that should have made the Churches allies, not enemies. The Latin Church was *the* Church, and, as Pope Gregory VII had asserted, what the Pope of the Latin Church said was the final word, even against other branches of the church. Over the next several centuries this religious intolerance was turned more and more frequently against the Jews living in Western Europe and against heretics within the Church itself.

This intolerance is ironic in light of the Church's changing view of God. The older, harsh, patriarchal view of God the Father was giving place to "the loving self-abnegating son of the New Testament, with his weeping and charitable mother" (Cantor 252). Peter Damiani, a contemporary of Gregory VII and advocate of this view of God, was one of the forerunners of the mystics who attested to their personal experiences of God over the next several centuries and who brought a heightened emotional involvement to religion that other men and other times would see spill over into fanaticism and mob violence (253).

This "to the people" piety, rooted in emotionalism and the failure of the Church to meet the needs of the growing bourgeois, became a general trend during the thirteenth century. Failing to find solace and stability in the organized Church, some people began to seek answers and assurance elsewhere. Numerous heretical sects offered answers to people eager to find some. Orthodox groups, such as the Dominican and Franciscan friars, who sought to carry the word of God from town to town received support from the Church in the hope that their preaching would help counteract heretical teachings. In spite of their efforts, the problem of heretical sects became so acute, and the attempts to quell heretical belief so ineffective, that the Church was eventually forced to take drastic countermeasures. The Church's answer came in the form of that "grim symbol of the medieval Church at its worst: the Inquisition" (Hollister 184).

The mendicant groups represent the last wave of monastic fervor to sweep Europe during the Middle Ages. Hollister sums up the change that was to follow,

> Popular piety remained strong, particularly in northern Europe where succeeding centuries witnessed a significant surge of mysticism. But in the south a more secular attitude was beginning to emerge. Young men no longer flocked into monastic orders; soldiers no longer rushed to crusades; papal excommunications no longer brought their former terror [195].

Religion's domination of the lives of the people was weakening. The world was changing and things that one used to be sure of were no longer as certain as they had been.

The weakening of the spiritual basis of the medieval world was evident in its highest representative as well. As the papacy became embroiled in the political maneuvering of the Western world, spiritual leadership waned. After Boniface VIII's death at the start of the fourteenth century, Philip the Fair installed the new pope, Clement V, at Avignon rather than Rome for fear of reprisals from Rome over the Boniface incident. There the papacy remained for 70 years until a schism between Roman and French popes occurred in 1378.

During the time when the center of papal authority was in Avignon, the Church gained legitimacy and acceptance by selling itself — literally. There was very little associated with the Church that could not be bought. In *A Distant Mirror*, her study of the fourteenth century, Barbara Tuchman itemizes some of goods and services for sale.

> Besides its regular revenue from tithes and annates on ecclesiastical income and from dues from papal fiefs, every office, every nomination, every appointment or preferment, every dispensation of the rules, every judgment of the Rota or adjudication of a claim, every pardon, indulgence, and absolution, everything the Church had or was, from cardinal's hat to pilgrim's relic, was for sale [26].

Perhaps most damaging to the Church and public was the sale of clerical offices which resulted in the investiture of "[p]riests who could not read or who, from ignorance, stumbled stupidly through the ritual of the Eucharist . . ." (27). How was the common man, for whom the Church offered the only road to salvation, to gain that salvation if his guide was as lost as he? "The unfit clergy spread dismay for these were the men supposed to have the souls of the laity in their charge and be the intermediaries between man and God" (27).

Further confusion was caused by the presence, for a time, of more than one pope. From 1378 until 1417, there were two popes, one in Rome and one in Avignon. The breach was not healed until the early fifteenth century after the whole affair had spun even further out of control and yet a third pope had been elected. At this point, the Holy Roman Emperor stepped in and convened the Council of Constance, whose representatives were wise enough not only to depose all three popes but to enforce the depositions. At last, "the schism was healed by the election of a conciliar pope, Martin V (1417–1431)" (Hollister 330).

The questions this schism raised were not simply theological or political ones. The division affected everyone who believed in the authority of the Church. If there were two popes, each of whom referred to the other as the Anti-Pope (or devil or Anti-Christ or other disparaging term), whose words were from God and whose from the devil? Whose mercy and absolution was efficacious and whose fruitless? Who represented the Church and Christ's salvation and who represented the short road to Hell? The answer became a political one and where you lived dictated who you believed, but the very fact that such a division could exist further weakened the authority of the Church.

The damage had been done, and the Church had lost much of its power in the struggle. People were overwhelmed by conflicting messages on how to achieve salvation and what was the "right" thing to believe. Mystical sects gained more and more adherents. William of Occam, an English Franciscan, raised serious questions about what could be known empirically and what had to be accepted entirely on faith. In Germany, Meister Eckhardt preached the value of a personal experience of God. The Brethren of the Common Life opened religion houses, unsanctioned by the Church, that taught the salvational value of belief coupled with hard work. In England, John Wycliffe exhorted believers to put the word of the Bible above the words of any earthly representative of religion and tried to make that Bible accessible to his followers by overseeing the genesis of its translation into English. In Germany, John Hus was advocating an individualistic religious belief combined with a form of nationalism. Some reformers, like Nicholas of Cusa, tried to work within the Church to salvage its dignity and spiritual strength. Too many factors worked against them, however, and they failed to convince the Church to make the changes that might have kept it unified rather than seeing it broken apart into the many Protestant groups of the Reformation.

The four centuries from the latter half of the eleventh century, when *The Song of Roland* was written down, to the latter half of the fifteenth century, when Malory's *Le Morte D'Arthur* was completed, were filled with conflict and confusion within the Catholic Church. In light of the religious instability surrounding them, it becomes reasonable to think that these people might have felt a need to hear and read about the archetypes utilized in some of the medieval romances, especially those tied to heaven, the afterlife, and salvation through the intervention of a god figure. Caxton's preface to his edition of *Le Morte D'Arthur* refers directly to this redemptive power of literature:

> And for to pass the time this book shall be pleasant to read in; but for to give faith and believe all that is true that is contained herein, ye be at your liberty; but all is written for our doctrine, and for to beware that we fall not to vice or sin, but to exercise and follow virtue; by which we may come and attain to good fame and renown in this life, and after this short and transitory life, to come unto everlasting bliss in heaven... [xxxv].

If the Church could not provide the needed assurance of Heaven, perhaps the romance, with its larger than life hero, its miracles, and its clearly delineated good and evil, could.

3

Pawns in the
Game of Kings

If the religious turmoil in the medieval world had been the only source of disruption, people could have turned elsewhere to seek security and order. Unfortunately, the rest of their world was no more stable than the Church. War and rebellion ravaged much of Western Europe for the greater part of the 400 years romance literature flourished. Society and technology underwent rapid changes that altered the way people saw themselves in relation to their world, and the plague decimated the population not once but several times.

Louis VII of France, having made a poor showing in the second Crusade, returned home to divorce his wife, Eleanor. Eleanor, who claimed Aquitaine as her own inheritance, promptly married Henry II of England, setting off the long struggle between England and France over possession of the Duchy of Aquitaine. This dispute between England and France escalated again in the 14th century. The Duchy was economically valuable to England, and England's presence on the continent was galling to the French. "[T]he English foothold within the realm was unacceptable. Every French king for 200 years had tried by war, confiscation, or treaty to regain Aquitaine" (Tuchman 72). Which means that for the same 200 years, the English and French people had their lives disrupted by the fighting, displacement, and heavy taxes that go along with war.

Even apparently neutral countries became embroiled in these long term hostilities, occasionally fueling the conflicts. Flanders, for example, found itself caught in the middle because, even though it turned to France for governance, it relied upon England for wool to keep its famous looms working.

In 1328, Edward III tried to claim the throne of France through his mother. France objected to the idea of an English king and invoked the "no succession to the French throne through the female" rule that they dusted off and applied whenever it was expedient to do so (Hollister 334). The ensuing war dragged on for ten years with very little gained by either side, until after more deaths and financial burdens for the populace, France and England signed a truce in 1347. Open warfare between these two nations stopped for a short period which spanned the outbreak of the plague, resumed in the 1350s, and continued in fits and starts until 1453, the protracted nature of the ordeal earning it the name The Hundred Years War.

As the fifteenth century began, the Hundred Years War had fifty more years to run. In England, Richard II had been deposed, Henry IV ruled briefly, and Henry V resumed the war with France, winning temporary control of Northern France (Cantor 519). France's King Charles VI was given to fits of insanity which became more frequent and more severe as the years went by. His inability to rule led to a power struggle between two French factions, Orleans and Burgundy, over who would have actual control of France (Huizinga 18). The French, therefore, were too busy fighting amongst themselves to do much about the English until someone unified and directed them, a peasant named Joan of Arc. Her military victories and her death at the stake galvanized France into action and, ultimately, victory (Hollister 338). The English returned home but had only scant years of tranquility before becoming embroiled in internal strife again as the York and Lancaster opposition broke out into the thirty year civil war dubbed the War of the Roses (335).

Matters were no more tranquil in other domains. As the 13th century began, Holy Roman Emperor Fredrick II of Germany was so eager to conquer and annex the Italian city-states he considered rightfully his that he neglected the German states he already controlled. In attempting to extend his holdings, Fredrick actually lost holdings as the German states rebelled against being used as the pocketbook to pay for the wars in Italy. The unconquered states in Italy rose up to help wrest control from Fredrick of those lands which he had previously conquered.

Rebellions sprang up in both the German states and the Italian and Fredrick lost them all. By the time of Fredrick's death in 1250, the back of the Holy Roman Empire was broken, and that empire was never to rise to a position of power again (Hollister 218–9).

The Black Death, too, drastically changed medieval life; killing quickly and indiscriminately, it honored no political, religious, or social boundaries. The Black Death, a combination of types of plagues, reached the Italian states late in 1347 and by 1349 had spread to the rest of Western Europe. An estimated one third to one half of the population of Western Europe, about 20 million people, lay dead by 1350. Outbreaks of the disease continued for more than a century, but the worst devastation generally occurred during the first two years after the disease reached a particular area.

The plague consisted primarily of two types of plague, one spread by fleas and the other by airborne germs. Both types thrived in densely populated areas, and as a result many towns lost 50 percent of their population, some towns even more. Rural areas might be passed by if no one carrying the plague fled there seeking refuge. If the plague did come to a small village, it could eradicate the entire population (Hollister 351). If a greater proportion of the poor succumbed, it was only because they lived in closer proximity than the wealthy and had no means to leave areas known to be infected with the plague. Ultimately, the plague would improve the lot of the poor by altering their social status, but that did not become evident until some years later.

The plague spread so easily and killed so swiftly that Christians were often left to fear for their souls as they lay dying. Some priests fled the illness, unwilling to risk their own lives. Priests who stayed to tend to their congregations could not minister to all those who fell sick because there were too many of them and the stricken died too quickly. Some priests authorized lay confession; some insisted that the true believer and penitent would find salvation through faith even without being shriven before death (Tuchman 94). Ultimately, Pope Clement VI "found it necessary to grant remissions of sin to all who died of the plague because so many were unattended by priests" (95).

People began to wonder if the end of the world was upon them. Some saw the plague as a punishment inflicted by God and wondered for which sins in particular mankind was being held accountable. The list of sins of which medieval mankind believed itself guilty was quite extensive, as a quote from Tuchman illustrates.

Primarily greed, the sin of avarice, followed by usury, worldliness, adultery, blasphemy, falsehood, luxury, irreligion. [...] Pity and anger about the condition of the poor, especially victimization of the peasantry in war, was often expressed by writers of the time and was certainly on the conscience of the century. Beneath it all was the daily condition of medieval life, in which hardly an act or thought, sexual, mercantile, or military, did not contravene the dictates of the Church. Mere failure to fast or attend mass was sin. The result was an underground lake of guilt in the soul that the plague now tapped [104–5].

Given this atmosphere of guilt and fear, it seems reasonable that one of the responses to the plague was a grassroots effort to placate God through acts of penance and abasement. Penitents set out in groups to walk to shrines to beg God's forgiveness. Sackcloth and ashes, tearing of hair and weeping, mortification of the flesh, all were offered to God by way of atonement (Tuchman 103). Believers willing to flagellate themselves into God's good graces became so common they traveled in groups which were referred to as the Flagellants.

Extreme behavior became common. People who could afford to do so fled to the countryside or to areas where the plague had not yet struck. This was a double-edged sword. It might save one's life, or the fleeing individual might bring the plague to an area that had been free of it and ensure his or her own death and that of many others. Families deserted infected members. Priests refused to attend the sick; legal clerks refused to make up wills. The dead became so numerous they were buried in mass or shallow graves and eventually they began to be left in the streets. Fearful they might die at any moment and aware that the social fabric was in such tatters that reprisals were unlikely, people began to indulge in all sorts of licentious and criminal behavior (Tuchman 100). Not all of the responses to the plague were contemptible, however; it also brought out the virtue in people. Many individuals selflessly nursed the sick and dying even though to do so was to put one's own life at risk (96–7).

Negative factors like war and disease were not the only causes of significant changes in medieval life. Innovations in agriculture were drastically changing the way food was produced and the amount that could be produced. Hollister attributes the increased productivity to:

the revolutionary developments in agricultural technology: the three-field system which spread across much of northern Europe, the windmill, the water mill (by 1086 there were over 5000 water mills in

England alone), the heavy, wheeled plow, the horseshoe and improved horse collar which transformed horses into efficient draught animals, and the tandem harness which made it possible to employ horses and oxen in large teams to draw plows or pull heavy wagons [146].

Although, as Hollister points out, these innovations developed over the course of centuries, the cumulative effect found expression in the Middle Ages (146).

The impact of these changes was more far-reaching than food production and an attendant population increase. The heavy plow pulled by horses required a different field shape than the old square field of the scratch plow. A different field configuration called for increased land clearing. The heavy plow needed the combined horses of several farmers and resulted in cooperative farming efforts rather than subsistence farms plowed by one family with a team of horses or oxen. Horse transportation also meant the farmer could live farther away from his fields, and since the new style of plow meant the farmers had to work together, logically they began to group their homes together, creating small towns that could now support a church and a small merchant class. Towns increased general safety as well, since they could be more readily defended than isolated homes (White 142). Towns also meant people had to learn new ways of social interaction.

Unfortunately, the agricultural economy which had expanded to the feasible limits of the time in an effort to feed the growing population was unable to make up the shortfalls of the abbreviated growing season resulting from the Little Ice Age which began at the start of the fourteenth century and lasted for four centuries. Average temperatures dropped, bringing cold and rain, and twice freezing the Baltic Sea within a space of five years. Heavy rains compounded the problem of the new colder climate's shorter growing season, and the ensuing crop failures caused famine throughout much of Europe by 1315 (Tuchman 24).

Attitudes altered as conditions of life altered. Where previously there had been a one on one connection between the peasant and the land he cultivated, there was now a breach, a shift from taking from nature what was needed for survival to a taking from the land whatever could be gained from it. Lynn White, author of *Medieval Religion and Technology*, sees this as a core attitudinal shift, "No more fundamental modification in man's relation to his environment can be imagined: he ceased to be nature's child and became her exploiter" (145).

There had been a long established division of society into three levels; Cantor refers to them as "those who fought, those who prayed, and those who labored" (237–8). With the increase in concentrated population centers, there came an increase in the number of people who provided skilled work in exchange for cash rather than for property or the obligations common to either landowners or serfs. The new bourgeois class had no clearly defined social position, no political clout, and no allegiance to anyone save the guilds of which they were a part. The bourgeois *did* have lots of money and a desire to make displays of monetary status, perhaps in lieu of political and social status. Said displays tended to take the form of buildings— homes, walled enclosures to protect their businesses, and cathedrals to proclaim their piety (Cantor 238 & Hollister 147).

The status of the peasant changed as an aftereffect of the plague because the death of such a large part of the population resulted in a labor shortage. Some peasants were dispossessed and starved, but many found that they, laborers, were a valuable commodity in short supply. The reciprocal bonds and obligations of serfdom became outdated. Nothing was certain any longer, not even one's social standing. Landed nobility looked for peasants willing to pay rent to till their land and began to pay the peasants cash for their labor in return. The peasants began to see their value and use the shortage of manpower as a means to procure higher wages (Hollister 352). The nobility, while willing to use the peasants to maintain their own status and wealth, were not in favor of sharing that wealth and fought the wage increases. The strife between the classes ignited a series of peasant rebellions which, in Hollister's words, "bore witness to a society in which classes struggled bitterly for their share of a declining wealth" (353).

Distribution of wealth was also having an impact on the structure of the family, particularly in France. The practices of parting out land to sons and daughters and gifting the Church with land had fragmented many great holdings throughout the years. Some families' holdings dwindled until they were able to claim little more than a name and a sword (Gies 123–4).

In an effort to retain what lands and power they held, some of the nobility began to practice a system of "impartible inheritance." The entire estate and the right to marry would be given to one son, often, but not always, the eldest (Gies 125). In time, this system was replaced by the more familiar system of primogeniture, the inheritance of all by the eldest son. The solidification of familial holdings under one son led to strengthening of the power of the lesser nobility and the mustering of a force connected by blood under one roof rather than a scattering of roofs. At the same time, the authority of the king and other overlords was weakening. The result was a world filled with pools of autonomous power (128–9).

This new system of inheritance and marriage created a group of landless younger sons who had no real role in their society and no prospects. A younger son might find a wealthy heiress to marry, find a home within the Church, or gain recognition through feats of arms in hopes of being awarded land or position (Gies 143). Limiting the number of sons who could marry had a profound effect on the marriageable female population as well. Daughters who were not fortunate enough to find husbands had as few options as their non-heir male siblings, the chief ones being to become a man's mistress or go into a convent or beguinage (136, 144).

Competition for marrying off one's daughters became fierce and children were often betrothed in the cradle. Consent became an issue, and an individual who had been betrothed in childhood or infancy could refuse to agree to the marriage once he or she reached adulthood (Gies 139). The Church was taking a hard line against divorce (or more accurately against annulment since the Church did not officially allow divorces) on any grounds other than incest, and the rules on what constituted incest were clarified to decrease the number of contested marriages and increase the pool of eligible marriage partners (140).

The legal codes by which people lived were shifting as well. The problems within the Church gave the secular powers sufficient latitude to develop a political system less dependent upon the Church. The widespread increase in knowledge of law allowed for an alternate means to control a country's population. Extensive study of the *Corpus Juris Civilis* by Justinian, copies of which had found their way back into circulation after over five centuries' absence, provided a framework for the construction of codified laws and the judicial apparatus to enforce them (Cantor 308).

The move toward secular administration of government was bolstered by the English example hammered out in the struggles between the existing Anglo-Saxon system of governance and administration and the Norman one brought to England by William the Conqueror and later refined and augmented by King Henry II (Cantor 398).

While the continent was inclining more toward the Justinian code, the idea of secular administration and governance was common to all. Nonetheless, individuals might find themselves unsure what rules they had violated and which court, civil or ecclesiastic, would be trying them.

Seemingly irrevocable change was occurring in other areas of life as well. Technology was shifting its emphasis away from what manpower could do to ways to augment manpower. Water and wind provided the means for increased mechanization, especially mills of various sorts. The spinning wheel was invented, and machine spun yarn began to find its ways into even the fine cloth of the Flemish. Eyeglasses were invented and the rudiments of a mechanical clock were developed even though no finalized design was put into use (White 80–2).

Technology was changing the tenor of battle. The use of longbows, while considered ungentlemanly in some quarters, was unquestionably effective and helped the English gain some of their initial victories over France. Gunpowder and cannons were a minor part of warfare at the beginning of the Hundred Years War, but their presence was increasing, and by the middle of the fifteenth century smaller guns that were usable in battle were being created (White 112). They were cumbersome and hard to reload, but they were making plate armor and knightly training passe (Hollister 353). Even the once clear military hierarchy was being called into doubt; with a longbow or a gun, a peasant could be as deadly in battle as a knight.

The knight was becoming an emblem rather than a warrior:

> But while the feudal knight was vanishing from European armies, he was, [sic] becoming ever more prominent in art, literature, and court ceremonial. The fifteenth century was an age of elaborate shining armor, fairy-tales castles, coats of arms, and extravagant tournaments. Knighthood, driven from the battlefield, took refuge in fantasy, and an age of ruthless political cynicism saw the full flowering of a romantic code of chivalric ethics [Hollister 353].

Appropriately, Malory's *Le Morte D'Arthur*, finished in 1469, can be seen as a reprise of the romances written earlier in the Middle Ages. Like the institution of knighthood itself, *Le Morte* is an attempt to relive the best of the "good old days," days gone, but fondly remembered, perhaps more fondly remembered *because* they were gone.

Society was in a near constant state of flux. In any given year, it was difficult to know who was in power and who was not, whether the plague would bypass your village or wipe it out, and whether the weather combined with your new agricultural equipment would provide an abundance of crops or barely enough to scrape by until the next harvest. Huizinga provides a succinct summary of the probable mood of the late medieval period:

> Bad government, exactions, the cupidity and violence of the great, wars and brigandage, scarcity, misery and pestilence — to this is contemporary history nearly reduced in the eyes of the people. The feeling of general insecurity which was caused by the chronic form wars were apt to take, by the constant menace of the dangerous classes, by the mistrust of justice, was further aggravated by the obsession of the coming of the end of the world, and by the fear of hell, of sorcerers and of devils. The background of all life in the world seems black [30].

The rapid, dramatic, and widespread change typifying these centuries is a common thread which, in part, accounts for their use of romance literature as a means to cling to hope for the future. From these years of foment and uncertainty came the bulk of the medieval romances: *The Song of Roland, King Horn, Havelok, Amis and Amiloun, Boeve of Haumtone, Guy of Warwick,* the lais of Marie de France, Wolfram von Eschenbach's *Parzival,* Crétien de Troyes' Arthurian romances, Gottfried von Strassburg's *Tristan and Iseult,* and Guillaume de Lorris and Jean de Meun's *The Romance of the Rose.* When life presents one with nothing but uncertainty, it is appealing to turn to a form of literature that promises that the bad king will always be defeated in the end, that God will correct injustices, and that the knight who lives virtuously will win the lady of his dreams and the lands and wealth he needs to survive.

4

Five Centuries Later, Still Looking for the Light

The early twentieth century, when science fiction was in its infancy and then — in the form of the numerous science fiction magazines— in its adolescence, provides more than ample tension and distress to warrant the archetypal response it elicited. The hope-inspiring property of romance literature and the world's need for literature which inspired hope was apparent to some modern science fiction and fantasy authors. Olaf Stapledon, for instance, begins the preface to his book *Star Maker*, by acknowledging the harsh realities of his pre–World War II world. Writing in March 1937, the British science fiction writer observed, "At a moment when Europe is in danger of a catastrophe worse than that of 1914 a book like this may be condemned as a distraction from the desperately urgent defence of civilization against modern barbarism" (7). His answer to that anticipated criticism, however, was to remind the reader that stepping back and looking at "our turbulent world against a background of stars" may allow us to see our current problems more clearly and awaken "the resolute will to serve our waking humanity" (8, 9).

Distress and danger are certainly evident in the history of twentieth century America, and it is to America that the reader must look since science fiction is generally considered to be an inherently American genre. Fantasy, too, tends to find its best reception among American audiences. The United States may not have been the place where all of the earliest science fiction and fantasy works were written, but it is the place they were best received and where the forms were nurtured and grew. Even The Lord of the Rings, written by an Englishman, found its most enthusiastic home in the United States, as evidenced by high sales figures and the pirated U.S. paperback edition which hit American bookshelves in 1965. That unauthorized Ace edition sold approximately 100,000 copies in the first year, an impressive figure which nonetheless pales before the sale of one million copies of the authorized U.S. edition which followed. The Lord of the Rings became "The Book, surpassing all previous best-sellers" (Carpenter 260).

Whether the world seems a grim or joyous place has much to do with where one stands within that world. Science fiction and fantasy are written primarily with the general reading public in mind, not the "literary" public; this is a feature it shares with the romance literature of the later Middle Ages. Since the readers of science fiction and fantasy are, by and large, the average people of our society, it is the history of those people that is here presented. Many readers may find the events in this chapter to be familiar territory. This is the history of their own times, and the history related here happened to and around many of the readers' family members. Some may even have happened during the readers' own lives.

As the century began, the United States was fighting a war to subdue the Philippine Islands, land many factions in the United States did not even want. The brutal subjugation of the islands and their non-white inhabitants threw the racial bias of the United States into high relief, even as its gave the lie to U.S. denials of empire building (Zinn 26, 28). Aggression continued until 1911, leaving the citizens of the U.S. only a small breathing space before the start of World War I in 1914. This was to become the pattern of the twentieth century for the U.S.: a war, followed by a brief lull, then another war. Except that the U.S. wars involved different nations each time, the appellation "Hundred Years War" might be as apt for twentieth century America as fourteenth and fifteenth century England and France. The longest period during which the U.S. was not openly at war was the twenty-one year space between the first and second World Wars. For ten of those twenty-one years, however, the country was plunged in the depths of the Great Depression, so while there were no ongoing military hostilities, there were economic ones. After World War II came Korea, then Vietnam, Grenada, Panama, Desert Storm, and the NATO intervention in Bosnia following close on each others' heels. There was never a span of more than eight years of peace from 1945 until the end of the century.

Besides the wars in which the United States was an active and overt presence, there were a number of wars around the globe in which the U.S. was either a minor or covert presence or a concerned bystander. The U.S. aided the Greeks in their civil war in the 1940s, became entangled in the Bay of Pigs fiasco in 1961, sent troops to Nicaragua in the 1970s, and responded to various African countries' requests for assistance with regime changes throughout the century. The Russian Revolution which resulted in the formation of the Union of Soviet Socialist Republics in 1922, the Cuban Revolution which put Castro and his government in place in 1959, and the Chinese Revolution which spawned the Communist Republic of China in 1949 may not have actively involved the U.S., but the establishment of those governments affected U.S. history for decades.

War became both more impersonal and more horrifying as the century went on. Tanks rolled across the battlefields of World War I, flattening terrain and personnel alike. Mustard gas in World War I paved the way for later use of the rainbow of chemicals which characterized warfare in Vietnam, Agent Orange being the most well-known and, possibly, the most destructive. Airplanes became an increasing presence in warfare. The First World War's courageous men in their fragile two and three-winged aircraft were replaced by men in sturdy, single-winged metal bombers on which the flyers painted women to remind them of home and bombs to chronicle successful missions. Aircraft also made possible the most devastating occurrence in warfare in the twentieth, or perhaps any, century, the destruction of Hiroshima and Nagasaki with atomic bombs. As the century progressed, propeller-driven fighter planes were replaced by jet aircraft and helicopters, both of which kept getting faster and more maneuverable. Communication methods improved, as did tracking. Commanders could make strategic decisions and give orders from farther away from the front lines, and soldiers could be deployed faster and more selectively. Weapons' range and accuracy increased, allowing death to be dealt from greater and greater distances. It was no longer necessary to see the people you were killing. Modern fighter jets, for example, can destroy targets which are not close enough for visual contact and can only be seen on a radar screen. Death is no longer even limited to the years during which the war takes place; chemical weapons and nuclear bombs cause illnesses and defects that kill long after the resolutions of the wars in which those weapons were employed.

War was, for the mainland U.S. citizen, something that happened elsewhere. For the citizen living in America in the early 1900's, however, there were often other pressing problems. The inequities in the economic arena were a particular sore point. The boom in industry which had brought unfathomable wealth to a few, had brought near serfdom to many, and the many were beginning to object. Working conditions were deplorable, hours long, workers expendable, and business owners, for the most part, only interested in profits, not in the people who made those profits possible. Workers, pushed to a point where they had little left to lose and everything to gain, began to strike. Horrifying tragedies like the Triangle Shirtwaist Company fire, in which 146 workers perished because they were trapped in the building, spurred the workers to demand safer working conditions and restitution for families of workers killed through company negligence (Zinn 38–9).

Unions began to organize. If you were a skilled male worker, you would probably join the American Federation of Labor (AFL). The exclusion of women, unskilled laborers, and non-whites from the AFL left plenty of room for the creation and rapid growth of the much more radical Industrial Workers of the World, the I.W.W. or Wobblies (41). Between the AFL and the IWW, workers were gaining leadership and power. Strikes became commonplace and unions began to support each other's strikes. Employers brought in armed guards, strikebreakers, police, and soldiers in an effort to force the workers back to their jobs or replace them and continue production (49).

The cost of resistance began to outweigh the cost of capitulation, however, and many industries began to accede to some of the workers' demands. Pressured by strikes and by new government regulations, companies began to shorten the workday and work week, eliminate some of the more dangerous hazards of the work place, lighten the work load on child laborers, and provide workmen's compensation (Zinn 51, 63, 70). Although these were significant advances, the lot of the average person was still hard and, outside of literature, there was little promise of a better future.

People living in the first decades of the twentieth century were searching for answers to an untenable economic situation. Despite minor improvements in the status of workers and a brief blush of wealth following World War I, the economy was unstable and the stock market crash of 1929 "brought the whole economy down with it" (Zinn 111). The depression that followed the crash affected everyone. "Industrial production fell by 50 percent, and by 1933 perhaps 15 million (no one knew exactly) — one-fourth or one-third of the labor force — were out of work" (111). People had no work, no money, no means to get money, nowhere to turn.

> There were millions of tons of food around, but it was not profitable to transport it, to sell it. Warehouses were full of clothing, but people could not afford it. There were lots of houses, but they stayed empty because people couldn't pay the rent, had been evicted, and now lived in shacks in quickly formed "Hoovervilles" built on garbage dumps [112].

Local assistance programs were established and some communities tried to take care of their own, but the help offered was inadequate to the need. To make matters worse, few people felt safe from the possibility that they could be the next to join the ranks of the unemployed and homeless. The fear of unemployment and homelessness had lasting effects for some. My own parents remained frugal long after such frugality was necessary in their lives because they feared another Depression. Echoing through their lives and the lives of their children were such adages as: "If you can't afford it [meaning if you haven't got the ready cash to pay for it], then you don't need it" and "Use it up, wear it out, make it do, or do without." Neither owned a credit card until well past the age of 70. Many of their generation lived this way. Hope for relief in the future may have been all some of these people had to help them survive the privations of the Depression.

The Socialist party was central to the IWW and to much of the labor unrest. Leaders such as Eugene Debs urged employees to work together to defeat the employers. Barriers of race and gender were less significant than the barrier of low economic status; the employers were the common enemy. The Socialists strove to place power in the hands of the masses. They reminded the working people that if they refused to work, the entire system would shut down. Without their labor, there would be no profits and the employers would be weakened. This could only work if the people maintained a united front, and this was the Socialists' goal. The strength of this appeal became increasingly evident as Socialist candidates began to be elected into public office (Zinn 54–5).

When Socialism turned out not to have all the answers to heal society's ills, some people turned to Communism for answers. The overthrow of corrupt "masters" reveling in wealth obtained through the labor of the impoverished masses had an obvious appeal, as did the redistribution of possessions in more equitable proportions amongst the populace. Communism continued to offer a segment of the population hope for a better economic future until the Cold War instilled a fear of the U.S.S.R., and hence communism, a fear which allowed Senator Joseph McCarthy to create a modern American version of the Inquisition as he searched for Communists under every bed and invented them when his efforts were not sufficiently rewarding.

The plight of the working class brought other areas of social inequity to the country's grudging attention as well, the two most prominent being the status of blacks and the status of women. People like W.E.B. Dubois began to demand that blacks be given the rights they deserved, "the right to vote, the right to enter the militia, to be on juries," and even more basic rights such as the right to make a living and support their families and the right not to be lynched just because of their color (64). Race riots occurred. Even though battalions of black soldiers had fought and died for the U.S. in World War I, the country continued to deny them the opportunity to exercise the voting rights which had been granted them by the 14th and 15th Amendments. Although the National Association for the Advancement of Colored People (NAACP) had been founded in 1910, little changed for African-Americans until the 1950s.

The 1950s and 1960s brought many freedoms to African-Americans, but those freedoms came at a high cost. Civil rights protesters were jailed. People — both black and white — who took action to try to eliminate segregation and ensure all people the vote, regardless of color, were threatened, hindered, harassed, and received death threats; some were even killed. In 1954 the Supreme Court ruled that segregated schooling was unconstitutional, but the first gradual attempt to integrate a school in 1957 in Little Rock, Arkansas required the presence of federal troops to allow nine black students to enter the school. Martin Luther King, Jr. spoke out for peaceful change through passive resistance like the strike against the bus companies who required blacks in sit in the back, but other blacks were not willing to wait for change. More militant blacks, like Malcolm X, advocated the use of violence and called for a rejection of the white world rather than a cooperative melding with it. Significantly, both King and Malcolm X were assassinated. Apparently, it didn't matter if desegregation came peacefully or violently, change was the issue; some people were willing to do anything to prevent the change to a less racially biased society.

Race riots erupted throughout the 1960s; the Watts riots in Los Angeles, for example, left dozens dead and interracial tensions high. Although the relationship between the races became less volatile by the end of the 1960s, the tension was always there just below the surface waiting to explode into violence as it did, again in Los Angeles, when a black man, Rodney King, was brutally beaten by four white police officers. The lines were not drawn just between blacks and whites, and not all encounters between races were negative, but the degree of racial unrest did contribute to the turmoil in twentieth century America and added to the need for healing archetypes in literature. In fact, such literature has traditionally been one way in which to demand rights for all sentient beings in the universe and to speak against discrimination in ways subtle enough to avoid censure by the political machine.

Women, too, were asking why they should support a system of government which did so little for them and did not even allow them the right to vote. Changes that benefited the workers in industry helped many women since they comprised one fifth of the labor force in 1910 (Zinn 40), but deeper, more comprehensive changes were needed to really alter the status of women. The women's movement sought more than just the vote and improved economic conditions; they wanted "recognition as equals in every sphere, including sexual relations and marriage" (57). Women won the right to vote when the 19th Amendment was ratified in 1920, but in many other ways — access to employment, equal pay for equal work, access to higher education — women remained second-class citizens until the 1960s. My oldest sister graduated at the top of her class in 1957 and applied to one of the top East Coast schools. She was accepted by the school, but denied admittance to the engineering program — not because of her grades but because she was female.

It is difficult for many young female students of the 2000s to come to grips with the idea that it is only within the last forty years that women have gained the freedoms these young students assume as their birthright: the freedom to speak their minds, the freedom to own and drive their own cars, the freedom to obtain their own housing and pay for that housing and its related bills with money the young woman earned herself in a career of her own choosing, the freedom to choose a partner and to leave that partner and choose a new partner, the freedom to say "no" in the marriage bed. Many of these freedoms were not legally prohibited before the 1960s, but most were socially prohibited. These changes, too, did not come easily. Some women became activists, burning their bras and holding rallies in protest of unequal treatment of the sexes; others took offending persons or companies to court and fought their battles for equality in the courtroom rather than on the streets.

Society was changing rapidly and people were struggling to adjust to changes which some would, at times, have preferred were not occurring. Technology, too, was changing, and at a pace that was arguably even faster than the social change. People had to keep adjusting as inventions were created and scrapped within a generation. The technological advance which had the most frightening effect on the twentieth century was the atomic bomb. From Fermi's splitting of the atom in 1942, it was only three years until tests and then the use of an atomic bomb. Nuclear weaponry provided humankind, for the first time in its history, with a means to eradicate all life on the planet — human, animal, and plant — and render the planet uninhabitable for an indeterminate period into the future. The implications of a weapon that could kill so indiscriminately on such a large scale were shattering. The deaths resulting from the use of such a weapon were not even confined to the time and place of the dropped bomb. The atomic bomb forced people to recognize not only their own mortality, but the mortality of their world, and to ask if there really are boundaries in the field of knowledge that should not be crossed. Even the threat of another such bombing could be used as a political bargaining chip; the stockpiles of such weapons ultimately led to the standoff between the United States and the U.S.S.R. known as the Cold War.

That such a bomb could be dropped was a result of rapid advances in aviation. The first heavier-than-air flight took place in 1903, the first trans-Atlantic flight in 1927, the first jet planes flew in 1944, Chuck Yeager flew through the sound barrier in 1947, and the Concorde cut across the Atlantic on its first supersonic passenger run in 1976. In 73 years, mankind not only left the ground but created the machinery needed to carry hundreds of passengers through the air at hitherto unfathomable speeds. A similar timeline can be constructed for mankind's departure from the cocoon of his own planet's atmosphere. Goddard began testing his first rockets in 1914. By 1957, the U.S.S.R.'s Sputnik had been launched into space. Manned spaceflight was achieved in 1961 when Soviet astronaut Gagarin entered space in Vostok I. Eight years later, Neil

Armstrong walked on the moon and proved once and for all that space was not unconquerable. Science fiction had long predicted man's voyage to the moon, and the achievement of that goal spurred writers to expand their horizon to the stars.

The telephone, the radio, the television, the moving picture, and the phonograph all evolved rapidly in the twentieth century, so rapidly that the original creators might not recognize their own creations' offspring. People keep having to upgrade their user skills. A phone need not be cranked now, but it also doesn't begin to work when you lift the receiver from the cradle (some modern telephone users might even wonder what a cradle is). The face of the phone, which used to consist solely of ten numbers dialed by finger, has shrunk in size but multiplied in complexity. Now the user has to negotiate sixteen or more buttons, each about the diameter of a pencil eraser, which turn the phone on and off, allow it to send and receive, access a menu which can be used for a variety of functions, move forward and backward through information, change the volume, and play games, or even take pictures. Depending on the phone, it can also be used to link to your computer. This is just one piece of equipment in the technological arsenal in the average person's life. There are many such, and each seems to make the world simultaneously more and less complicated and, most emphatically, more stressful.

Computers have become the household item of the 2000s as the TV was in the 1960s. The microchip technology developed in the late 1950s, and repeatedly improved upon since, has allowed for smaller and faster computers and computer-hybrids, those items which existed before computers but which now incorporate them, such as cars. Virtual reality exists alongside reality, and the pathways of the World Wide Web are more familiar to some people than the streets in their own towns. Increasingly realistic games blur the distinction between the physical world and the cyberworld. Improved prosthetics are even blurring the lines within the physical world as people begin living their lives with the possibility of synthetic parts rather than just transplants. A quick look at a list of current articles on bioengineered prosthetics reveals such items in testing as an artificial retina for the eye, digital memory aids, and microchips that can be plugged into the brain.*

---

*These items all came from a quick scan of the abstracts of the articles provided by a sort for "prosthetics" done on the BasicBIOSIS database on July 25, 2005.

Medical knowledge advanced from the discovery of penicillin in 1928 to the first heart transplant in 1967, from the first X-rays five years before the start of the century to the CAT scan in 1971. The nation progressed from refusing to allow women access to safe birth control to making a range of contraceptives readily available, from condoms to the Pill to the "morning after" pill. The first test-tube baby was born in 1978, and the first cloned mammal, Dolly the sheep, was born in 1997. Vaccines eradicated many of the lethal diseases of the early century — polio, measles, rabies, tetanus. For all this medical advancement, however, some diseases and ailments continued to threaten life on the planet. Influenza killed millions in 1918, and in spite of vaccines and medicines to counteract many symptoms of flu, new strains continue to evolve and to kill. Cancer has continued to defy any definitive cure, and, according to a United Nations report cited on the Black Coalition on AIDS website, AIDS killed over 19 million people worldwide between 1980 and the end of the century.

The last decades of the century brought economic troubles again. Fuel supplies were curtailed; for awhile, people had to line up at gas pumps on alternating days to buy limited amounts of fuel. When fuel became readily available once more, the prices began to rise in leaps and bounds, from 35¢ a gallon in the early 1970s to over $1.00 per gallon in 1999. Fuel costs were but one example of the rising cost of living; many families found that they could not afford to meet their bills unless more than one member worked. An individual working forty hours per week and making minimum wage might well find he or she could not afford housing and the other basics of life.

The difficulties of life in the twentieth century could easily have led people to turn to God for assistance. Unfortunately, God himself was no longer a certainty for twentieth mankind. In the late nineteenth century, in his book *Thus Spoke Zarathustra*, Nietzsche had declared that "God is dead" (12), and many people believed him. As Karen Armstrong observes in *A History of God*, humankind has had increasing difficulty accepting the "ignoble servitude" and "unworthy dependence" which are a part of many religions, particularly Christianity (352). In fact, she claims that "by the end of the [19th] century, a significant number of people were beginning to feel that if God was not yet dead, it was the duty of rational, emancipated human beings everywhere to kill him" (346).

Nietzsche argued that the Christian God limited mankind's growth and that without God, "human beings would have to become gods themselves" and thereby enter a "newer, higher plane of human history" (Armstrong 356). Sigmund Freud simply dismissed God as a father figure, essential for the growth and psychological development of immature humans, but unneeded by mature adults. He felt that the ethical values which had formerly been instilled by religion would henceforth be provided by science, "the new *logos* which would supplant God" (357). The question of God's existence extended beyond scholarly haggling. The Nazi treatment of fellow humans in the death camps challenged many people's belief in the possibility of God. "If God is omnipotent, he could have prevented the Holocaust. If he was unable to stop it, he is impotent and useless; if he could have stopped it and chose not to, he is a monster" (376).

The twentieth century could easily be described as "the century born to woe," a phrase that Barbara Tuchman actually used to characterize the fourteenth century (25). Many of the woes of the fourteenth century would sound familiar to anyone who had lived through the twentieth century — war, famine, pestilence, environmental disasters, social upheaval, religious uncertainty, rapid technological change. In phrases almost as bleak as the ones Huizinga used to describe the close of the Middle Ages, Karen Armstrong summarizes the close of the twentieth century:

> For decades we have lived with the knowledge that we have created weapons that could wipe out human life on the planet. The Cold War may have ended, but the new world order seems no less frightening than the old. We are facing the possibility of ecological disaster. The AIDS virus threatens to bring a plague of unmanageable proportions. Within two or three generations, the population will become too great for the planet to support [Armstrong 377].

Some modern authors, like Marge Piercy and George Orwell or playwrights like David Mamet, feel we must confront the bleakness of our world and accept it. But to accept this flawed world without any hope of bettering it is to admit that we cannot be more than we currently are, and very few science fiction writers would accept that view of the world. It is because some people still believe, as their predecessors believed so many centuries ago, that mankind can be more than he is right now, that there is hope for the future. If all the future could offer was more war, more disease, more hatred, and bigger and more lethal weapons, why bother? Why would anyone want to continue living if

Orwell's projected future, "a boot stomping on a human face — forever," were the only one? Many people need to believe that the future offers something better than the present or that in some other dimension humankind managed to evolve into something more admirable. Science fiction and fantasy provide views of those possible alternative futures or alternative worlds. just as medieval romance literature did for the people of the Middle Ages.

5

The Hero

"Some are born great, some achieve greatness,
and some have greatness thrust upon them."
— William Shakespeare,
Twelfth Night, II.V.159.

Having argued that a societal need for such literature existed and still exists, it is appropriate to move on to the consideration of how medieval romance literature, science fiction, and fantasy provide hope to the societies in which they were created. Those forms of literature are part of a greater body of romantic literature that also includes folktales and fairy tales. The distinguishing characteristics of this mode of literature are the type of hero, the balance between plot and characterization, the degree of "realism," and the ways in which they utilize archetypes. The choices the author makes in these areas determine how the resulting literature will be classified, how it will be received by the public, and who is likely to read it.

The story begins, as any good romance should, with the hero. Art, according to Aristotle in his *Poetics*, is an imitation of life or nature (7) and humans are the "objects of imitation" (11). For Aristotle then, the hero is the human who is representing or imitating humankind in the work of literature. While the plays about which Aristotle was writing had few enough characters to limit the term *hero*, modern literature has peopled the metaphorical stage with casts of dozens and, at times, even thousands. One or two characters still tend to take the preeminent place(s), however, and onto them devolves the status of heroes. The Aristotelean concept of "hero" provides us with three possible representations of man: man as he is, man as better than he is, or man as worse than he is (11).

Literature, according to Frye, can be divided into five modes based upon the relationship of the hero figure to the average human being and the human world. If the hero is vastly above the level of both mankind and his world, the hero is considered to be divine and the story a myth (*Anatomy* 33). If the hero is fully human, but "superior in *degree* to other men and to his environment," the story is classified as a romance (33). If the hero rises above the average man but not above his environment, he is the hero of a work in the high mimetic mode; if he rises above neither but is simply an average man, he is the hero of a low mimetic work. Lastly, if he is inferior to the average man, the work is considered to be ironic (34).

Examples and additional qualifications are given for each of these modes. For the romance mode, which is the one that applies to the works under consideration, Frye adds that the romance hero operates by rules slightly different from the ones most people are familiar with in their everyday world. In the realm of the romance hero,

> the ordinary laws of nature are slightly suspended: prodigies of courage and endurance, unnatural to us, are natural to him, and enchanted weapons, talking animals, terrifying ogres and witches, and talismans of miraculous power violate no rule of probability once the postulates of romance have been established [33].

Therefore, our romance hero is not only superior to other men, he is superior to his world and can manipulate it in ways that the average human reading or hearing the story remains incapable of doing.

To take an example from literature, this means that Amis, in the early medieval romance *Amis and Amiloun,* can kill his two children and use their blood to heal Amiloun of leprosy, yet have the children rise unscathed from their beds the next day. The miraculous cure is, of course, attributed in part to the virtue of Amis and Amiloun and the strength of their bond of friendship, as is the survival of the children. Even at the age of fifteen, Amis and Amiloun were described as "the doughtiest that rode with shield and spear" (Rickert 4). Their prowess sets them above their contemporaries, as does their friendship, which is such that Amiloun agrees to fight a battle for Amis even though he has been warned that he will be struck with leprosy as a result. They are both *of* their world and beyond it, not gods, but exceptional men.

The science fiction hero, too, must be superior to his fellowman and his world. Aldiss, writer of fiction and criticism including several books of science fiction criticism, considers the issue of characterization in his book *Billion Year Spree: The True History of Science Fiction.* He reminds us that, while the hero can be Everyman, he cannot be the ordinary man. "[T]he more powers above the ordinary that the protagonist enjoys, the closer the fiction will approach to hard-core science fiction. Conversely, the more ordinary and fallible the protagonist, the further from hard-core" (8). The hero must be sufficiently like the reader to engage his sympathies and promote identification, but, at the same time, the hero must be sufficiently superior to the average man to stand out as someone who can "get things done," whether this is due to intellect, physical prowess, or moral superiority.

Which powers or abilities the hero has are less important than that he has them. Sir Gawain is not always depicted as the strongest knight of the Round Table, but he is a model of chivalry and, as such, above the average man. Aragorn, in Tolkien's The Lord of the Rings, is both a man of high moral fiber and also a descendant of kings. Ebling Mis in Isaac Asimov's *Foundation and Empire* is a brilliant man capable of solving problems no one else can solve. What they all have in common is their larger than life quality set against the background of their human fallibility. The ultimate romantic hero is Christ, fully human and therefore subject to the Devil's temptations and the death of the body, yet fully God, therefore able to resist the Devil and rise from the dead. The simultaneous man/God nature of Christ sets him apart from other god figures. Take away either part and He loses his value as a hero we can emulate, someone showing us the way.

Gawain cannot be perfect, because we are not perfect. If he is to teach us that we can reach beyond ourselves and be more than we are, his successes must be obtainable ones, obtainable for us as well as himself. If he has no flaws, he becomes a god, not a man, and the story shifts from romance to myth. If Frodo Baggins walks straight through the three books of The Lord of the Rings to the pits of Mordor and blithely tosses the One Ring into Mount Doom, he is no one we can be; virtually none of us are so free of doubt, so able to resist the lure of power.

Yet heroes cannot be average men either or we will not believe in their deeds. We know there are those among us who rise above the rest and do more than is expected; the hero of the romance needs to be one of those if he is to show us that we too can rise above, "if only"—if only we follow God more closely, if only we believe in ourselves, if only we believe in our technology, if only we move to a new planet or country.

In a modern science fiction work, the additional qualification of the hero needing to cope with a world running by rules somewhat different from our own may fall under the heading "marvelous" or "fantastic" rather than "miraculous," but it is present, and the hero's ability to survive or surmount such a world helps identify the work as a romance. When Hober Mallow, the adventurous, spacefaring trader who ultimately founds a line of merchant princes in Asimov's *Foundation*, seeks to learn the strength of the dying Empire, he offers as a bribe one of a multitude of handheld nuclear devices, a personal forcefield with an atomic power source the size of a walnut. While it might be easy for modern man to *imagine* nuclear science progressing to the point where atomic reactors can fit in the palm of one's hand, it has not happened yet so it is still a marvel. Modern society's belief in the "truth" of science paves the way for the reader to accept this example of the marvelous as the strong religious foundation of the western European world of the Middle Ages lent credibility to the miracle of healing in *Amis and Amiloun*.

The romance hero and his relationship to his world are evident in fantasy as well. In fact, the definition of fantasy provided in Chapter 1 is very similar to Frye's assessment of that hero/world relationship. Fantasy was defined as a work in which a different set of rules has been substituted for the rules of our physical world, perhaps allowing for the use of magic or for human-sized cats to walk upright and rule planets. Whatever the changes, once the rules of the fantasy world have been set down, the world adheres to them. There are all manner of unusual folk populating Middle Earth in Tolkien's Lord of the Rings trilogy, but once the characteristics of a being have been set down, the reader can recognize one when it appears. Hobbits are always shorter than men; they do not suddenly grow to giant-size, even if doing so would allow them to escape a peril. Rivendell's elves may possess magic, but that magic has limits and those limits are not exceeded.

Frodo Baggins may initially seem to violate the requirement that the hero of a romance be superior to the average man, but on closer consideration, it becomes apparent he does not since he is not human and therefore cannot be judged by human standards. By hobbit stan-

dards, he is unusual. He is not content to stay in his hobbithole growing a garden, eating six meals a day, and visiting with his neighbors; he
wants to see the world, meet new peoples, have an adventure. Ultimately,
he discovers that he is superior both to other hobbits and to many
humans because he is able to resist for so long the lure of evil exerted
on him by the ring of power he carries.

While the hero's role is important, he often remains a somewhat
undeveloped character. One of the criticisms leveled against science
fiction is that it provides inadequate character development and lacks
psychological depth. Kingsley Amis, writer and critic, agrees with the
assessment, but does not agree that it is a negative factor in the writing;
he feels that the "specifying, distinguishing, questioning form of char-
acterisation [sic] to which general fiction has accustomed us" would set
the tenor of science fiction works "awry" (127). The focus in science
fiction and fantasy is not on the character but on the action or the idea.
Amis even goes so far as to call "idea" the hero of much science fiction:
idea "occupies the position given in ordinary fiction to matters of human
situation or character" (137).

Rather than developing an in-depth character portrait which reveals
the psychological profile of an individual, romance works seek to present some larger, more universal truths about human life so that readers
can learn from them or use them to work through their own psychological dramas. Frye likens this function of romance literature to dreams.
As with the dream, "its limits are not the real, but the conceivable"
(*Anatomy* 119). Dreams deal in wish fulfillment and the facing and conquering of terrors. We do not ask the people in our dreams to be fully
rounded characters or for the dream to provide extensive psychological
analysis of such characters; we simply ask them to exist and play their
necessary roles.

Amis extends his argument against extensive character development in science fiction to the point of claiming that the use of stock
types is essential because we are dealing with unknown and unfamiliar
worlds: "an added reference-point or reassurance to the reader can be
furnished by treating character conservatively and limiting interest in
it; it must be shown quickly that the familiar categories of human behavior persist in an unfamiliar environment..."(127). Amis' argument may
not apply in all cases, but, nonetheless, keeping the characters relatively
undeveloped allows them to stand as archetypal images and lets the
writer, and the reader, focus on the ideas being promulgated.

In an attempt to tap some cultural, or even universal, archetype, the author of a romance deprives the character of some individuality but allows him to become Everyman. This Everyman status does not mean the character has been lowered to the level of the common man (this would turn the writing into low mimetic literature), but instead means he is being held up as an example of what a human can do under given circumstances with maximum ability and effort. Erich Neumann, drawing on the work of Jung, says of the hero:

> [He] is the archetypal forerunner of mankind in general. His fate is the pattern in accordance with which the masses of humanity must live, and always have lived, however haltingly and distantly, and however short of the ideal man they have fallen[...] [131].

The significant idea here being that mankind, like the hero, refuses to give up and continues to believe there is an ideal for which to strive.

The great irony, of course, is that even though the characters of romance do not have well defined personalities, they are clearly and stubbornly individuals. This individuality is essential to personal growth, for the hero and for all humankind. Modern man needs to return to a sense of self, of wholeness, an individualness that ancient man possessed as part of his life and experience but modern man has lost, as Jung points out in his works. No one needed to tell Odysseus to be himself; he would not have understood. He might even have asked, despite his penchant for disguising himself, who else he could be. No need either to tell the knight of the medieval romance to be himself, as he rode out into battle with his individual symbol emblazoned on his shield, his distinctive color choices, his personally named sword and charger (Roland and his horse Veillantif and sword Durendal are a good example). The only time the medieval knight could be anyone else was when he was enchanted, where losing himself was part of the evil — as in Marion Zimmer Bradley's *The Mists of Avalon* where Arthur was enchanted and had Excalibur stolen from him and used against him — or when he deliberately obscured his identity by wearing featureless solid colored armor — as Lancelot does once he is so well known that other knights are reluctant to compete against him. Even when enchanted or disguised, however, a man's fighting style was often distinctive enough to betray his true identity.

Gone are the days when one looked into one's opponent's eyes while dealing a death blow with a weapon that put one literally within arm's length; modern man has moved to impersonal mass murder via weapons one can drop or shoot from miles away without risk to one's self or first-hand knowledge of the resultant destruction. In the last decades of the twentieth century, people often dressed in clothes that not only showed no individuality, but did not even reveal gender. Many school teachers are admonished to tailor their lessons to the masses, the middle ability students, rather than challenge students to rise to higher standards. Small wonder in a world where mankind seems to be sinking to the lowest common denominator that man seeks to return to or move forward to a time and place where one individual and his efforts could make a perceptible difference in the universe.

As Jung put it, "There is only one remedy for the levelling effect of all collective measures, and that is to emphasize and increase the value of the individual" (*Flying* 97). It is not surprising that the hero or heroine of science fiction or fantasy is, more often than not, a misfit or a loner, a person to whom individuality is of paramount importance. While many times the hero is in search of self, it is often the hero's very understanding of the importance of self that sets him off from others in the science fiction or fantasy world he inhabits. The hero is that person who can "remember his own soul and his own wholeness" in the face of "the danger of mass-mindedness" (Jung, *Flying* 101). Jung is referring here to the "wholeness which we have lost in the midst of our civilized conscious existence, a wholeness which we always were without knowing it" (100).

In Ray Bradbury's *Fahrenheit 451*, the main character, Guy Montag, thinks he is a good follower of the collective mentality until he realizes that he does not really buy the party line. He is troubled by what he is doing, and he begins asking questions that reveal to him that he no longer accepts the rules of his society. Question askers are always a danger, and Montag is forced to flee. When he reaches the rebels' hiding place, he learns that each person has memorized his or her favorite book so as not to let those books die out. Seeing each person as a book underscores the theme of individuality. Each book is different and hence each person's individuality is emphasized both in personal taste in choosing the book and because each person's knowledge incorporates a work that differs from every other person. Ironically, the people become known as their books rather than by their names.

Genuine selfhood cannot be created by the crowd, defined by the crowd, or invested in the crowd because the mass consciousness is too fickle. The hero of a modern mimetic work (high or low depending on your opinion of the main character) may erroneously believe that identity is determined by the crowd. Take the case of the main character in *The Bonfire of the Vanities*, Sherman McCoy. He begins the book believing he is one of the "masters of the universe"; he accepts this definition of himself because that is how he has been cast by the media, his associates, and his social peers. When he is plummeted to the depths and the media labels him scum later in the book, he accepts that revised image of himself without question because he has no "self" distinct from the one that has been constructed by those around him.

Sir Gawain undergoes a similar fall from perfection in *Sir Gawain and the Green Knight*. At the beginning of the tale, Gawain had believed himself to be the perfect knight his society told him he was. During the course of the story, Gawain learns he is a flawed man when he fails the test of the green girdle. Upon his return to Arthur's court, his peers take the girdle and make a joke of it, turning it into a new fashion and praising him as a hero. At the end, when faced with the ideal societal version of who he is or his own tarnished but real version, Gawain chooses to accept the self he knows to be the true one. The difference between Gawain and Sherman McCoy, who does eventually construct a self separate from the societal images of him, is that Gawain possesses a strong internal sense of self to begin with and McCoy has to build one.

The heroes of science fiction and fantasy and medieval romance literature may not always be sure of who they are, but they are not usually willing to accept blithely the pronouncement of identity made by others. Lancelot has no illusions about his own physical strength, bravery or valor; nor does he lie to himself about his moral purity. He knows he is among the fallen because of his love for Guinevere. When the Grail is refused him, he laments but he never claims a mistake has been made. Similarly, *Star Wars'* Luke Skywalker knows, long before anyone else tells him, that wearing the clothes and carrying the light saber may make you look like a Jedi knight, but they do not make you one.

Individuality is extremely important to romance literature. These works are not about what the average human can do, the human who is but one of millions. The works are about what one person can do, one who pushes beyond what he thought was possible, who discovers the good and accepts the bad in himself. Often, as in the case of Luke Skywalker, it is only through the confrontation with one's own weaknesses that one can move on to gain the power or insight needed to complete the task at hand. It is by being a person, a whole distinct person that one is able to succeed. Some of the novels in science fiction and fantasy's humorous vein are based on this very idea — the hero is missing some crucial part or quality and therefore success is never a certainty.

Thus far, the term "hero" has been taken to mean the protagonist or first actor in the drama or story. Jungian psychology, however, defines the hero in a slightly different way, a way that is relevant to the romance mode because of the mode's affinity to dreams and the archetypal. Joseph L. Henderson, a Jungian psychologist, describes the hero's story as follows: "his miraculous but humble birth, his early proof of superhuman strength, his rapid rise to prominence or power, his triumphant struggle with the forces of evil, his fallibility to the sin of pride (*hybris*), and his fall through betrayal or a 'heroic' sacrifice that ends in his death" (*Man & His Symbols*, 101). Often there is a mentor or guardian associated with the hero (101), not unlike the helper V. Propp describes as a standard folktale component in his *Morphology of the Folktale*.

As the self explores the individual's strengths and weaknesses in order to create a cohesive, integrated personality, so the science fiction and fantasy or medieval romance hero is led through a series of tests that determine his ultimate strength and the integrity of his society. The hero is often unaware of his or her own heroic abilities at the start of the story and grows into this knowledge. Others may believe the hero capable of the task that has fallen to him, as Gandalf believes in Frodo, but testing permits the hero to prove his worth to the skeptics and to himself.

As Henderson explains, the hero can be seen through four faces which represent the four stages of growth: the Trickster, the Hare, the Red Horn and the Twin. The first is an infantile stage in which physical gratification dominates the person or personality (103–4). At the end of each stage, the person is moving closer to social integration. A literary example of a character at this stage, borrowed from mythology rather than romance, would be the Norse god Loki. While science fiction and fantasy works and medieval romances rarely depict a hero who remains at this stage throughout the work in which he or she appears, sometimes the story begins as this stage is being left behind, underscoring the fact that the hero is progressing toward a more mature self in the work.

When we first meet Frodo Baggins he is participating in a huge banquet being held to celebrate his uncle Bilbo Baggins eleventy-first birthday. Frodo has inherited his uncle's property, including an impressive wine cellar, and has had seventeen years to settle into the creature comforts of his new life, when duty—in the form of a wizard named Gandalf and a ring with evil powers—tears him from this cozy life and thrusts him out into the world. A similar thing happens in *Foundation*, but on a galaxy-wide scale. The galactic empire has become so materialistic and desirous of its own creature comforts that it has collectively forgotten how to think original thoughts; only a small group has been pushed out of the "nest" (actually two small groups as we discover in subsequent volumes) and forced to eschew physical comforts and learn to think for itself.

The knight, too, must leave the world of comfort, the castle and all it holds, in order to find the adventure that will make him a true knight. Tale after tale tells of knights sleeping out in the forest or taking refuge in a hermit's hut for the night. In *Sir Gawain and the Green Knight*, Gawain first encounters the Green Knight at the end of a Christmas feast that has been in progress for "full fifteen days,/ with all meats and all mirth that men could devise" (Tolkien, *Sir Gawain* 20). Gawain has to leave this world of privilege and luxury in order to embark on his adventure. He departs at the beginning of November, after a feast held in his honor, and enters a drastically different world, a world where he has to suffer severe privation during his month plus search for the Green Knight's abode: "Well-nigh slain by the sleet he slept ironclad/ more nights than enow in the naked rocks" (41).

In the Hare stage, we see the nascent social being. Here, the hero is an agent of transition. He is not yet a mature adult character, but he has transcended the purely physical needs of the Trickster and is creating social structures (Henderson 104–5). Alvin, the hero of Arthur C. Clarke's *The City and the Stars*, is such a character. He manifests a number of the general hero characteristics—unnatural circumstances surrounding his birth, early evidence of his unique abilities, and the separation from the crowd that those unique abilities cause—but he exemplifies the Hare stage of the hero's development as well because his primary goal in *The City and the Stars* is to rejoin the fragments of a fractured civilization into one society. When he discovers that there is a civilization living outside of the walls of the city which he had hitherto believed to be the extent of life on his planet, he wants to bring together the civilization he finds outside the city with the one he left inside. He is clever enough to find a way to exert his will even though the forces of both sides are against his plan and seek to prevent the contact.

A number of medieval romances introduce the hero to the story when he is at the Hare stage. Many times such stories begin when a young man who has been shielded from any knowledge of knighthood sees a knight for the first time and is overcome with a desire to become a knight. This is the premise of *Parzival* and of *Sir Libeaus Desconus*. In each case, the young man rejects the idyllic but infantile world of the mother and goes off to find his place in the adult/male world.

At the Red Horn stage the hero has reached a level of maturity and social awareness but still has to pass one or more tests to prove himself. The mentor often joins the story at this point. This stage seems to be the one upon which the preponderance of romance literature, new and old, dwells. The hero sets out on a quest which, whatever its stated purpose and role in the narrative, is at its core a test of self-worth. The ability of the hero to overcome obstacles, achieve his goal, and either return to his society — for the betterment of all — or die for his society — a necessary sacrifice — determines his value as a hero and as a person.

In Ursula LeGuin's science fiction novel *Rocannon's World*, the hero, Rocannon, is tested — several times. He is tested for bravery when he has to join in an aerial fight on flying tigers (the striped, fanged variety) using primitive weapons unfamiliar to him, for endurance when he is captured and put in the fire by a group of native rebels, and commitment when his friend is killed. Rocannon would gladly give his own life to save the world he is on. He has little to lose; he is stranded on the world with none of his peers, no way to get home, and no possibility of rescue for at least eight years. What he is reluctant to relinquish is the life of his companion and friend, which of course makes the friend's life the price of success. His friend Mohein is the typical brawny barbarian swordsman type, but in this work he fills the role of companion and sacrifice rather than hero. In fact, Mohein and the Fian, the *Rocannon's World*'s version of the little people, serve as Rocannon's mentors.

The final stage, the Twin, is the one at which man must come to grips with the shadow side of himself and accept that both the black and white, male and female parts of his personality are necessary to make him a whole being. At this stage, hubris can put the hero in the position of needing to offer himself as a sacrifice in the flesh or symbolically. (106). Ender Wiggins, from *Ender's Game*, has to accept the killer, male part of himself that acted as commander of the wargames which destroyed the alien lifeforms he had come to understand. At the same time, he fosters the female nurturing side of himself by taking on the responsibility for reestablishing the lifeform on another planet. This is but one example of the fusion of disparate parts of the self that can be found in science fiction and fantasy.

When the individual has successfully progressed through all of these stages, he reaches a point of unity and wholeness at which it is no longer needful for him to go fight dragons or other foes. At this point, most romance works end. The personality has been melded together, no further work is needed. As Henderson puts it, when the hero is victorious in his battle with the dragons of his own trickster side and parental limitations, "we see the full hero image emerging as a kind of ego strength ... that has no further need to overcome the monsters and the giants" (119).

Similar to this testing by combat or strength is the initiation ritual, often also a test of strength, but at other times a test of cleverness or endurance. This is differentiated from the hero myth by the ultimate outcome. The hero will nearly always achieve his goal, even if the achievement of same is followed by death. The initiation ritual asks the applicant to offer up voluntarily his position in life, his sanity, and possibly even his life with no guarantee that his efforts will result in a successful outcome. The only hope held out to the initiate is the hope of rebirth if his death is demanded. The hero myth is focused on the result, the initiation rite on the attempt (124).

The other option for ego unity is to turn away from social integration toward transcendence. This is a step toward maturity as man attempts to rise above societally limiting patterns of behaviors and existence to something higher (146). Symbols of this transcendence tend to be birds and other emblems of flight, including the modern day equivalents, planes, spaceships, and rockets (156).

The explanation for why science fiction and fantasy novels and medieval romances focus on the individual may lie in this Jungian connection. If works in the romance mode are symbolic representations of the ego striving toward and achieving integration and totality, then the works are presenting the process of individuation which by definition can only deal with one person's story at a time: "It is, moreover, useless to cast furtive glances at the way someone else is developing, because each of us has a unique task of self-realization" (von Franz, *Man & His Symbols*, 167). This is not to say that there is no similarity between experiences, because human problems are human problems, but each person has to find the right ways to surmount his or her own barriers to wholeness. Nonetheless, reading works that depict another's process of individuation may be psychologically beneficial because although our answers are not someone else's answers, anyone's story may help shed light on our own.

The romance hero presents the reader with a series of paradoxes. He is endowed with special abilities that allow him to transcend his world to some degree. Yet, at the same time, he is a man like any other man. His "gifts" may set him apart from birth and put him on the hero's path described by Henderson, or they may remain latent in his character until some need calls them forth. He is a unique individual, and he is Everyman. He is expected to face every challenge and strive for success, and yet ultimately success may mean that he must fail or die in order to win. Confusing as all of this may seem, it is true to the human psyche of which the hero is the archetypal image. His struggle is the human struggle. His victory is our victory, and in his refusal to admit defeat and lay down his sword, no matter how bleak his prospects, is our hope.

6

Lights, Camera, Action

While character, particularly of the hero, is important in science fiction, fantasy, and medieval romance literature, it is nearly always subordinated to plot. Every work of literature must include some degree of characterization and plot development in order to be considered good literature, but the balance between those elements of literature shifts from book to book and from type of literature to type of literature. In romance literature, because the hero has to be seen in relation to his world as well as his fellow beings, it is essential that he be seen interacting with those beings and that world. His success or failure depends on his doing something. As Aristotle argued, in the discussion of tragedy in his *Poetics*, "character determines men's qualities, but it is by their actions that they are happy or the reverse" (27). It is also by the hero's actions that we know ourselves to be reading a romance.

Looking at several works in detail will reveal some of the characteristics of how plot is utilized in romance, whether medieval or modern. A variety of works will be mentioned briefly, but the emphasis will fall upon Malory's *Le Morte D'Arthur*, Arthur C. Clarke's *Earthlight*, and the last book of Guy Gavriel Kay's Fionavar Tapestry, *The Darkest Road*. In these works and others of their types, character is usually subordinated to plot. Because of that, one of the most important aspects of the hero is his or her ability not only to take but, often, to initiate action. Indecisiveness and inaction are undesirable and often dangerous qualities in the hero. These are not ordinary worlds the characters are inhabiting but worlds in which the influence of the supernatural or miraculous is being exerted and that influence often has an effect on the action or the need for action.

In any medieval romance, it is not who the hero is as much as what he does that matters. In *Le Morte D'Arthur*, for example, Arthur is the king; he holds the highest position in his society, but the emphasis in the tales is on the other knights, particularly Lancelot and Gawain, because as knights they are able to go out into their world and act; Arthur is often forced to remain at Camelot, governing. Even Gawain, however, is not really a personality as much as an image in the sense medieval theologians argued man was an image of God, an imprecise reflection of something else. In some tales, such as "The Siege of Benwick" in *Le Morte D'Arthur*, Gawain has characteristics of the ancient Celtic sun-god, his strength waxing and waning with the rising and setting sun. In other tales such as *Sir Gawain and the Green Knight*, Gawain, not Lancelot, is the exemplar of chivalrous behavior in Arthur's court. In that tale, Gawain is punished for failing at chivalry when, believing it will save his life, he keeps the magical green girdle to himself when he should have handed it over to his host. Other depictions of Gawain are far from virtuous. In "The Loathly Lady," Gawain rapes a young girl and as punishment is sent out on a quest to learn what women really want or return and be put to death at the end of a year. All of these portrayals are Gawain, but all provide different images of him. He is a character being used to make a point, but the exigencies of the plot determine the way Gawain is presented in any particular tale. This is not to say characterization is nonexistent or poorly done, as Gawain at his most chivalrous would still not be mistaken for Lancelot, rather plot is given the preeminent place.

Turning to science fiction, we have Clarke's *Earthlight*, in which we are introduced to Bertram Sadler, the narrator, who has been recruited as a reluctant spy and sent to the science colony on the moon to discover who has been leaking important secrets to the planet colonies. The action does not center around Sadler's search for the spy, however, but around the war that looms over the divided human race, the spectacular battle that occurs between Earth and the planet colonies, and the aftermath of that battle. The identity of the man for whom the spy was searching is not revealed until the final five pages of the novel. Thirty years after the fact, Sadler visits Professor Robert Molton to confirm, solely for Sadler's own personal satisfaction, the theory that Molton may have been the leak.

The important information being provided at this point in the novel is not that Molton was the leak, but that he leaked the information in order to maintain the balance of power between the planet colonies and Earth in order to force the two governments to seek peace rather than continue to escalate hostilities. Molton's reflections end the novel:

> Professor Molton smiled as he watched them [a group of children] racing toward their bright untroubled future — the future he had helped to make. He had many consolations, and that was the greatest of them. Never again, as far ahead as imagination could roam, would the human race be divided against itself [155].

This is not an isolated example. Any of Asimov's Foundation books would provide a sense that character is important, but primarily important because the characters make the plot unfold. In fact, according to the theory of psychohistory explained in the Foundation series, when a hero is required, the society that needs him will spawn him and he will take the action necessary to push that society in the correct direction.

James Gunn, critic and writer of science fiction, emphasizes the differing approach to plot development as a fundamental characteristic distinguishing mainstream fiction from science fiction and fantasy. Gunn's contention is that mainstream fiction is not only set in the present, but frozen in the present, seeing humankind as the end result of an evolutionary process. The focus is on people's interactions themselves not what those interactions can bring about.

> Mainstream fiction's preoccupation with the present reflects an apparent desire to freeze reality in its current state, and a belief that everything that has happened or is likely to happen is of little importance except as it reflects on the present.... To put it another way, the concentration by mainstream fiction on social interactions seems to incorporate the conviction that the most important, if not the only important, aspect of existence is the ways in which people relate to each other [par. 16].

Gunn feels that science fiction, on the other hand, concentrates on humankind's adaptability, presenting humans as still evolving rather than at an evolutionary plateau, and on humankind's ability to "choose a course other than that instilled by its environment" (par. 9).

Medieval romance seems to conform to Gunn's assessment of science fiction rather than his depiction of mainstream fiction. Numerous times in a romance, characters are confronted with a choice between following the dictates of their environment or stepping up to a higher "evolutionary plateau" by acting in accordance with God's laws rather than man's. This can be seen in Joseph Bédier's retelling of *The Romance of Tristan and Iseult*, which the author himself attributes to earlier versions by Béroul, Thomas of Built (the Anglo-Saxon poet), Eilhart von Oberg and Gottfried von Strassburg. In this version, when King Mark is informed of the whereabouts of the two lovers, Tristan and Iseult, he sets out planning to kill them. He finds the two asleep, fully clothed, with a sword lying between them. Tristan and Iseult have been lovers but on this occasion resisted their carnal impulses, and the result is that King Mark spares them.

> Does not all the world know that a naked sword separating two bodies is the proof and the guardian of chastity? If they loved each other with mad love, would they lie here so purely? No, I will not slay, for this would be treason and wrong: and if I wakened this sleeper and one of us twain were killed, men would speak long of it and to our dishonour [75–6].

King Mark then exchanges Tristan's sword for his own and a ring Iseult is wearing for one she gave to him so they will know he found them and spared them. Arguably, King Mark is acting according to his environmental programming when he spares the lovers to keep himself from being dishonoured, but in the context of the larger story, his exacting revenge would most likely not have been seen as dishonorable by anyone other than himself. He is choosing to be better than the average person, and, whatever his rationalization, it is his own choice.

When the lovers awake and find the evidence that King Mark has found them and spared them, they, too, are prompted to take a nobler course of action. Tristan petitions King Mark to receive Iseult back into his court without dishonor, and Tristan agrees to leave the region to dispel suspicion about his relationship with Queen Iseult. Unfortunately, Tristan is unable to maintain this higher level of behavior and backslides, causing additional heartache before he is forced to flee.

Fortunately for the Christians among humankind, they are judged not just by their success in overcoming their human frailty but also by the sincerity of their efforts to do so. Therefore, Lancelot is vouchsafed a vision of the Grail even though he may never attain it. To Christ only was given the ability to resist the Devil's temptations without a stumble or second thought.

Operating in the belief that we can choose to be other than we are,

Gunn argues science fiction presents existence as "a search for humanity's origins, its purpose, and its ultimate fate" (par. 17). A look at the preceding description of science fiction's aims— a search for origin, purpose, and fate — reveals the eternal questions of religion and philosophy. In that context, it becomes easy to see why there are so many gods in science fiction works, whether human gods, technological gods, or alien gods. Humankind is searching for answers, and science fiction and fantasy are two of the modern search routes, as mysticism and holy crusading were two search routes for medieval man.

Because of the importance of the search and of the element of change in science fiction, "plot remains at the heart of science fiction" (Gunn, par. 19), as it does in medieval romance and fantasy: in a romance novel, plot means action. The action may be as simple as riding off on a charger or a rocketsled to make a name for oneself or as complex as going back in time to alter one essential event to make the future come out a particular way. Only infrequently are these contemplative novels. In the medieval romance novel, even the religious figures take the appellation "warrior for Christ" literally. The priests may be seen sitting in a chapel praying for the souls of the knights who are going into battle, but just as often they are out slaying pagans. In *Song of Roland*, Archbishop Turpin blesses the French before the battle, absolves their sins, and assures them that "If you should die, blest martyrdom's your guerdon;/ You'll sit on high in Paradise eternal" (95). Six stanzas later, Turpin is plunging his lance into Corsablis of Barbary.

If there is a contemplative aspect to the work, it tends to come near the end the work and the end of the hero's life. Guy of Warwick is not a cleric, but he ends his adventures fighting for God. Guy retires to a hermitage at the end of the story but not until he has proven himself the best of the best in all categories—jousting, battle, monster killing, and defending the faith. Lancelot, too, follows this path. He rises to the peak of his knightly prowess, takes his love for Guinevere as far as he can (and perhaps a bit beyond), seeks and is denied the Grail. Then, at the end, when Arthur is dead, the Round Table is broken, and Guinevere has joined a convent, he turns to the contemplative life. When he sees Guinevere for the last time, he tells her:

> God defend but I should forsake the world as ye have done. For in the quest of the Sangreal I had forsaken the vanities of the world had not your lord been. And if I had done so at that time, with my heart, will, and thought, I had passed all the knights that were in the Sangreal

except Sir Galahad my son. And therefore lady, sithen ye have taken you to perfection, I must needs take me to perfection, of right [Caxton, *Le Morte* 529].

Shortly thereafter, Lancelot joins the Bishop of Canterbury and serves God "day and night with prayers and fastings" (530). Some years later he is made a priest. But the life of prayer is not a life of action, and the medieval romance is a literature of action. Lancelot becomes a priest and within three short chapters, in a book containing over 530 chapters, the story ends.

The two knights referred to above are following an order that is seen reflected some years later in a 1591 hymn by Giovanni Pierluigi da Palestrina:

> The strife is o'er, the battle done;
> The victory of life is won;
> The song of triumph has begun.
> Alleluia [*The Hymnbook*, 182].

That these words refer to Christ's passion would only have rendered the knight's actions more appropriate in a world that revered the *imitatio Christi*. No matter that the knight's battles were with sword and shield and Christ's battle was symbolic, the order was action first, introspection second, if at all. The typical knight rode off into his adventure and continued from adventure to adventure until the storyteller got tired or the story ended. The important thing was the adventure and what it meant.

According to Frye, "[t]he essential element of plot in romance is adventure.... At its most naive it is an endless form in which a central character who never develops or ages goes through one adventure after another..." (*Anatomy* 186). The romance hero is not a hero who sits on a rock and dictates 300 pages of personal reflections. He is a hero who does things. Sometimes the doing itself is the essential factor in the story. Sitting by indecisively is the way to bring disaster down upon yourself. If a world is waiting for you, it will come find you whether you are ready for it or not.

In Guy Gavriel Kay's Fionavar Tapestry Trilogy, the characters are drawn through from one reality to an alternate reality because their presence is needed in the alternate world. This idea is not unique. Often a fantasy or science fiction story will involve the passage from one world or reality to another where the hero or heroes find themselves forced to take an active part in the happenings of the new world or perish. Typically, the person or persons thus transported are able to tap underused or unknown reservoirs in themselves that allow them to make a serious attempt at fulfilling their expected role and, sometimes, to succeed. When the reluctant hero tries to flee his responsibility to the new world in which he has been unceremoniously deposited, the work becomes a humorous story, a parody of the genre of which it remains a part. The title of Simon Hawke's *The Reluctant Sorcerer* speaks for itself.

Reluctant would as accurately describe Gawain's initial involvement in the adventure of the Green Knight. In *Sir Gawain and the Green Knight*, Gawain is the hero, in part because he does recognize the need for action when most of his fellow knights do not. After issuing the challenge of his "Christmas game," "to strike a strong [axe] blow in return for another," the Green Knight ridicules the knights of King Arthur's court for their inaction (Stone 31).

> "What, is this Arthur's house, the honour of which
> Is bruited abroad so abundantly?
> Has your pride disappeared? Your prowess gone?
> Your victories, your valour, your vaunts, where are they?
> The revel and renown of the Round Table
> Is now overwhelmed by a word from one man's voice,
> For all flinch for fear from a fight not begun!" [32].

Arthur offers the first response to the Green Knight's challenge, but Gawain steps up to remind the king that it is the knights' responsibility to protect him, and the young knight seeks the honor of standing in Arthur's stead. When it comes time for Gawain to seek out the Green Knight and face the reciprocal blow, he is not eager to go, but he recalls that knight's role is one of action, and he gears himself up for the encounter, saying to the other knights, "Whether fate be foul or fair,/ Why falter I or fear?/ What should man do but dare?" (Stone 42). Inaction gains one nothing; success can only follow action.

Science fiction has been referred to many times as a literature of ideas. As science fiction writer Samuel Delaney said in a *New York Times* article on the paucity of intellectual science fiction movies, "They [Hollywood producers and writers] always say they have a good idea for a story, but in science fiction what you need is a good story for an idea, a story that will dramatize the idea" (Beale, par. 6). Writers and critics have struggled to determine whether the label is a positive or negative one. To some critics calling science fiction a literature of ideas is a harsh criticism because it suggests that literary concerns are ignored in the interest of getting the point across to the reader. While some less talented writers in the genre have taken refuge behind the smokescreen that their work is significant because it is "profound," most capable writers are adept enough to incorporate both ideas and literary quality into their work. Other critics feel "literature of ideas" is a useful and positive label because it conveys the multivalent nature of the writing.

Science fiction and fantasy novels are like philosophy in action. Have an idea for how the world could be or should be? Write it down as you think it should be, and you have a philosophical treatise. Put it into practice and create a world where it can work, and you have probably written a science fiction or fantasy novel. Even in novels that are clearly didactic or philosophical, such as Suzette Elgin's paired novels, *Native Tongue* and *Judas Rose*, the characters are not sitting around discussing the deficiencies of their society; they are actively attempting to alter the social fabric. The two novels present a society which is suffering a severe inferiority complex because all of the aliens with whom the world comes into contact are superior to human beings. The society suppresses women and they appear to accept the status quo while covertly subverting the dominant social mode by creating and spreading a "woman's" language among themselves and to the aliens. The action is subtle but it is, literally, world-changing.

In fantasy, too, the need to act and determine one's own fate is key. One of the most powerful moments in Kay's Fionavar Tapestry series comes near the end of the last book, *The Darkest Road*, when King Arthur, who has been trapped in a cycle of penance which forces him to relive the massacre of the innocents he decreed in an effort to kill Mordred as a baby, is told that he has the choice to break the cycle.

> And Arthur said, in that silver light, in that silence, his voice an instrument of bone-deep self-condemnation: "Twiceborn, how could it ever change? I had the children slain."
> "And have paid full, fullest price," Paul replied without hesitation [393].

He had not considered the possibility until one of the outsiders suggested it, but once aware of the choice, Arthur realized the truth of Paul's earlier comment on fate: "We are not slaves to the Loom, not bound forever to our fate. Not even you, my lord Arthur" (393).

Arthur steps into a waiting boat, breaking the cycle and changing his own future and with his Guinevere's and Lancelot's because his action opens the way for the miracle to extend to them as well. Guinevere joins her lord in the boat, and they both turn to look at Lancelot. Arthur holds out his hand and calls Lancelot to come with them.

> For a moment, Lancelot did not move. Then something long held back, so long denied, blazed in his eyes brighter than any star. He stepped forward. He took Arthur's hand, and then Guinevere's, and they drew him aboard. And so the three of them stood there together, the grief of the long tale healed and made whole at last [397].

Arthur has altered not only his own and his friends' lives but also the future of his world, by simply choosing his own fate rather than acting in the way he thought had been laid out for him.

Like the folktale or the medieval romance, the success of a science fiction or fantasy novel may depend heavily on the ability of the story-teller to spin a captivating yarn. The primacy of plot calls for quality storytelling. There is, after all, only one story ever told in any fantasy novel (and arguably any science fiction novel), the story of the fight between good and evil. It is *how* the story is told that determines the quality of the work. The same idea developed by two different writers will come across differently, even to the same audience. The first book of Terry Brooks' Shannara series, *Sword of Shannara*, struck some read-ers as too derivative of Tolkien's Lord of the Rings, as science fiction author and critic Frank Herbert points out in his review: "Brooks spends about half of this book trying on J. R. R. Tolkien's style and subject mat-ter. The debt to Tolkien is so obvious you can anticipate many of the developments" (par. 2). According to Herbert, those imitative sections of the book lack substance. Herbert does note, however, that during the course of the book Brooks learns the very lesson mentioned above about the quality of the telling and by the end, when Brooks discovers his own style, the writing improves (par. 5).

A sample from the second book of the Shannara series shows that while Brooks' style has become more completely his own, he has still not succeeded in finding one which successfully blends with his subject mat-ter. Consider the following two passages, one written by Brooks and one written by Tolkien. Both passages describe how a sacred elven tree played a part in the history of the respective novel's people. Tolkien's telling is powerful and potent; Brooks' telling is awkward and flat, failing to cre-ate the sense of history and dignity Tolkien achieves.

Tolkien's writing sounds rich and mystical. The phrasing is archaic, befitting the subject matter, and the wording is spare but evokes a sense of power. The selection resonates with cadences from the Bible and other ancient writings.

> There in the courts of the King grew a white tree, from the seed of that tree which Isildur brought over the deep waters, and the seed of that tree before came from Eressëa, and before that out of the Uttermost West in the Day before days when the world was young.
> But in the wearing of the swift years of Middle-earth the line of Meneldil son of Anárion failed, and the Tree withered, and the blood of the Númenóreans became mingled with that of lesser men. Then the watch upon the walls of Mordor slept, and dark things crept back to Gorgoroth [*Fellowship* 321].

The second passage, from Terry Brooks' *The Elfstones of Shannara*, is more straightforward and modern in structure, and it uses less descriptive wording. The passage does not evoke the majesty and depth that Tolkien's does. Only at the very end of this passage do we hear faint echoes of the authority of the ancient bard recounting legend.

> But the story of the Ellcrys and the Forbidding wasn't just a story — it was the foundation of everything that was truly Elven, the most important event in the history of his people.
> It had all taken place long ago, before the birth of the new world. There had been a great war between good and evil — a war that the Elves had finally won by creating the Ellcrys and a Forbidding that had banished the evil Demons into a timeless dark. And so long as the Ellcrys was kept well, so long would the evil be locked from the land [3].

Brooks has his characters claim that this event is tremendously important, but then glosses the story in a matter of lines. No names or places or dates are given in the great war between good and evil; the description of the ancient war which prompted the action described in the passage is so non-specific that it could be lifted from Brooks' novel and placed in many other fantasy novels. If the subject matter were less mythical or magical, this stripped down modern version might be fine, but as a recounting of a culture's mythology, the tale is better told in Tolkien's style. Brooks' later works are better as his style has evolved. In addition, his style was always a more appropriate fit for the humorous tales he wrote, such as *Magic Kingdom, For Sale — Sold*.

The manner in which the story was told was all important in the

Middle Ages as well. The love triangle at the heart of the Arthurian cycle was not new when Malory compiled *Le Morte D'Arthur*, but his presentation captured the human imagination and caused the story to endure. His version is the one most familiar to modern readers, many of whom first discover the works he utilized to create his compilation through reading *Le Morte D'Arthur*. The Arthurian tale has been reworked into countless modern versions, but while the language and structure of the retellings may be more accessible to 20th and 21st century readers, Malory's version remains the most powerful.

One of the characteristics of the best tellings is the *truth* of the story. Truth does not refer here to the accuracy with which the author captures the facts and features of the physical world in which we live, but the accuracy with which the author captures the essence of the world he or she has created, an essence that often includes psychological or social elements that are quite human, no matter what manner of creature or world is portrayed.

The romance mode, as explained by Frye, is characterized by interaction between the real and the supernatural. The hero is expected to encounter things like magic swords and dragons and two-headed monsters as a matter of course. Such is the nature of the romance world, according to Frye: "each mode of literature develops its own existential projection.... Romance peoples the world with fantastic, normally invisible personalities or powers: angels, demons, fairies, ghosts, enchanted animals, elemental spirits like those in *The Tempest* and *Comus*" (*Anatomy* 64). Science fiction, populated with extraterrestrials, androids, and experimental humans, fits right in, as does fantasy with its myriad of magical creatures from elves and witches to hobbits and ghatti.

These characters are not fantastic simply for novelty's sake. One of the questions many science fiction and fantasy books try to answer is how the average human would react to meeting the other residents of the galaxy. More accurately, the books typically concern themselves with the response of the better than average human, the hero. The average human would probably call the police or the FBI and be thrilled that the unusual being went away never to be seen again. The hero, on the other hand, is expected to make contact with the unusual being and either kill it or establish some sort of rapport with it.

The question of how we would react to beings unlike ourselves is not a new one. It is a logical next step from the medieval knight who had to progress from fighting other humans to fighting supernatural beings like dragons, the Green Knight, or Amorant, the giant Ethiopian whom Guy of Warwick defeats. To be the best, the knight had to prove he was able to conquer things beyond the human realm because they were embodiments of evil and his triumph over them signaled the knight's favor in the sight of God. In the medieval romance, the hero's options were more limited; he interacted with the being as he interacted with any challenge, he fought it. If God was on his side, he emerged victorious; if not, he died. What he did not do was refuse to act.

Action dominates the medieval romance, science fiction, and fantasy. Rather than languish in the stasis of the present, these works try to show that change, adaptation, evolution, or whatever else the action may be called is essential to our own and society's growth toward perfection. As Marion Zimmer Bradley has one of her characters say in *City of Sorcery*, "But no one is perfect. Perfectable [sic], maybe, in the fullness of time. Not perfect" (353). "Perfect" is an existing condition, the present, the unchanging, the utopian. "Perfectable" is a goal, and reaching a goal requires action, the decisive, independent action of the hero, the individual. The goal may not be achieved, as Lancelot learns to his sorrow when he is denied the Grail, but only one who strives has any chance of success. Striving is action, and action is plot. Therefore, to achieve its own goal of providing humankind with the hope of a better future, romance literature tends to be plot driven, not character based.

7

Archetypes, or Why Does
This Seem Familiar?

Before exploring other archetypal images used in romance literature, the importance of those images and their function in the literature under consideration needs to be addressed. Modern usage has allowed the distinction between archetype and archetypal image to become unclear. The distinction is important, however, and worth preserving. The universal patterns by which humans respond to certain stimuli — mother, death, the need for knowledge, the need to explain our presence in the universe — these are archetypes. Archetypal images, on the other hand, are the means of expression humans devise to try to capture the essence of these fundamentally inexplicable and irreducable instinctive reactions— the Earth Goddess, the grim reaper, the wise owl, the Great Chain of Being — these are archetypal images.

Jolande Jacobi explains the archetype as a "disposition" to arrange or represent stimulus in a particular way; "archetypes are not inherited representations, but inherited *possibilities* of representations" (52). It may be inferred that this is Jung's theory, not just Jacobi's, since Jacobi's explication of Jung's work in the former's book *Complex/Archetype/Symbol in the Psychology of C. G. Jung* bears a foreword by Jung himself stating that Jacobi has clearly and accurately represented Jung's theory of archetypes. The archetype is not a manifestation of physical reality, but rather, as Jung puts it, "how the psyche experiences the physical fact"

(*Archetypes* 154). The power of this "collective psychic substratum" is such that "the psyche often behaves so autocratically that it denies tangible reality or makes statements that fly in the face of it" (155, 154). This is often seen in stories in which the fantastic elements seem inherently right and real even though they are a physical impossibility — Peter Pan flying, for instance, or Alice being able to fall down a rabbit hole into Wonderland. Or *The Odyssey*, of which Winston Weathers says in *The Archetype and The Psyche*, "even with all its fantasies, it is tremendously real and believable" (17). Archetypes are so deeply imbedded in our minds that until the need arises to tap them, they remain in our subconscious and we are blithely unaware of their existence.

The archetypes remain constant, but the symbols used in the attempt to express them are influenced by the individual's personality and external world in which he or she lives (74). The mother archetype may find expression in an Earth Goddess, a bowl, the Virgin Mary, the sea, a dragon, a fertility rite, a witch, or a garden. The association of each of these images with the mother archetype is a human effort to capture, even fleetingly, the essence of what "mother" is, but the archetype at the core of all of these symbols does not change in spite of the apparently contradictory nature of the symbolic representations.

Because archetypes are, as Jung describes them, "manifestations of processes in the collective unconscious" rather than anything that has ever been part of the conscious mind, it is not possible to make connection between a specific physical fact and the archetype (156). Instead, interpretation remains necessary and all that can be arrived at is an "ultimate core of meaning" which "may be circumscribed, but not described" (*Archetypes* 156). As a consequence, any image/interpretation that captures the essence of the archetype rings true.

> every interpretation that comes anywhere near the hidden sense (or, from the point of view of the scientific intellect, nonsense, which comes to the same thing) has always, right from the beginning, laid claim not only to absolute truth and validity, but to instant reverence and religious devotion. Archetypes were, and still are, living psychic forces that demand to be taken seriously, and they have a strange way of making sure of their effect [156].

The archetypes persist, despite modern man's efforts to pretend they are unneeded. Their power can be illustrated quickly by reference to several popular science fiction films. Luke Skywalker, the young man aspiring to Jedi-hero status in the Star Wars movies, elicits a gut level sympathetic response from the audience at the same time some of the audience's intellects may be rejecting the whole thing as "hokey." He is the knight going off on the quest; the self in search of identity. E.T. wanting to go home, in the movie *E.T.: The Extra-Terrestrial*, grabs hold of the viewer's psyche at a level so deep he or she may not even realize the link has been forged, but it is there. Few are the viewers who could honestly say they were not rooting for the ugly little creature to get its wish, and NASA be damned. The story builds on the same archetypal desire for home that *The Odyssey* does and, because of E.T.'s childlike qualities, our ingrained tendency to protect our young.

In the healthy individual, according to the Jungian view of the mind, the psyche is involved in the "continual synthesis of something conscious with its unconscious opposite" (Cohen 27). Universal archetypes are lifted from the unconscious as the individual confronts something in his or her life that calls for a personal response that evokes the pattern of that particular archetype. A variety of images may be used to express the archetype, but the archetype retains its inexplicable, primal quality. Which archetypes you draw upon and how you utilize them in the formation of your character, determines who you are. "The process of a known and an unknown yielding a higher understanding, Jung called *individuation*, since it represents the unfolding of a particular personality out of a vast field of possibilities" (27–8).

Romance literature, in which classification science fiction and fantasy may be placed, can help bring the archetypes in the collective unconscious to the attention of the conscious since such literature is filled with archetypal images. Obviously, this lifting of archetypal material from one level of consciousness to another will only apply if the psyche exposed to the literature is open to the message. Nonetheless, the presence of so many archetypal images in romance literature increases the likelihood that an image the psyche is seeking to bridge the gap between conscious and subconscious may be available when needed.

Ironically, the *psychological* mode of artistic creation, as Jung calls it, is not the medium by which this gap is bridged. In these works, the psychological components of the characters and their behavior have already been scrutinized by the author and little room has been left for interpretation by the reader (Jung, *Modern Man* 154). "This material is [...] given an expression which forces the reader to greater clarity and depth of human insight by bringing fully to his consciousness what he ordinarily evades and overlooks or senses only with a feeling of dull discomfort" (155). This explanation corresponds to Gunn's description of mainstream literature as literature locked into the here and now. In both of these views, the literature is preoccupied with exploring why specific characters are the way they are and act the way they act, not the larger issues of why humans act this way and what it means for the world.

Most mainstream fiction would fall into this category; these are the stories of "love, the environment, the family, crime and society" (156). In such a story, "[e]verything that it embraces— the experience as well as its artistic expression — belongs to the realm of the understandable" (156). Scant interpretation of the psychological implications is needed; everything is spelled out for the reader. Mainstream fiction as described here would encompass everything from *Madame Bovary* to the latest Danielle Steel novel, all of which concentrate on revealing our psychological motivations and responses to us rather than letting us discover them for ourselves in our reactions to what we have read. While not all such works wrap the issues up in neat little packages by the last page, the psychological parameters are usually clearly defined and we are more often left to judge at the end rather than to interpret. Kate Chopin's *Awakening*, for example, gives us all the psychological information we need to understand Edna Pontellier's plight. The ending suggests that she commits suicide, but whether or not she did and whether or not her action was justified are up to the reader to decide based on the evidence provided.

Jung places greater value on what he calls *visionary* novels, novels in which fundamental human experiences are tapped and shaped and left to the individual to interpret. These visionary works are stories that break the bonds of everyday human experience.

> The experience that furnishes the material for artistic expression is no longer familiar. It is a strange something that derives its existence from the hinterland of man's mind — that suggests the abyss of time separating us from pre-human ages, or evokes a super-human world of contrasting light and dark. [...] It arises from the primordial depths; it is foreign and cold, many-sided, demonic and grotesque. [...] But the primordial experiences rend from top to bottom the curtain upon which is painted the picture of an ordered world, and allow a glimpse into the unfathomed abyss of what has not yet become. Is it a vision of other worlds, or of the obscuration of the spirit, or of the beginning of things before the age of man, or of the unborn generations of the future? [...] [*Modern Man* 156–7].

Jung does not specify science fiction and fantasy in this description of visionary literature, although he might have since *Modern Man in Search of a Soul* was published in 1933 when science fiction was gaining in popularity. The emphasis on the unknown, other worlds, and the future, however, opens the way to a strong connection to science fiction and fantasy, even as the mention of the spiritual and the demonic combined with the image of a world split into light and dark conjures up the world of the medieval romance. The strength of such intuitive links is increased by considering several of the works that Jung did specifically cite as visionary literature: Dante's writings, Wagner's "Der Ring des Nibelung" [derived from the medieval German *The Song of the Nibelungs*], and Rider Haggard's *She* fantasy novels (157).

The writer, or for Jung, artist, who creates visionary literature is responding to imbalances in the society around him by countering them with the appropriate archetypal images necessary to restore equilibrium. The "seeds" of each archetype exist at all times in every human, but they "do not appear in the dreams of individuals or in works of art until they are called into being by the waywardness of the general outlook" (171). By expressing the balancing archetypes in his work, the writer/artist answers "the spiritual need of the society in which he lives" (171). Perhaps this is why in our more spiritually insecure age, many of the science fiction and fantasy novels have gods or godlike figures, and why these two forms of literature in which there is always a hero and the world is usually divided into good and evil have gained in popular readership in the last three decades when the general public has so few heroes available to them.

Visionary literature, the Jungian category to which many works of medieval romance, science fiction, and fantasy belong, is not concerned with the individual even when it is written about an individual. Exploring the individual experience is a feature of Jung's *psychological* literature. Visionary literature concerns itself with human existence in its entirety: "This is why every great work of art is objective and impersonal, but none the less [sic] profoundly moves us each and all" (172). And, that is why many people are uncomfortable with such literature. Reason, order, and science do not explain away the needs addressed or the forces confronted. The reader must look at humanity unmasked and in so doing risk the chance of seeing himself, which is a fearsome thing for most people. As Jung observed, "This confrontation is the first test of courage on the inner way, a test sufficient to frighten off most people, for the meeting with ourselves belongs to the more unpleasant things that can be avoided..." (*Archetypes* 20).

Jung claims that archetypes and their expression through rites and rituals provide a psychological defense system necessary to help people cope with the world around them: "This was the purpose of rite and dogma; they were dams and walls to keep back the dangers of the unconscious, the 'perils of the soul'" (*Archetypes* 22). When we dispense with confronting these archetypal elements of our psyche on the symbolic level, preferring the logic and order of the "rational" view of the world, we upset our psychological balance. On the individual level, when the psyche cannot follow the natural course of confronting and synthesizing elements of the collective unconscious, mental illness ensues (39–40). On the cultural level, societal illness occurs in the sense that the society loses its soul — "whose loss is always and everywhere, even among the civilized, a moral catastrophe" (154).

Science fiction and fantasy provide an alternate approach to working through the contents of the collective unconscious. Fantasy allows readers to hark back to a time when these archetypal images were projected out onto the world and dealt with directly; often this time period is the medieval one. Beowulf, for example, can confront the fear of the archetypal Great Mother by conquering Grendel's beast mother and later by defeating the dragon, another of her symbols. This is not to say that life was "better" during that time period, but there were fewer layers of psychological armor hindering the individual from confronting his archetypal needs. Modern man has to find psychological equivalents to monsters and dragons because our world no longer accepts such things as even quasi-real entities. Alternatively, the reader is taken to a world in which those archetypes manifest and are battled in person. Science fiction is rooted in those same images but tries to explain them away using science and logic. The method differs, but the literature deals with the same human needs. Contemporary images of the archetypes must conform to the changing world in which they find expression; in so doing, the new interpretation of the archetype is able to preserve the past while acknowledging the primacy of the present (157).

Simon R. Green, author of contemporary fantasy, has taken up this question of what happens when the rational and fantastic compete for human acceptance. Green's book *Beyond the Blue Moon* is written from the point of view that man *can* escape the psychological need for archetypal expression. This stance falls neatly into the behavior of the scientific intellect observed by Jung: The archetype "remains unknown and not to be fitted into a formula. For this reason the scientific intellect is always inclined to put on airs of enlightenment in hope of banishing the spectre once and for all" (*Archetypes* 157).

In his novel, a fantasy set in a quasi-medieval world, Green has the two heroes of the book discuss the fate of their world with the Magus, a wise man/worker of magic (one of the fundamental archetypal images Jung identified and wrote about). Fisher, one of the heroes, asks about Chaos Magic, and the Magus replies that it is simply an "attempt to produce a magic that works like science" (234). He mocks it because it is a "pathetic" attempt to hold onto the old way of doing things by disguising it in the trappings of the new way. In his opinion, science and magic are mutually exclusive and the growth of one way of dealing with the world will cause the demise of the other. As the Magus puts it:

"No, within the next dozen generations or so magic will be gone, and the world will be a safer, duller place. All the myth and wonder of the world will be replaced by gadgets and mechanisms. Clever, but essentially soulless. No dragons, no unicorns..." [234].

Hawk, the other hero, points out that the loss of those positive magical beings will also mean the loss of all the negative magical beings, such as demons. The Magus applauds Hawk's perception and adds that the loss of those evil creatures is a major part of mankind's desire to rationalize his world:

"As man learns to control his world through science, so the greater threats to his existence will be banished. You banished the Demon Prince through the Wild Magic of the Rainbow, but he can still return. He is a Transient Being, one of the never-born, the soulless, the stalkers on the edge of reality, a living personification of an abstract idea. As such, he can never be destroyed, as long as magic exists. Ideas are immortal. But replace magic with science and he cannot return, because this whole plane of existence would be closed to him and his kind. He could not exist here; the scientific laws of the universe would not permit it" [234].

The problem with this logic, according to the Jungian view of humankind, is that man cannot escape his essential nature: "Anyone who succeeds in putting off the mantle of faith can do so only because another lies close to hand. No one can escape the prejudice of being human" (*Archetypes* 63). Nor, Jung adds, can mankind escape the essential nature of the universe, "He [man] ought never to forget that the world exists only because opposing forces are held in equilibrium. So, too, the rational is counterbalanced by the irrational, and what is planned and purposed by what *is*" (94). To dispel the irrational is to create an imbalance that will need to be corrected at some future time.

Since every archetype has its good side and its evil side, both must be present for the world to function and for man to attain and maintain mental health. If the externalized manifestations of evil are banished from society due to the progress of science and other disciplines, then man is forced to internalize those manifestations, or demons, instead. In the medieval world, mankind was able to acknowledge its demons as essentially the evil side of itself. Churches were often decorated with panels depicting both the joys of Heaven and the torments of Hell so people would be constantly reminded that the "Right" was a choice each man had to make within himself. God could only be called upon to aid you if you had already chosen to walk the path of righteousness. Sinners were free to take themselves to Hell if they so chose. This is evident, too, in morality plays such as *Everyman*; no one and nothing can save Everyman except his own deeds.

While the medieval person might have phrased it in terms of God and Satan fighting for control of a man's soul, not the dark and light sides of man fighting for ascendancy, there was, even in medieval times, an awareness that the enemy you must conquer is often yourself. In *Sir Gawain and the Green Knight*, the real challenge is not whether Gawain is man enough to show up on the first day of the next year to expose his neck to the Green Knight's axe. The challenge is whether he can resist the seductive qualities of, first, the lady of the castle and, second, the offer of a means to render himself invulnerable to physical harm, an offer that forces Gawain to violate the agreement he has made with the host.

Even when the enemy is someone other than oneself, it is easy to see that enemy as the dark side of mankind. In *Song of Roland*, the Emir's troops include many fantastic and horrible creatures: giants; men with "huge and hairy polls,/ Upon whose backs, all down the spine in rows,/ As on wild boars, enormous bristles grow;" (lines 3221–23); and "Sons of the desert, a wild and godless clan;/ [...]/ Harder than iron their hide on head and flanks" (lines 3247–49). Even though the enemy might be "misguided" in terms of his religious belief, or even inhuman or evil, he is not powerless. Indeed, he must be as strong and valiant as oneself or defeating him brings no honor upon one. This sentiment is clearly expressed in the same author's assessment of the Emir, regarding whom the French remark, "Were he but Christian, God! what a warrior!" (line 3164).

Modern man does not have the outlet of making his demons real and defeating them, unless he does it symbolically, so those demons become part of him instead. This is one reason for fantasy literature (and other forms of romance literature). It puts the "bad guy" back on the outside where he or she can be dealt with in an appropriate way without one's having to accede consciously to the fact that the bad guy is, in fact, part of oneself.

As Green's depiction of the movement toward science and away from magic in *Beyond the Blue Moon* illustrates, however, logic and rationality are means of mankind freeing itself from its own fears and limitations. When the two heroes confront the Demon Prince, he gloats because he believes he cannot be defeated; like any archetype, he is an idea and can take as many forms as mankind chooses to cast upon him.

> "Strictly speaking we're neither good nor bad[...]. Those are human terms, human limitations. We are archetypes, reflections of what's on man's inner mind. We are the shadows humanity casts. We are the physical manifestations of abstract concepts, forces, fears, and preoccupations. Neuroses and psychoses, given rein to run free and potent in the mortal world. We are the rod you made for your own back" [456–7].

At this juncture, the Magus, who is taking humanity's part, responds that, "Humanity is entering, or creating, the time of the rational mind, and soon he will have no use for such as us anymore" (457).

Green seems to believe that man's rational mind can eradicate the need for archetypes and all of their attendant images. Moreover, he has the Magus equate rejection of the archetypes and magic with mankind's maturation:

> "I have lived a very long time in the world of men, and seen reason slowly replace superstition. I have watched the world become a better place as the wild madness was controlled and put aside. It just got in the way of humanity's maturing.
> "They'll be so much better off without magic, with all its temptations and perversions of hope and ambition" [459].

Jung, too, addresses this possibility, but he contends that mankind cannot survive without archetypes and their images. For Jung, archetypes and the irrational are essential to mankind's psychological well being. If we are ruled entirely by reason, we become one-dimensional (*Archetypes* 94).

If our ever-so-rational world were able to convince itself that archetypes did not exist, then according to Jung, "we would have to invent them forthwith in order to keep our highest and most important values from disappearing into the unconscious" (93). Not only can we not escape from our irrational side, ignoring or denying it would force it to find other ways to intrude itself upon our consciousness, ways we would be ill equipped to combat because we would deny the very existence of such phenomena. By tapping the archetypes and conveying images of them in literature, science fiction and fantasy, like other forms of romance literature before them, including medieval romance literature, allow the reader to participate in the rituals that enable the psyche and the soul to maintain balance and sanity.

Certain archetypes seem to appear repeatedly in romance literature: the quest or journey sequence, the child, the wise old man, the great mother, the treasure of immense value that is only won through heroic effort. They are handled differently in the literature of different ages, but the choice of which archetypes a society reverences in its literature reveals that society's values. The modeling of literary images upon similar archetypes, therefore, suggests a bond between the ages based upon the nexus of values and potentially the societal occurrences that precipitated the rise of those particular archetypes from the collective unconscious to the conscious. Interpretations of some of the archetypes and their presence in the types of literature under consideration will be explored in the chapters to follow.

8

There and Back Again:
The Archetypal Journey

One of most common and most obvious archetypes in romance literature is the hero's quest or journey. The journey furnishes the narrative structure for many of these romances, medieval and modern. A look at several works from medieval romance, science fiction, and fantasy will disclose the presence of the standard quest sequences. The action proceeds through one of the common orders: the folktale cycle outlined by Propp, the seasonal cycle, or the sacrificial cycle of birth, life, death, and rebirth. Clarke's *The City and the Stars*, Bédier's *The Romance of Tristan and Iseult*, Tolkien's *The Hobbit*, LeGuin's *The Left Hand of Darkness*, Bradbury's *Farenheit 451*, and the anonymous medieval romance, *Sir Orfeo*, will be used to illustrate these structures and the archetypal quest.

The structure of the romance is similar to that of the folktale, the literary form from which Frye believes romance literature is descended (*Secular* 15). Vladimir Propp's *Morphology of the Folktale* explains the folktale structure as he understood it based on his analysis of 100 Russian folktales. The typical structure Propp identifies follows a basic pattern subject to a quantifiable array of variations. In its most basic form the order is as follows: initial situation, departure, complication, first move, second move, resolution. First move includes such actions as the acquisition of a magical object, meeting a helper (magical or otherwise), encountering the villain and overcoming same, and return. Second move and third move, often applicable as threes are popular in folk tales, are similar to first move but in the last, of however many moves are presented, the resolution is final and no further adventures ensue (119–127).

To see if Propp's structural requirements applied to science fiction as well, a science fiction novel was selected at random from a library collection and analyzed. The book, Clarke's *The City and the Stars*, fit the structuring technique well (and the novel also proved to conform to a number of the other characteristics of romance literature under consideration in this study). In the initial situation, the hero is introduced. In *The City and the Stars*, the prologue introduces the city of Diaspar — a major entity in the novel, and Chapter 1 introduces our hero, Alvin. We have barely met Alvin when we learn that he has reached the age of majority for people in his society and his parents are taking their formal leave of their role in his life and sending him out on his own. This corresponds with Propp's second function — the departure — which is paired with an interdiction. Alvin's interdiction is cultural rather than specifically from his parents or specific to him: he is warned not to try to see what lies beyond the city limits. Of course, this is precisely what he sets out to do and eventually does.

The complication is how to leave the city. First move begins as Alvin breaks the interdiction and overcomes the complication with the aid of two helpers, one in the form of a man called Khedron, whose formal role in the city is Jester — the person of misrule and disorder, and the other in the form of the Central Computer. Alvin is transported via a "magical" (advanced science) means of transport to the "village" Lys, where he meets the woman, Seranis, who functions briefly as the villain. She questions Alvin about his world and tells him a little about her world. He freely answers her questions and then learns that Seranis wants him either to stay eternally in Lys or return to Diaspar with his memory modified. Alvin escapes aided by a robot he found on his explorations and prevents the "villain" Seranis from erasing his mind. When Alvin returns to Diaspar, he must prove himself worthy through testing, done in this story by the Central Computer. Alvin passes the test, returns briefly to confront the inhabitants of Lys, and convinces the council that contact between Lys and Diaspar is not only inevitable, but desirable.

Alvin has achieved his goal — in part. Second move begins as Alvin strives to learn how mankind came to the position they find themselves in at the beginning of the book. The story continues as Alvin once again seeks to fulfill a lack, once again leaves home — this time leaving the planet as well, encounters danger, receives aid, and finally discovers the answers he wants. He returns to the planet and the resolution is reached. The folktale would usually end in a marriage, but this novel stops just short of that, leaving Alvin longing for love and for a world where children will once again be born, not created by computer program. This structure follows Propp's guidelines very closely, departing only in functions omitted or repeated, a practice that occurs in folktales as well.

With a bit of imagination, it is easy to see the seasonal parallels to Propp's order and recognize it as a version of archetypal cycle of life, death, and rebirth. Spring arrives, the grain pushes green tendrils through the soil. There is too little sun, or too much, too little rain, or too much, or just enough. The farmer tends the crops or neglects them. Gods receive acceptable or unacceptable offerings and the crops flourish or wither. Eventually, the crops are harvested, and sustenance is provided for another year. If it is a particularly good year, a second harvest may follow the first. Winter arrives. Those who followed the rituals and made appropriate offerings survive on the rewards of their efforts; those who have failed the appropriate gods suffer or starve. In the spring, the entire process resumes, and any society which took heed of the lessons learned during the preceding year should prosper from the new knowledge it has acquired.

The appeal of this order is so powerful that some medieval romances used actual, not just symbolic, seasonal parallels as a sequencing device. *Parzival*, for example, proceeds from spring to spring, "from a first Pentecost when Parzival is made a knight in name to a seventh Pentecost when he becomes truly a knight in spirit" (Mustard and Passage *l*). The central tale of the Bédier version of *The Romance of Tristan and Iseult* not only begins in the spring but follows a seasonal progression. King Mark is being pressed to take a wife and father an heir. He resists until Tristan himself joins the barons in urging that the king wed. The time of year is revealed by the pair of "building swallows" who drop the golden strand of hair they had brought to weave into their nest. King Mark agrees to marry the woman from whom the golden hair came, and Tristan sets off to win Iseult for King Mark. On the journey from Ireland to Tintagel, Tristan and Iseult drink the magic love philter intended for Iseult and King Mark. By summer, the two strands of the plot have ripened fully; King Mark and Iseult are husband and wife and Tristan and Iseult are lovers.

Although they cannot prove the alliance, the barons at King Mark's court plant a suspicion of it and the suspicion grows until, in the fall, when the grapes are ripe and the trees are covered with fruit, King Mark banishes Tristan from the castle. The autumn of Tristan's relationship has begun. The king and knight are reconciled briefly, but further accusations are made and Tristan is obliged to flee. He manages to have Iseult, who has also been accused, rescued from the castle and the two take up residence in a hut in the woods, staying there from late fall through the winter into spring, but the relationship never flourishes with its former beauty; winter has arrived. The seasons pass many more times, morality and obligation ultimately dividing Tristan and Iseult, until one spring when Tristan dons the disguise of a pilgrim and finds his way to Iseult a final time.

Late spring is the last time Iseult sees Tristan alive. When he leaves, he knows his death is near. Spring is the time of rebirth, but not necessarily rebirth in the mortal world. At times, the hero and/or heroine must die in the spring to be reborn into a new immortal life. When she sees her lover dead, Iseult dies of grief. Their new life together in the immortal realm is symbolized by the briar that burgeons forth from Tristan's tomb, arcs over to Iseult's tomb, roots there, and cannot be displaced or destroyed.

This familiar seasonal sequencing is followed in *The Hobbit* and *The Lord of the Rings* as well, which should probably surprise few people, given Tolkien's knowledge of medieval literature. *The Hobbit*, from which this chapter borrowed its title, can be used to illustrate. Gandalf appears at Bilbo Baggins' doorstep one morning "just before May" and involves him in an adventure, the like of which has not touched the Shire before. After a bit of confusion, Bilbo ends up rushing off unprepared, to do something he has never done and has no idea if he can do. This is his spring, a time of new beginnings, growth, and discovery.

As spring gives way to summer, Bilbo begins to discover that there is more to him than he would have expected. He manages to escape from trolls and help ransack their treasure, but he still really just wants to go home, and probably would if not for his pride. Each time conditions, weather or safety, become unpleasant Bilbo is apt to wish for home: "He was thinking once again of his comfortable chair before the fire in his favourite sitting-room in his hobbit-hole, and of the kettle singing" (55). Whether he wishes it or no, Bilbo is expanding his knowledge of the world. Mid-summer is spent with the elves, creatures which hitherto had been mere myths to Bilbo.

Autumn has begun when Bilbo has the experience that is the turning point in his journey. He has been parted from the dwarves, and he is sitting under a tree dreaming of home. He awakens in time to kill a giant spider that has been wrapping him in its silk.

> Somehow the killing of the giant spider, all alone by himself in the dark without the help of the wizard or the dwarves or of anyone else, made a great difference to Mr. Baggins. He felt a different person, and much fiercer and bolder in spite of an empty stomach, as he wiped his sword on the grass and put it back in its sheath [154].

Bilbo's behavior in this instance is a harvest of the knowledge and experience gained thus far on his journey. The old Bilbo might have called for help or waited for reinforcements, but the new Bilbo is ready to tackle problems head on.

Putting on the ring of invisibility he has acquired, he sets out to find the dwarves. He not only finds but rescues them, and once they are all safely away from the spiders, it becomes apparent that Bilbo is now an accepted member of their company rather than someone along on sufferance. More than that, they begin to turn to him for leadership.

> [Y]ou can see that they had changed their opinion of Mr. Baggins very much, and had begun to have a great respect for him (as Gandalf had said they would). Indeed they really expected him to think of some wonderful plan for helping them, and were not merely grumbling. They knew only too well that they would soon all have been dead, if it had not been for the hobbit; and they thanked him many times [163].

Between his own actions and their praise, Bilbo has come to believe in himself, perhaps even to believe he is "a bold adventurer" (163). This confidence is not just a facade; using the wits, luck, and magic ring the dwarves see as his assets, Bilbo is able to help them escape from the wood elves and reach Lake-town, the town nearest the mountain and dragon-guarded treasure that are their goal.

In keeping with the seasonal construction of the storyline, the adventurers reach their goal at the onset of winter: "They were come to the Desolation of the Dragon, and they were come at the waning of the year" (195). The dwarves are beginning to despair of ever getting inside the mountain when Bilbo puts all the clues together, solves the riddle of the door, and calls for the key just in time to gain them entrance before the opportunity is lost. With the opening of the door, winter has begun. The dwarves and the hobbit try to find a way to evict the dragon and repossess the treasure, but they are unsuccessful. Ultimately, the dragon becomes angry enough to smash the hillside over the secret door and fly off to Lake-town to punish its inhabitants for helping the invaders who are now trapped in his mountain.

True winter, with its bloodshed and death, has descended. The dragon demolishes much of Lake-town before the beast is killed by one of the Lake-town men. The destruction is blamed on the dwarves stirring up the dragon, and the Lake-town inhabitants set out to demand a fair share of the treasure in return for their trouble and the slaying of the dragon. Thorin, the dwarf who has resumed his rightful position as King under the Mountain, refuses to share the treasure and both sides prepare for war. War is only averted by the appearance of a mutual enemy, the goblins. Thorin and many others amongst the dwarves, the Lakemen, and the elves, who had come to the aid of the Lakemen, die before the goblins are defeated. The treasure lust that had blinded Thorin to offers of peace seems not to have fallen upon the other dwarves, and ancient alliances with the Lakemen are reestablished.

As spring returns, Bilbo heads home. On May 1st, Gandalf and Bilbo reenter the valley of Rivendell, home of the Elvenlords. There they rest and recover from their trials and travails. But home is calling Bilbo and he is soon back on the road to the Shire. On June 22 he arrives at his hobbit-hole. He settles back into his life, but he is never the same hobbit, a change he sees as a positive one.

> Indeed Bilbo found he had lost more than spoons — he had lost his reputation. It is true that for ever after he remained an elf-friend, and had the honor of dwarves, wizards, and all such folk as ever passed that way; but he was no longer quite respectable [285].

Most of his fellow hobbits are unsure what to make of a hobbit who owns sword and mail, writes poetry, and consorts with elves. Bilbo himself finds the life of the Shire richer and more pleasurable because of the experiences that had taken him away from it. He lives a long happy life in the Shire and eventually retires to Rivendell to live with the elves.

Seasonal sequencing is not limited to the older, medieval works or the fantasy works that emulate them. LeGuin's science fiction novel *The Left Hand of Darkness* follows this order as well. The story begins in spring, "the twenty-second day of the third month of spring" to be precise (8). The main character, Genly Ai, is watching a parade and blissfully unaware that his diplomatic mission to the planet Winter is about to put his life in peril. The native Gethenian, Estraven, who has been sheltering Genly is about to withdraw his protection because Estraven's political position has changed and will endanger Genly. Genly is one day from informing the Karhidish king that there is a whole universe full of beings beyond his planet, information the king does not want to hear, and the king's reaction will cause Genly to set out on a journey to Orgoreyn, one of the planet's other inhabited regions, to see if his message will get a better reception there.

Genly experiences a brief summer and fall with the Orgota before his message regarding the universe garners him a place in a backcountry prison workfarm. He is rescued by Estraven and the two set out across the glacier to escape Orgoreyn and return to Karhide. Their winter journey is harsh even for a planet that is geared toward brutal weather, and their attendant emotional and psychological journeys are not much more pleasant. For Genly, this includes coming to terms with the sexuality of the Gethenians, a people who have evolved into true hermaphrodites. They are sexually neutral unless they are in "kemmer," a hormonal cycle not unlike the seasonal sex cycles of many Earth mammals. When a Gethenian is in "kemmer," its gender is determined by a variety of factors including whether the individual's partner has begun to develop one or the other gender's characteristics. One partner develops into a male and one into a female; any given individual may assume either gender's role at different times in his/her life.

Estraven, the Gethenian who has saved Genly and is accompanying him over the glacier, has always seemed male to Genly, based on Genly's own cultural preconceptions. When Estraven comes into "kemmer" during their journey, however, s/he develops female sexual characteristics because Genly is male. The two have become close friends during their travels, sharing stories of their lives and beliefs, but up until this point Genly did not really understand what it meant to be Gethenian. The two do not engage in sexual contact, but the shared experience and the stories they have told establish a rapport that had not been there before and Genly is finally able to accept Estraven as s/he is. The journey across the glacier was harsh and sterile physically, but emotionally the trip nurtured the seeds of understanding which blossom when the two companions return to civilization.

They survive and come down from the glacier on the ninth day of the last month of winter — 17 days before the return of spring. By the twelfth day of that month, they have reached Karhide, and at the very onset of spring, Estraven skis into the gunfire of the border patrol, sacrificing himself so that Genly will be able to accomplish his mission. A few weeks later as spring begins in earnest, the interplanetary ship on which Genly had come to Winter lands, confirming beyond doubt the existence of other beings in the universe and drawing Winter and its people into that community. The planet Winter is aptly named, as it has been isolated from the springlike forces of growth that the representatives of the greater universal community bring upon their arrival. The physical climate will remain wintry, but the newcomers have initiated a Spring in the social climate.

Genly returns to Karhide, to his diplomatic position, but not to the self he had been before his trip across the glacier. After months of feeling like an outsider on the planet, he experiences the unnerving sensation of feeling alienated from his own kind when the ship lands and he is reunited with them.

> [T]hey all looked strange to me, men and women, well as I knew them. Their voices sounded strange: too deep, too shrill. They were like a troupe of great, strange animals, of two different species: great apes with intelligent eyes, all of them in rut, in kemmer.... They took my hand, touched me, held me.
>   I managed to keep myself in control, [...]. When we got to the Palace, however, I had to get to my room at once [279].

Genly has journeyed out both from his own world and from the part of the world to which his mission brought him. He has been tested, not by fire, but by ice and been reborn as a different person who is part of his new world as he had not been previously. Like Bilbo, Genly decides that the understanding he has gained more than compensates for whatever he has lost.

LeGuin consciously incorporates archetypal images in her works, a practice she writes about in several essays in her non-fiction collection, *The Language of the Night*. But even in works where the images are not as obvious, many authors utilize these archetypes. In *Fahrenheit 451*, for example, the season in which the story is set is autumn, an appropriate seasonal image since the world Guy Montag inhabits is a world winding down to death, or winter. The sequence of events that Montag himself experiences, however, can be seen as following the spring, summer, fall, winter, spring (or birth, growth, decline, death, and rebirth) pattern.

When the reader first encounters Guy Montag, he is cheerfully performing his job — burning books.

With the brass nozzle in his fists, with this great python spitting its venomous kerosene upon the world, the blood pounded in his head, and his hands were the hands of some amazing conductor playing all the symphonies of blazing and burning to bring down the tatters and charcoal ruins of history [3].

It is a time of innocence for Montag. He does his job, he does it well, and he does not ask questions. Interestingly, the first time the reader sees him, Montag is working in conjunction with the image of the Dragon, the fire hose, the enemy who must be defeated in order to reach selfhood. Later in the book, the venom this python spits will be used to kill the man who was once Montag's supervisor, an act that will force Montag to flee his city in search of refuge and a new life.

Montag's spring is signaled by the young woman he meets on the way home. Montag is intrigued but disturbed by seventeen year-old Clarisse McClellan. She thinks about things and asks him to think, really think, not just accept what he has been told is true. When Montag meets her for the first time some seasonal dislocation is apparent even to him, although the indicators are more appropriate signs of summer than spring: "there was the faintest breath of fresh apricots and strawberries in the air" (6–7). She makes him look at the world around him as he has not done in a long time.

"Bet I know something else you don't. There's dew on the grass in the morning."

He suddenly couldn't remember if he had known that or not, and it made him quite irritable.

"And if you look" — she nodded at the sky — "there's a man in the moon."

He hadn't looked for a long time [9].

Montag is being awakened to his world and given a chance to grow, both properties of archetypal images of spring, brought by a youthful or spring figure.

The summer of his increasing knowledge begins after Montag's conversations with Clarisse. Arriving home, Montag discovers that his wife, Mildred, has taken a overdose of sleeping tablets. His innocence is ripped away by her act and its implications.

As he stood there the sky over the house screamed. There was a tremendous ripping sound as if two giant hands had torn ten thousand miles of black lines down the seam. Montag was cut in half. He felt his chest chopped down and split apart [13].

He understands then the emptiness of the life he and his wife have been living, and the emptiness of the lives of most of the people in their society. The paramedics who come to revive Mildred comment that they see nine or ten such attempted suicides a night.

Up to the meeting with Clarisse, Montag has floated along in his life, never asking if it, or he, had any purpose. Mildred's sole entertainment is participating in the life of the TV family in the insipid programming that is piped in to three full-wall screens in their home. Now he is on a crusade to find something that will engage them in life, something that will keep Mildred from preferring death. Although he does not read them, he begins to bring home books when he goes to start the fires, he starts to question his job and wonder how others feel when their books are burned, and he begins to fear the Mechanical Hound who can track people down and kill them when so instructed.

Montag's autumn comes quickly. The day after he watches a woman set fire to her own house with herself in it rather than allow the Firemen to take her books away from her, Montag refuses to get up and go to work. Beatty, his captain, shows up and tries to talk Montag through the reaction to the previous night's fire. Beatty knows Montag has stolen a book but attributes it to common curiosity and gives him 24 hours in which to burn the book. Once the chief has left, Montag tries once more to make contact with his wife, but she is too brainwashed by the TV to listen, until Montag begins pulling books out of the ventilator shaft. Then she responds, by seizing a book and trying to stuff it in the kitchen incinerator. Montag restrains her, turns off the TV, and sits and begins to read to her. But she is impervious. She does not want to hear; she wants mindless laughter and display, not words she has to puzzle over to extract a meaning.

Winter is coming. Montag can feel it. He seeks out a retired English professor he had talked to once in the park, and asks the man to help him understand the books he is trying to read. Faber, the professor, asks what has brought Montag to this point, and Montag replies: "I don't know. We have everything we need to be happy, but we aren't happy. Something's missing. I looked around. The only thing I positively *knew* was gone was the books I'd burned in ten or twelve years. So I thought books might help" (82). Faber calls him a romantic, which seems apt for a man who sees his world as it is but knows that world is lacking and sets out to find a way to improve both his world and himself. Montag believes books hold the answers, but Faber explains that it is not the books themselves that are the lack, but the ideas, the detail, the life in the books that we have lost. The professor explains that books can only help if three conditions are met: "Number one, as I said: quality of information. Number two: leisure to digest it. And number three: the right to carry out actions based on what we learn from the intersection of the first two" (84–5). Montag knows he has condemned himself at this point, and he finds a freedom in that awareness: "That's the good part of dying; when you've nothing to lose, you run any risk you want" (85).

Winter descends. Montag returns home and unplugs the wall-screens in an effort to get his wife and her friends to talk about real things instead of the TV family. They founder in the silence and then begin to make inconsequential chit-chat. Montag tries another tack, he reads to them, but they don't *want* to be reached. He goes to work and hands over a book for Beatty to burn. Like Lady Macbeth, Montag feels like his hands are drenched in blood and he cannot get them clean. The question is whether the guilt that stains his hands is from plucking the book from destruction initially, allowing the woman to immolate herself, handing the book over for destruction, or facing and accepting his own part in the destruction of years' worth of lives and books.

Montag is both surprised and not surprised when the alarm they respond to that night is at his own home. Mildred, whose secure existence in the mindless world of the TV family has been threatened, has turned him in. Montag is required to burn his own house and books, which he does. He acts like man in a fog until he realizes that his friends are at risk of exposure too. He is willing to risk his own life, but not their lives, and when Beatty becomes a threat to them Montag turns the kerosene hose on Beatty and then sets him aflame. His final act as fireman is to burn the Mechanical Hound that has been loosed on his trail. Then he runs. First, he runs to the professor, but he realizes the danger he has put the man in and he leaves in order to draw the Hound away and extinguish his trail in the river.

The river washes away the scent of him, and he changes to the extra clothes Faber loaned him. Montag is baptized and reborn. Because the police cannot afford to have people think a dangerous criminal like Montag has eluded them, a scapegoat is killed and proclaimed to be Montag. In the eyes of his world he has died, literally. In many ways, Montag *is* dead, and what survives is a man who carries in his head the Book of Ecclesiastes. He joins a group of other exiles who are keeping literature alive in their heads against the day when the world may recognize the need for it once more, like seeds stored underground awaiting the warm rains of spring. As the Book of Ecclesiastes, which Montag has now made part of himself, reminds us, "To everything there is a season" (165). This is Montag's spring, his rebirth.

In addition to providing narrative structure, the hero's journey also provides an archetypal foundation for redemption and psychological equilibrium. Reading about the hero's journey out into the world is not unlike reading about rebirth rituals many societies and religions use. The god is born, lives, dies, and is reborn. The story of Christ fits this pattern. He is born in midwinter of humble but worthy parents, sought by a jealous foe who would destroy him before he could grow, escapes that fate, and lives a quiet, uneventful life until maturity. The season of Christ's birth is problematic since the description in the Bible has prompted many scholars to set his birth at midsummer rather than midwinter. Midwinter makes more sense from an archetypal point of view, however, as he is like a seed in the ground, waiting for the right time to grow into the role ordained for him. At approximately age 30, Christ begins preaching a way of salvation that did not mesh with any part of the status quo. He wanted people to live good lives, assume responsibility for their own salvation, and think for themselves rather than simply buy the party line. Such revolutionary ideas typically lead to the same conclusion in any age or place, death.

Christ's crucifixion occurs in the spring, the time of rebirth. He is the sacrifice needed to ensure the successful harvest, in this case a harvest of souls who chose to follow the guidelines for salvation He provided. In the Christian myth, Christ combats death and wins, earning the right to return to Earth briefly and then to Heaven for eternity. His victory also holds out hope to the believer that only one's body will perish while one's soul passes on to a form of spiritual immortality. Most of the elements of the hero's quest surface in Christ's life and teachings: the hero sets off on a quest, is initiated into a new life, must leave part or all of his old life/self behind, and returns. Ideally, the hero returns alive, but, dead or alive, he has achieved something that would not have been achieved had he not embarked on his journey.

Following the most basic daily and seasonal archetypes of death and rebirth, of the sun and of plant and animal life, mankind created archetypal images of death and rebirth among the gods and among select, privileged heroes. Mortal man can only join in this cycle symbolically through rituals, such as the Christian rite of Holy Communion. Although the participants in rebirth rituals, unlike the gods, cannot in actuality die and be reborn, Jung suggests that participation in such a ceremony does affirm their belief in "the permanence and continuity of life, which outlasts all changes of form and, phoenix-like, continually rises anew from its own ashes" (*Archetypes* 117). Readers of medieval romance literature, science fiction, and fantasy, like the observers in the ritual are not active participants, but they too reap the psychological benefits of the rebirth process by living through the hero's experience with him.

Medieval romance literature, drawing on the Christian tradition and the traditions of the druids and the Celts and various other earlier religions whose beliefs either bore some similarity to these religions or influenced them in some way (belief in Mithras for example), has the death and rebirth images woven right into the stories. The story of *Sir Orfeo*, a revision of the Orpheus story conflated with Celtic fairy tales, tells of Sir Orfeo, who loses his wife to the king of fairies. His wife is as good as dead to the mortal world; people tend not to return from the fairy kingdom. Orfeo gives up his kingdom to his steward and wanders for ten years as an itinerant harper until one day he sees his wife riding in a fairy troupe. Although he is aware of the risk, he follows her back to the fairy hall where his skill at the harp so impresses the king that Sir Orfeo wins both his own and his wife's freedom. They return to the mortal world and pick up the threads of their lives (Gibbs).

The cycle of death and rebirth figures prominently in other romances as well. In *Amis & Amiloun*, Amis' children die so Amiloun can be healed, but, miraculously, the children are alive the next day. In *Athelston*, the falsely accused knight and his family walk through fire and emerge unscathed. Possibly the best known promise of rebirth in medieval romance literature, which remains unfilled but anticipated, is the famous inscription on Arthur's tomb near the end of Malory's *Le Morte D'Arthur*: "HIC IACET ARTHURUS, REX QUONDAM REXQUE FUTURUS. Here lies Arthur, king once and king yet to be" (Brewer 148).

Religious belief in resurrection has become less popular in the twentieth and current centuries and there is a concurrent drop in the overt presence of such death and rebirth scenes in literature. Some fantasy and science fiction characters *are* allowed to participate in an actual death and rebirth experience, but for most characters the death and rebirth remain symbolic. Perhaps the best known example of the former in fantasy literature is Tolkien's Gandalf, who plunges into the abyss while battling the Balrog in the depths of Moria, allowing his companions to escape with their lives.

> With a terrible cry the Balrog fell forward, and its shadow plunged down and vanished. But even as it fell it swung its whip, and the thongs lashed and curled about the wizard's knees, dragging him to the brink. He staggered, and fell, grasped vainly at the stone, and slid into the abyss. "Fly, you fools!" he cried, and was gone [Fellowship 430].

This is the last the companions see of Gandalf for a considerable time; all believe he has perished. In a manner of speaking, he has, as the Gandalf who later rejoins a small group of the now sundered companions is not the Gandalf who left them. Like the precious metals the dwarves once worked there, Gandalf has passed through the fire in the depths of Moria and emerged purified.

> "Yes, I am in white now," said Gandalf. "[...] I have passed through fire and deep water, since we parted. I have forgotten much that I thought I knew, and learned again much that I had forgotten. I can see many things far off, but many things that are close at hand I cannot see" [Two Towers 125].

He has also experienced things unknown to the world above, battled the Balrog a second time, and been nursed back from the brink of death by the elven Lady, Galadriel of Lothlorien (133–5). Gandalf the Grey has become Gandalf the White, embodiment of the powers of good in Middle-earth in the Third Age. He is changed; he has even forgotten the name by which the companions called him, but he is content to assume it once again, when he is greeted by it. "'Gandalf,' the old man repeated, as if recalling from old memory a long disused word. 'Yes, that was the name. I was Gandalf'" (125). In that guise, the wizard has come, to provide the companions with a resource they sorely need, hope. "'I have spoken words of hope. But only of hope. Hope is not victory'" (132). Yet, as Gandalf and the others know, there can be no victory if there is no hope.

Examples of the death and rebirth cycle can be found in science fiction as well. The main human character in Clarke's *2001: A Space Odyssey*, Dave Bowman, undergoes a transformation out in space beyond Jupiter after he unplugs HAL, the computer that has tried to remove all the humans from the mission and take over. In the movie version of *2001: A Space Odyssey*, Dave's transformation into a completely new life form is symbolized by the image of a baby superimposed on a backdrop of stars. The transformation itself is expressed through an impressive (for the time) artistic and cinematographic display accompanied by the moving strains of "Thus Spoke Zarathustra" (a work Jung placed in his visionary category of art).

Frank Poole, another character from *2001*, underwent a more prosaic death that was not revealed until Clarke wrote *3001: The Final Odyssey*. Poole's space suit developed an air leak and he was frozen by the cold of space. He remained dead until he was recovered and revived in the year 3001. When Rip Van Winkle wandered bewilderedly down from the mountains after twenty years, he found his world changed but still recognizable. Poole's "return" to his world after 1000 years is much more disorienting. Poole discovers a world he barely recognizes, run on scientific principles he has trouble comprehending even though he is a scientist.

Symbolic death and rebirth are much more common in science fiction and fantasy than literal death and rebirth. Frodo Baggins, the hobbit hero of The Lord of the Rings does not die, although he has several near-death experiences. The purpose of his journey is atypical, rather than archetypal; his quest is to get rid of a treasure, not obtain one, but the journey itself fits the rebirth cycle of life, death (real or symbolic), and rebirth. During his travels he loses much he values, including friends and his innocence, and gains much in knowledge and experience. He learns about his own strengths and limitations, accomplishes his goal with the aid of a helper, learns compassion, faces the sad fact that the world is not willing to pass hobbits by even when hobbits would be delighted to have the world ignore them, and, at long last, returns home a very different hobbit than the one who left.

His return to the Shire is important because evil times have at last reached into its cozy confines and the experience and courage of Frodo and his hobbit companions are needed to evict the lowlife element who have taken over their beloved Shire. With Frodo and Sam's return, the Shire's inhabitants learn that the quest has been completed and the hero has survived. An effort is made to return to the peaceful existence that shaped all of their lives before the Dark Lord reached out for the ring of power, but even for those hobbits who never left the Shire the world cannot slip back into the innocent past. Frodo finds it impossible to resume his old life. He has taken a wound in the shoulder that never completely heals and, like the knights who went on the Grail quest, he has been through many things about which he cannot speak to any but the companions who shared his journey.

He has been spared from physical death, but has suffered a spiritual death that can only be healed by passing across the sea to the west with the setting sun, out of the world he loves into the unknown world, to the refuge to which the elves return when life weighs too heavily upon them. Frodo's attempt to explain to his closest companion, Sam, why he cannot stay in the Shire testifies to the price the hero must pay for his journey and return.

> "But," said Sam, and tears started in his eyes, I thought you were going to enjoy the Shire, too, for years and years, after all you have done."
>
> "So I thought too, once. But I have been too deeply hurt, Sam. I tried to save the Shire, and it has been saved, but not for me. It must often be so, Sam when things are in danger: some one has to give them up, lose them, so that others may keep them" [*Return* 382].

Yet in the loss, there is a gain. As Frodo said, *he* cannot stay in the Shire, but because of him, there is still a Shire for others. What he has bought with his body and his soul is a future for the others, a chance for the next adventurer to set off on his archetypal journey.

9

Will Wonders Never Cease?

Sensationalism, love of adventure, technological audacity, intellectual curiosity may appear to be sufficient motives for our futuristic fantasies, but the impulse to spin such fantasies ... springs from an underlying cause, namely a situation of distress and the vital need that goes with it [Jung, *Flying Saucers* 14].

The "vital need," in general, is a need for unity. This unity is most often achieved through "a reorientation to the prevailing canon [of collective unconscious values shared by a society] and a reunion with the collective" (Neumann 371). Less frequently, it may occur when "the archetypes break through the creative person into the conscious world of culture. It is this deeper-lying reality that fertilizes, transforms, and broadens the life of the collective [...]" (377). If balance cannot be regained within the social structure as it exists, then a new balance must be sought.

These two options inform the archetypes treated in this chapter and the ones that follow. The archetypes mentioned include: the marvelous or miraculous, which requires the reader to accept new ways of seeing; the child hero, who stands for innovative problem-solving and futurity; the wise old man, who represents the accumulated wisdom of the ages and the reasoning power of the individual; the mother, who stands for new life, for security and suffocation, protection and infantilization; and the transformation, which melds all of the variables together into an integrated personality/society.

One of the archetypes shared by the various types of romance literature is the presence of the miraculous or marvelous. Granted, the marvelous is an essential component of the romance mode of literature, but it is also more than that. The presence of the marvelous is an affirmation of the generative side of the human psyche. The shadow creates horrors and abominations that inspire terror and despair. The optimistic side of the psyche creates wonders and marvels. Both need to appear in romance literature, but ideally — and we are dealing with idealized situations — the terrors will be vanquished and the marvels will prevail. In this way, the turmoil of the outer and inner worlds can be calmed, and the individual, and society, can resume belief in the continuity of his culture or world; in other words, the characters and the readers are offered hope.

Not only are the marvels expected, they are needed, according to Jungian psychology. For the human psyche to complete itself and become a whole self, it requires that the unity-seeking "religious instinct" free itself from the psyche's baser instincts for power and sexual gratification (*Flying* 46). Only when this has been accomplished is it possible to turn one's energies to molding a finished self from the disparate parts of the psyche. Unfortunately, humans are quite resistant to elevating themselves out of their psychological ruts, and "Only something overwhelming, no matter what form of expression it uses, can challenge the whole man and force him to react as a whole" (48).

The marvelous, the wonder-inspiring can be the catalyst of just such a reaction. Jung addresses this connection in relation to people's need to invent U.F.O. stories:

> Should something extraordinary or impressive then occur in the outside world, be it a human personality, a thing, or an idea, the unconscious content can project itself upon it, thereby investing the projection carrier with numinous and mythical powers [148–9].

Jung had already drawn the parallel to medieval stories of magic and myth earlier in the same book (83), and anything that involves evoking wonder can be applied to a large chunk of science fiction and fantasy as well.

The marvels and terrors in this type of literature fall into several different categories — magical, sacred, man-made, natural, and supernatural. Fantasy tends toward the magical, and science fiction toward the man-made, but underneath it all, there is a sameness to the experience of the marvelous that binds them all together. This is the sense of wonder, the sense that something extraordinary has happened and because of it one will never be the same. Spectacle is easy; it only has to stimulate your senses. Wonder is difficult; it has to engage your mind or touch your soul.

Asimov, among others, has described the importance of this sense of wonder. He sets science fiction in a tradition dating back to ancient stories and myths which he claims fill similar emotional needs now as they did then, "the satisfaction of the longing for wonder" (*Asimov on SF* 101). He elaborates on this by explaining the limitations of the various types of wonder involved.

> The difference is that the ancient myths and legends fulfill those needs and meet those goals against the background of a Universe that is controlled by gods and demons who can in turn be controlled by magical formulas either in the form of enchantments to coerce, or prayers to cajole. Science fiction, on the other hand, fulfills those needs against the background of a Universe that is controlled by impersonal and unanswerable laws of nature which can in turn be controlled by an understanding of their nature [101–2].

Wonder is essential; what changes is where we find the wonder.

As more and more of the world became known, the wonderful and marvelous kept being pushed farther and farther afield. As Clareson notes in his essay, "The Emergence of the Scientific Romance," exploration of the world had revealed that the supposedly exotic was not much different than the known world.

> And so the idealized kingdom once more was pushed beyond known frontiers. So long as great portions of the world remained unexplored, it could be placed on an island, in a valley beyond the next range of mountains, in one of the polar regions or inside the Earth itself. But as the Earth was ever more fully mapped, the writers who sought such lands were forced, increasingly, to rely upon the scientific romance [*Anatomy of Wonder* 45].

One such world to which a writer could always turn, no matter how well known the physical geography of Earth was becoming and how little mystery it retained, was the world of Fairy (Faërie). Tolkien underscores the importance of the world of Faërie to the Fairy Story in his essay "Tree and Leaf" found in *The Tolkien Reader*. As he makes clear, fairy stories are not predominately stories about fairies; they are rather stories that draw "upon the nature of *Faërie*: the Perilous Realm itself, and the air that blows out of that country" (38). He acknowledges that the sense of what Faerie is cannot be reduced to an adequate definition. "Faërie cannot be caught in a net of words; for it is one of its qualities to be indescribable, though not imperceptible" (39). Some glimmers of definition shine through, glimmers that show the strong emphasis on the marvelous. "Faërie itself may perhaps most nearly be translated by Magic — but it is a magic of a peculiar mood and power, at the furthest pole from the vulgar devices of the laborious, scientific magician" (39). The marvelous must exist in the story and it must be presented as marvelous, not explained away as a dream sequence or illusion. The Faërie land's influence must be felt, and the story must seem to be real within the secondary world created in the novel (42).

This abides by the "rules" of reality to which archetypes conform. The realism of the story being told need not apply to the physical world of the hearer or reader, but it must conform to the psychic world. Flying is fine; the psyche accepts flying as a form of locomotion and freedom. If the soul can fly, why not the body? Wings can take a variety of forms, large and leathery, gossamer and petite, feathered and functional. People may fly in rockets, planes, or helicopters, on carpets, brooms, airsleds, rocket skates, winged horses, dragons, or tigers. Flight may be conferred by magic incantations, fairy dust, imbibing a specific potion or substance, or holding onto a flight-capable creature. Standing in one's backyard flapping one's arms in the usual flight simulating fashion, however, is not going to be credible to most readers even though it is no less incredible than most of the other options listed. It does not *feel* right. The wonders may be improbable, but they must be believable, as contradictory as that sounds.

Romance literature provides many wonders. For the knights of the Round Table seeking the Grail, miraculous occurrences abound. Knights with extraordinary strength or special abilities are so numerous as to be mundane, as are dragons. A sword in a stone floating on a river is unusual enough to qualify as a marvel, however, and fulfills Arthur's requirement of seeing "some adventure" before he will eat at a holiday gathering. Upon the sword that pierces the stone is written, "Never shall man take me hence, but only he by whose side I ought to hang, and he shall be the best knight of the world" (Caxton 373). Arthur urges Lancelot to draw forth the sword, but Lancelot has the intelligence and humility to concede that he is not the one so named. In fact, he realizes that if he should try to draw the sword and fail, as he expects to do, he would "receive a wound by that sword that he shall not be whole long after" (373). Lancelot also foresees the start of the Grail quest in the coming of the sword.

The Middle Ages being a time of Christianity in Europe, the devil and God are seen as instrumental in many of the wonders. When Sir Bors meets a fair lady and she insists that he accept her as his lady and lover or she and all of her gentlewomen intend to plunge from a high tower to their deaths, he stands fast in his belief that it would be morally wrong for him to lie with her. He refuses to lose his soul for the temptresses' lives. The women do eventually leap from the tower and fall to the ground, but when Sir Bors crosses himself to ward off any evil their self-destructive action may prompt, the entire castle vanishes amidst "a great noise and a great cry, as though all the fiends of hell had been about him" (417). Wisely, Sir Bors' immediate response is to raise his hands to the heavens and thank God for his deliverance.

Galahad, of course, is a wonder from start to end. Any perfect man must, of necessity, be a wonder in our imperfect world. His perfection brings to him a variety of extraordinary experiences that usually center around holy objects or persons. Galahad and his companions are fed from the Sangrael in a sanctified event during which Joseph, the first bishop of Christendom, blesses the host of the sacrament causing it to become the actual person of Christ. The Christ sacrament then picks up the Grail and offers it to Galahad and his companions, Sir Percivale and Sir Bors. After this adventure Galahad inships and travels to the castle of the maimed king, where he performs a miracle of healing by touching the king with the bloody spear that had pierced Christ's side. Additional miracles follow: healing the lame, being succored by the Grail while imprisoned, converting a pagan and being set to rule over his city after his death (Caxton 442–4).

The final miracle in which Galahad is involved is his death. On the selfsame day one year after Galahad has been crowned king of the pagan city, Joseph of Aramathie appears before the three companions and bids Galahad come to him and see "that which thou has much desired to see," a final view of the Sangrael (444). Having attained his highest goal in life, Galahad petitions God for death. "Now, blessed Lord, would I not longer live, if it might please thee, Lord" (444). This is granted him, and his soul is borne to heaven amidst a host of angels. At the same time, God takes back the holy objects that had been the object of the great quest.

> Also the two fellows [Sir Percivale and Sir Bors] saw come from
> heaven an hand, but they saw not the body. And then it came right
> to the vessel, and took it and the spear, and so bare it up to heaven.
> Sithen then was there never man so hardy to say that he had seen the
> Sangrael [445].

Such is the nature of the medieval miracle. God is given credit, but
sometimes even in the tales themselves, there seems to be a blurring of
the Christian and the pagan. It is no secret that the Grail can as easily
be accounted for through Celtic mythology as Christian, a topic explored
at length in Roger Sherman Loomis' *The Grail: From Celtic Myth to Christian Symbol* and a number of other studies of the Grail.

Some miraculous objects are too tempting for authors to leave them
in the realm of medieval literature. The Siege Perilous is one example.
This seat in which none but the correct man could sit without peril is
intriguing simply because of that property. But, what happens if the
wrong man does sit in the seat? Does he die? Does he vanish? If he vanishes, where to?

Andre Norton provides an answer to this question in *Witch World*,
the first book in the series of the same name. In her novel, the Siege Perilous is a stone of power like unto the menhirs that comprise Stone-
henge. It has come into the hands of one Jorge Petronius who provides
the stone's services to others for a fee. He explains to Simon Tregarth,
who is considering buying those services, what the stone can do.

> "But in Cornwall there was another stone of power — the Siege
> Perilous. It was one rumored to be able to judge a man, determine
> his worth, and then deliver him to his fate. Arthur was supposed to
> have discovered its power through the Seer Merlin and incorporated
> it among the seats of the round table. Six of his knights tried it — and
> disappeared" [11].

Tregarth scoffs at Petronius' story, dismissing it as "a fairy tale for kids,"
but his own desperation — he is being hunted by assassins— drives him
to chance the stone, possible life over certain death. And, he who has
always been a soldier finds himself in a world at war, a world that has
need of soldiers. Wonders may only be for children's tales, but in this
case, Simon finds himself transported inside a children's tale he cannot
escape.

Other wonders await him there to compensate for what he has left
behind. Witches exist in the world to which he has been transported,

witches who can affect people's actions and thoughts and command the elements all through the use of concentrated will and the life power that lies in the land. Perhaps most startling to Tregarth is the discovery that he has this witch talent in small measure. Traditionally, only women possess the talent in the world he has entered. Due to his unexpected ability, he is a wild card against which the Witches' enemies will have no defense because there has never been one like him to defend against. He has become a wonder himself.

Technology provides wonders and marvels, too. The anti-gravity device invented by Lone in Theodore Sturgeon's *More Than Human* is invented to help a farmer plow his fields. Lone has no comprehension of the magnitude of what he has invented with the help of the others in his group entity. Later in the book, the ramifications of the invention are considered, and it is found to be so potent a catalyst for disaster that the group entity decides to destroy what it has made.

> "Well, he asked Baby what effect it would have if this invention got out and Baby said plenty. He said it would turn the whole world upside down, worse than the industrial revolution. Worse than anything that ever happened. He said if things went one way we'd have such a war, you wouldn't believe it. If they went the other way, science would go too far, too fast. Seems that gravatics is the key to everything" [208–9].

All of this fuss would be the result of one small machine, a gravity generator invented to allow a friend's truck to be used as a tractor (208).

Science fiction actually provides the author with free license to invent all of the wonderful things mankind does not have but would like, or thinks it would like. H. G. Wells gave us a time machine, Jules Verne a submarine, and E. E. "Doc" Smith rocket ships big enough to carry humans but small enough to be built of spare parts right in one's backyard. More subtle but impressive inventions include the still-suits of the Fremen of Dune which recycle all of the body's water and wastes into a liquid pure enough to be palatable and rehydrating although not particularly pleasant or refreshing. Asimov's Foundation series gives the world the Visi-Sonor, a musical instrument that makes audible sounds that pair with visual stimulation achieved by "stimulat[ing] the optic center of the brain directly without ever touching the optic nerve" (*Foundation and Empire* 139), personal atomic devices with generators the size of walnuts (shavers, personal force fields, garbage disposers), and the use of spectroscopic analysis of stars to calculate positions in space and allow space ships to make hundred or more light-year hops through hyper-space.

Human beings sometimes turn out to be the wonders themselves as they discover or tap unknown or little used human talents. The triplets of Simon Tregarth and his Witch World wife are able to communicate with each other telepathically over long distances and send a wordless warning of danger over even longer distances. The main characters in *More Than Human* all have psychic talents, as do the characters in Anne McCaffrey's *Rowan* books. *Foundation's* Hari Seldon does not claim any special mental abilities, but he develops a form of historical/sociological/psychological study based on mathematics that can accurately predict the behavior of large groups of people thousands of years in the future. These are all wonders that find their genesis in humans as we know them even now.

Some of the marvels attributed to humans relate to special abilities that identify an individual as supernatural in some way. The Reverend Mothers of the religious order of the Fremen of Herbert's Dune planet are born with the ability to ingest water that has been poisoned by the drowning in it of one of the young of the planet's impressive monster worm species. The Reverend Mother then realigns the molecular structure of the poison, rendering it harmless. There is a technical explanation supplied for the process, but it bears the stamp of the supernatural or sacred as well.

> She began recognizing familiar structures, atomic linkages: a carbon atom here, helical wavering ... a glucose molecule. An entire chain of molecules confronted her, and she recognized a protein ... a methyl-protein configuration.
> *A-h-h-h!*
> It was a soundless mental sigh within her as she saw the nature of the poison.
> With her psychokinesthetic probing, she moved into it, shifted an oxygen mote, allowed another carbon mote to link, reattached a linkage of oxygen ... hydrogen [355].

A drop of the water she has changed is introduced into the supply of poisoned water producing a chain reaction which neutralizes all of the toxin in the supply but leaves drug-enhanced sense perceptions and a mild euphoria in all who drink it. The ability to make this change in the water signals that a woman is Reverend Mother material. If anyone tries to drink the water and does not have the ability to change the poison, she dies and is weeded out of the gene pool. The mystical resonances of this change are heightened in the creation of a new Reverend Mother where the next step in the experience is a mind link with the existing Reverend Mother and the receipt from her of the entire race memory.

This extraordinary ability is given yet another twist in the novel. The ability to alter the water's chemical formula is a sex-linked characteristic, appearing only in females. No male has ever survived drinking the unchanged water, no male until Paul Atriedes, that is. Paul, the promised warrior/savior has the singular gift of being able to transform the water as the Reverend Mothers do. His experience is very different from theirs, however. When he drinks the water, a drop as compared to the sip taken by the Reverend Mother, he falls into a death-like coma for three weeks and is not roused from it until a second drop of the sacred poisoned water, the "Water of the Maker," is placed upon his lips. Then he awakens, unaware of the passage of time, but profoundly aware of the cultural memory of the Fremen, both of the memory passed down by the women and also of the memory to which only a male can gain access. He has converted the poisonous Water of the Maker into the mildly narcotic Water of Life, and he has converted the cultural memory as well, by reinvesting it with the male side that had remained locked away for so long.

The division between the world of what is accepted as real and the world of what is considered unreal used to be made of mist, as the title of Marion Zimmer Bradley's aptly named *The Mists of Avalon* implies. In the medieval world, many people believed that you could have a personal, physical relationship with God; mystics, both male and female claimed to have been ravished by God, to have felt God pour into them until there was no room for anything else. One could argue that they are speaking metaphorically, but the descriptions they provide to try and explain their indescribable experiences are couched in very human, very physical terms. In reading the writings of Mechthild of Magdeburg, Bernard of Clairveaux, and Hadewijch of Brabant, the reader encounters concrete sensory images that reveal that the mystics themselves considered their experiences real. Consider this description of "Union with God" written by Hadewijch:

> From the depths of his wisdom, he shall teach you what he is and
> with what wonderful sweetness the one lover lives in the other and

so permeates the other that they do not know themselves from each other. But they possess each other in mutual delight, mouth in mouth, heart in heart, body in body, soul in soul, while a single divine nature flows through them both and they both become one through each other, yet remaining always themselves [109].

Similarly, devils were believed to be real and able to enter human beings. Casting out devils was a physical process and required providing a physical place for the devil to enter in lieu of the human. If the devil could not be cast out, the human had to be killed in a way that would destroy the devil as well, the most popular choice being fire. When God and the devil can interact with humans, the door is open for other supernatural beings like dragons, fairies, elves, ogres, and trolls. The medieval Catholic Church certainly acknowledged that many people believed in these other beings; in fact the Church made a great effort to suppress such beliefs and recast all the evil supernatural beings into devils and all of the good ones into angels, whether the people wanted their supernatural beings converted or not.

Beowulf neatly captures this transition. Christianity makes a halting and uncertain appearance in the story in a way that links the power of the Church to the ability to defeat the monster. Grendel, however, is clearly a monster of the supernatural variety, who has not yet been Christianized into an evil spirit or devil, a transformation which Tolkien observed tended to happen to pagan monsters when Christianity took over a culture's mythology. "For the monsters do not depart, whether the gods go or come. A Christian was (and is) still like his forefathers a mortal hemmed in a hostile world. The monsters remained the enemies of mankind, the infantry of the old war, and became inevitably the enemies of the one God..." ("Beowulf: The Monsters" 22). Grendel is occasionally referred to as a "fêond" or fiend, but not a "dêofel" or devil. Although some modern translators do use the word demon to refer to the monster, there is not much evidence of Grendel's being seen as Satan. He is, instead, Cain's twisted descendant, a failed human.

As mentioned in Chapter Two, the end of the medieval period saw the rise of theologians like William of Occam and Gabriel Biel, who drew a line between things that had to be accepted on faith and things that could be proven empirically. Only Christian things were permitted in the faith category, and so fairies and dragons, unicorns and goblins, and all of the inhabitants of the populous supernatural world faded to mere childish imaginings through lack of empirical evidence for their existence. Things that could not be proven to exist were deemed not to exist, or to exist only in some people's imaginations. Over the centuries, religion has become divorced from science, and people who genuinely believe that there are such things as elves or visitors from outer space, or even angels and devils, often have their sanity called into question.

Because of the schism between the real and the supernatural worlds, the question of how "unreal" a book has to be before it is classified as science fiction or fantasy is an important question. Science fiction's unreality is, paradoxically, a possible reality. Dreams, drug-induced hallucinations, or psychotic episodes, which occur fairly often in modern fiction and cause some critics to lump those works in with science fiction and fantasy, are examples of the surreal. There need be no logic, no consistency, no law to the surreal experience. One can be able to speak Portuguese at the beginning of a dream and unable to do so at the end without anything having caused the change. Events in the surreal can be random and inexplicable.

The worlds created in science fiction and fantasy are not worlds that function by the physical laws governing twentieth century Earth revolving around the star Sol, but they are worlds that do function by rules of some kind. In science fiction, those rules are usually plausible extensions of our current physical laws. Alternate systems of physical laws are invented. A question such as, "What if there were a world where...?" or "What if *our* world were like this instead of this?" is posed, and in response a world is created in which these laws apply.

In Clarke's *3001: The Final Odyssey*, mankind has learned how to build skyscrapers up into the vacuum of space and connect them to each other in a halo circling the earth. Humans do not have the ability to create such architecture at this time, but maybe in 1000 years we will. This attitude concurs with the position and comments of one of the book's main characters, Frank Poole, who has been revived in the year 3001 and gets to see his "ancient" 2000's fantasies become another time period's realities.

> The tower dwindled away until it became a glittering thread against the blackness of space, and he did not doubt it continued all the way to the geostationary orbit, thirty-six thousand kilometers above the equator. Such fantasies had been well known in Poole's day: he had never dreamed he would see the reality—and be living in it [28].

Other laws, such as the law of gravity, remain unchanged in the book.

In his article entitled "Science Fiction and the Semiotics of Realism," J. Timothy Bagwell dubs the proposed scientific basis for the unusual "the explanation" and considers it one of the key features of science fiction. "SF is not obliged actually to explain unreality (that would be impossible), but rather merely to appear to explain it or at least accept thematically the presence of or need for explanation" (42). In Gregory Benford and David Brin's *Heart of the Comet*, for example, there is no explanation of how society progressed to the point where it could colonize a comet, but there are explanations of how the colonists made the comet habitable, explanations that sometimes involve yet-to-be-invented technology. Most science fiction readers would accept this. They only balk when the explanation seems to conflict with the known or with the world of the story as established by the author. Humans cannot walk around in a vacuum, so if human characters are walking on the moon with no oxygen supplies and the only rationale the author provides is that people have learned to breath in space, most readers will reject the story as nonsense. On the other hand, if the author adds any oxygen producing device, however strange, such as noseplugs which extract oxygen from the dust of the lunar environment, a majority of readers will find that sufficient and accept the story.

Fantasy is often singled out as unscientific because of the absence of this "Explanation": however, science and fantasy are not as dissimilar as many people would like to think. Modern science has a surprising element of "fantasy" in it, as Arlen Hansen notes in his article, "The Meeting of Parallel Lines: Science, Fiction, and Science Fiction":

> We tend to think of scientists as the ultimate realists—we call them "physicists" and "naturalists." Surely, we think, they have no truck with fiction or fantasy. Yet, like Maxwell in his allusion to an "imaginary substance," many theoretical scientists themselves freely acknowledge their indebtedness to fantasy. Their laboratories are fantasy worlds where electrons look like billiard balls and where black holes are as common as side pockets [52].

The laws by which worlds operate in fantasy novels are often quite far from the laws by which our known world operates, but it is possible to show that most fantasy worlds do have laws by which they operate. Kathleen Spencer refers to Andrzej Zgorzelski's theory of the reality of fantasy worlds in her article "Victorian Urban Gothic: The First Modern Fantastic Literature":

In the case of the fantastic, the initial signals indicate a fictive world based on objective reality, what Zgorzelski calls "a mimetic world model." The subsequent entrance of the fantastic element breaches this model and changes it into a different world, one following different laws. The genre of the fantastic, then, consists of those texts which "build their fictional world as *a textual confrontation of those two models of reality*" [88].

Tolkien's Middle-earth, for example, becomes real to us because it builds on our perceptions of the world we know, but it is fantastic because it transcends those perceptions. Middle-earth draws us in because of the juxtaposition of the known and the unknown. As Spencer observes, "... if we recognize and accept the world and its characters as realistic, and enter into their perceptions and experiences, we thereby make an emotional commitment to the text as verisimilar, we commit energy to believing in it" (90).

This verisimilitude need not be physical. In fact, it is often not. As Bagwell points out, "The truth of fantasy ... is almost always a psychological or cultural one" (46). Allegorical, he adds: "fantasy is not realistic, it is apt" (46). Hobbits are not human, but enough of their behavior is human that we humans can identify with them and be drawn into their stories. The Gethenians in *The Left Hand of Darkness* are androgynous beings and only sexually active during *kemmer*, yet the questions their sexuality raises are human questions, from how we would react to meeting a people like the Gethenians to what a comparison of their sexuality to human sexuality reveals about humans.

The most egregious violation of "reality" in the eyes of many hard science fiction readers is magic, despite Clarke's Third Law regarding technology and magic (quoted in Chapter 1), but magic has rules too. Just because a world has magic does not mean that anyone who walks into that world can start zapping people with spells. In most fantasy worlds, magical power must be achieved: either learned from another practitioner or from books or both, passed down through one's genes, or earned through prayer or some other form of preparation, often one with spiritual overtones. In a world where magic is hereditary, if neither of your parents' families has ever produced magicians and you were not adopted, you will not be a magician. The rules hold. In addition, there is a sense of "conservation of energy" in magic that smacks of the scientific (and, interestingly, also of the mystical). The practitioner of magic has to expend energy to make magic work. There are not limitless supplies to draw on, it can be used up, you can wear yourself out, people can deprive you of your power source, and you can render yourself incapable of using magic for a period of time by overextending yourself.

For us to relate to the fictional world, it must be familiar enough for us to care about; for the fictional world to be a romance world, it must include the supernatural or the super-real. In the medieval period, there seems to have been less resistance to the interaction of these worlds and therefore monsters and dragons appear in the medieval romance with no explanation necessary. This is not to suggest that everyone reading or hearing a medieval romance believed in such creatures, but it does suggest that their presence in a narrative was considered acceptable, perhaps even necessary. Who would the knight fight to prove his godliness if he had no supernatural beings to challenge? Any man can fight another man; only the superior man can defend himself against demons and monsters, with God's help, of course.

Science fiction and fantasy face a different challenge, one of modern skepticism. In each science fiction novel, the author must create some semblance of an explanation for those things that are not possible in our world or the audience will not accept the novel as a whole. How much explanation is needed has changed over the years as science has become more and more sophisticated. The old Doc Smith novels of spaceships built in the backyard out of scrap metal and ingenuity are read with humor now that we know what it takes to construct and launch a real spaceship, but the core idea of man venturing out into the unknown remains as powerful a human need now as it was then. Only the vehicle has changed, not the desire.

Fantasy novels dispense with "the explanation" and often retreat to a time in our own history, like the Middle Ages, where humans had not yet decided that what could not be proven empirically did not exist. Alternately, many fantasy novels are set on other worlds where the physical laws of Earth need not apply. The important thing is to make the reader believe in the world for the duration of the novel, whether or not that reader believes in the possibility of the existence of the fictional world outside of the novel.

In the words of Harry Levin, author of the critical article "Science and Fiction," "Storytellers have always acknowledged the double need to contrive a tale that is interesting — which implies being novel, strange, surprising — and to tell it with credibility so that it sounds like the truth"

(8–9). This feeling of truth is underscored by the archetypal images of the marvelous and miraculous even when the physical evidence is at odds with our known reality.

The presence of these wonders provides the reader with the means to rebalance his or her psychological world. If the current society in which the reader lives is inadequate to the individual's needs, alternative answers to those needs may be found in these works. The medieval romance does this through the promise of Heavenly rewards for superior moral and physical prowess—rewards the hero, and the reader, are given a preview of in the miracles recounted in the tale. The reader of science fiction may pin his or her hope on the promise of a better society sometime in the future which, like the medieval romance's Heavenly rewards, may not be attainable in this lifetime, but unlike those rewards, may come to pass in time for the reader's descendants to enjoy. Fantasy offers less obvious rewards. It does not offer a better future either on Earth or in Heaven, but it does provide the psychological elements, in the form of the archetypal images of wonder, that are needed to rise above the mundane and shape a stronger self. Each type of literature presents the marvelous in a different way, but the goal is always the same, to supply the psyche with the tools needed to cope with the present and help humankind achieve its future.

10

And a Little Child
Shall Lead Them*

Medieval romance, science fiction, and fantasy have long been associated with children. One reason for this has already been mentioned: the presence of archetypal images that draw on emotions rather than reason. The prevalence of the young within the stories, especially as images of the child-hero archetype, may also prompt readers to see this as literature for children. It is not. The literature instead seeks to reach the child in each of us, a child Jungian psychology places in the role of mediator or savior.

"Suffer the little children to come unto me" (KJV, Mark 10:14). With these words, Jesus admonished his disciples and other listeners to remember their true relationship to God, as children to father. Jesus continues, "Verily I say unto you, Whosoever shall not receive the kingdom of God as a little child, he shall not enter therein" (KJV, Mark 10:15). In Christianity, as well as other belief structures, children are often seen as closer to God or the gods than adults are. The child has not absorbed or accepted all of the biases and limitations of the culture into which he has been born. He is closer to the archetypes at the center of human existence and free to express those archetypes in a variety of images, not just the ones that his society has deemed appropriate. While he is not necessarily the blank sheet of paper of Lockean philosophy (Locke 620)

*KJV, Isaiah 11:6.

nor the blank slate of Aristotle, still the child represents a greater percentage of potential than accomplished fact.

Therefore, in order to attain the new, higher level of existence being proffered, we must become as children, shedding the supposed knowledge of the world and opening our minds to the new form of knowledge being offered. We must admit our ignorance and inexperience and allow ourselves to be taught. The man who already thinks he knows all that is worth knowing will not listen to wisdom because he feels there is nothing more for him to learn. Socrates makes this observation in the *Apology*:

> "Well, I am certainly wiser than this man. It is only too likely that neither of us has any knowledge to boast of; but he thinks that he knows something which he does not know, whereas I am quite conscious of my ignorance. At any rate it seems that I am wiser than he is to this small extent, that I do not think that I know what I do not know" [Plato, *Last Days* 50].

The child as archetypal image is the promise of the future. Like the future he is an unknown, both moldable to our purposes and beyond our control. He is simultaneously helpless and powerful:

> It is a striking paradox in all child myths that the "child" is on the one hand delivered helpless into the power of terrible enemies and in continual danger of extinction, while on the other he possesses powers far exceeding those of ordinary humanity [Jung, *Archetypes* 170].

The child is innocence and knowledge, inexperience and potential, product of the past and promise of tomorrow.

Contradictions are an important feature of this archetype, not just the good/bad duality of all archetypal images, but a deeper unification of opposites that makes the child archetype "a mediator, bringer of healing, that is, one who makes whole" (164). One aspect of this union of opposites is the image of the child as savior; the healer property of the child archetype includes the healing of the breaches in the culture or societal behavior that have caused the need for salvation. The child hero or god forges a new solution that transcends the earlier inadequate solutions.

The child finding the new answer to a challenge is analogous to the Jungian explanation of the way the mind solves thorny problems. When two solutions are posited and neither seems to provide a successful conclusion to the problem, a third solution derived from the irrational subconscious mind, a solution that "the conscious mind neither expects nor understands," is created and put forth (Jung, *Archetypes* 167). The conscious mind seeks to reject this new and unsettling answer while simultaneously admiring it for its creativity and aptness. Similarly, the child hero is scoffed at for his creative new solutions to old problems and his rejection of the status quo, while at the same time he is admired for seeing in a new way, a way that may solve a serious problem and enhance the lives of his peers (168–9).

It is the paradox of helplessness and power that seems to make the child an attractive candidate for the role of hero in many romances, medieval and modern. In the early medieval romance *Roswall & Lillian*, Roswall's innocence is both his downfall and his salvation. His youthful compassion prompts him to release some political prisoners from his father's jail, with the result that the boy is banished from his own kingdom, and his childlike trust of the family steward earns him only betrayal as the man robs Roswall of his possessions and the letters of introduction his parents had given him. The release of the prisoners that caused Roswall's exile, however, permits them to appear at the crucial moment to provide arms and a horse for the tournament in which he eventually has to fight to win the woman he loves.

Galahad is the extreme example of the child hero. He has to maintain a childlike purity and belief in order to be worthy to achieve the Grail. Not only is Galahad a youth himself, but through his belief in God he carries the power to rejuvenate others, as is shown in the scene with King Mordrayns near the end of "The Tale of the Sangreal."

> "Sir Galahad, flower of all knighthood, whose coming I have awaited for so long, welcome! I pray you take me in your arms and hold me to your breast, for you alone, true servant of Christ that you are, possess the virginity of the white lily together with the virtue of the burning rose: qualities of the Holy Ghost, by which my flesh shall be made young again" [Baines 425].

Galahad does as asked, and "the ancient king's flesh was made young again, before his soul departed from his body" (425).

This rejuvenative quality is in keeping with the role of the archetypal image in personality development. The child represents the urge toward self-actualization. Since the fully actualized Self is a constantly retreating goal, a person will always stand in the relation of child to adult in terms of the evolving self and the total personality. Jung explains the relationship of these two selves in the following way: "Where the Ego is total psyche at some particular time, the Self is its totality for all time" (Cohen 27). For one to be open and receptive to the world around one, especially to the new and wonder-filled worlds of fantasy and science fiction, one needs to be like a child. If one believes one has attained adulthood and therefore need not grow any longer, one will begin to stagnate.

In his book *The Dreams Our Stuff is Made Of: How Science Fiction Conquered the World* and also in his article "The Embarrassments of Science Fiction" included in the collection *Science Fiction at Large*, science fiction writer Thomas Disch belittles the genre for being comprised largely of what he considers children's literature in its intellectual, emotional, and moral scope ("Embarrassments" 143). He sees this as a liability of science fiction, and potentially of fantasy, but the very traits for which he condemns science fiction may, in fact, be the traits that make it valuable. The child character and the childlike or primitive perspective are actually assets in terms of the literature's archetypal value. Archetypes exert the strongest influence in the first years of life, according to Jung, "when consciousness is weakest and most restricted, and where fantasy can overrun the facts of the outer world" (*Archetypes* 67). If the child can establish the important "balance between the collective unconscious and the conscious personality" at a young age, "dangerous manifestations" of the archetypes are less likely to occur when he or she becomes an adult (Cohen 118). For those individuals who were unable to establish that crucial balance during their own childhoods, the child hero of the story offers a second chance. By living through the child's experience, the archetype is brought from the subconscious to the conscious level where it can be integrated into the self.

Ender Wiggins, of Orson Scott Card's science fiction novel *Ender's Game*, is a classic example of the characteristics of the child as hero. When the story begins, Ender is only six years old. He and his two older siblings are all geniuses, but only Ender has passed all of the tests and screenings to be accepted into the school that trains youth to become soldiers and commanders of the International Fleet, a starship fleet whose purpose is to protect Earth from invasion by alien lifeforms. While six may seem young to begin such training, six is exactly what the teachers want because it allows them to shape the child to the desired result. At the same time, part of Ender's appeal is his ability to come up with creative and unique solutions to problems. This takes us back to the contradictory nature of the child — biddable but still able to see the world in ways closed to most adults by their acceptance of limitations. Consider, for example, the number of children and teens who have broken into supposedly secure computer systems whose security was created by and vouched for by adults, simply because the youngsters did not know, or did not believe, that it could not be done.

Ender also has the empathetic skills needed to understand the enemy, an understanding essential to his future victory over them. The flaw in the plan is that if Ender develops empathy with the "buggers" he may not want to kill them, may even refuse to provide to others the information that would allow anyone to kill them. Because of this, Ender is kept in the dark about the reality of what he is doing. At ten, he is promoted to Command School and given command of many of the young people with whom he went through Battle School. Everything is set up as a game on a simulator, and they fight valiantly, believing they are merely practicing the skills they will need when they are called to active service in a few years. After months of "simulated" battles that break some of the young people and drive Ender to the edge of exhaustion and psychological collapse, a final "graduation battle" is conducted and, against 1000 to 1 odds, Ender blows up the bugger home world.

Only at this point do the adults running the command school reveal the truth of what Ender has been doing. Mazer Rackham, Ender's mentor and the hero of the previous war against the buggers, explains:

> "Ender, for the past few months you have been the battle commander of our fleets. This was the Third Invasion. There were no games, the battles were real, and the only enemy you fought was the buggers. You won every battle, and today you finally fought them at their home world, where the queen was, all the queens from all their colonies, they were all there and you destroyed them completely. They'll never attack us again. You did it. You" [327].

Ender is horrified. All the time he thought he had been killing blips on a screen, he had been killing living beings. At the age of eleven, he has become the hero of his planet and the destroyer of another planet's entire civilization.

The adults have shaped and twisted him to their own ends, and yet without his ability to step beyond what the adults could envision, the whole project would have failed. He had to be both pliable and independent, knowledgeable and ignorant. Mazer is the one who explains this to Ender as well:

"And it had to be a child, Ender," said Mazer. "You were faster than me. Better than me. I was too old and cautious. Any decent person who knows what warfare is can never go into battle with a whole heart. But you didn't know. We made sure you didn't know. You were reckless and brilliant and young. It's what you were born for" [328–9].

Ender, who "possesses powers far exceeding those of ordinary humanity" and who has been "delivered helpless into the power of terrible enemies" (both the buggers and the adults who were manipulating him), is the archetypal child hero (Jung, *Archetypes* 170). There is, however, another aspect of the child archetype, futurity, and Ender fulfills that aspect as well, ultimately confounding the adults' plans for a "bugger-free" universe. Because of the empathy Ender has with the buggers, the Queen has made a heroic last attempt to ensure the survival of her race. She has created a place on the bugger home world that copies a part of Ender's dreams and placed a treasure there that she believes Ender will find and protect, "the pupa of a queen bugger, already fertilized by the larval males, ready, out of her own body, to hatch a hundred thousand buggers, including a few queens and males" (351).

Because Ender has learned to understand the buggers better than anyone else and because the Queen has entered his dreams and discovered that Ender was unaware he was killing real buggers, the Queen has entrusted their survival to him. Her trust was well placed. Ender has not forgiven the adults who deceived him and he has not forgiven himself for being used; allowing the buggers to repopulate another planet is a way for him to make amends. He does not fear the buggers' reprisals because he knows that the two species were simply so different that neither recognized the other as an intelligent life form until it was too late to stop the war.

So Ender lifts the silken cocoon from its hiding place, receives mental images that instruct him in its care and hatching, and makes a promise to the bugger queen.

"I'll carry you," said Ender, "I'll go from world to world until I find a time and a place where you can come awake in safety. And I'll tell your story to my people, so that perhaps in time they can forgive you, too. The way that you've forgiven me" [354].

He keeps this promise by publishing a book of the words and images the hive queen had put in his head, "all the good and all the evil that the hive-queen knew," and signing it with the pseudonym Speaker for the

Dead (355). As the book ends, Ender is traveling through space with his sister Valentine searching for the right world on which to reestablish the bugger colony.

The adults in a romance work often confuse inexperience with inability. This error is a popular one for the young medieval knight to dispel. In story after story, the newly made knight asks the boon of the next adventure and is granted it. The person who comes seeking aid, usually a beautiful woman, scoffs at the young knight and asks for a better champion. The king upholds the young man's right to try his luck and the woman goes off with her young champion but spends much of their travel time belittling the man and complaining about the ill fate that brought him to her side. Inevitably, the young knight proves himself worthy of the task. This is, of course, a test of the young knight's manhood, a coming of age ritual, but it is also a reminder that the new should not be discounted as it may be able to overcome the old.

One of the more familiar versions of this tale is that of Percival, or Parzival. Parzival's mother has raised him in seclusion in the hope that she will not lose him to the knightly adventures that took his father from her. The young man is so sheltered that the first time he sees a knight he thinks the man is a god. Awestruck by the knight, even after he learns knights are not gods, Parzival begs his mother to let him go to King Arthur and become a knight. Reluctantly, she lets him go and his natural beauty, grace, and manners win him entrance to Arthur's court and the coveted chance to be a knight. Parzival's first battle is less than knightly as he kills his man with an arrow, which is not a knight's weapon; however, the dead knight's armor does provide the youth with what he needs to look the part. Parzival is so ignorant he has to get someone to help disarm the dead knight, show him how to don the armor, and explain to him the use of the sword and the value of the spear. Nonetheless, Parzival goes on to become one of the three knights who achieve the Grail.

Another well-known tale is that of Beaumains, who turns out to be Sir Gareth, the brother of Sir Gawain and nephew of Arthur. A lesser-known tale in the same vein is *Sir Libeaus Desconus*. The young man is Sir Gawain's son, a fact the reader or listener is aware of but the young man is not. Therefore, the audience is prepared for this young knight's success based on his parentage. The other characters have to base their reactions on the knight's behavior. He is as green as anyone can possibly be. He has lived a simple life with his mother, who called him only

Beau-fis or Fair Face, and he never questions his life until the day he finds a dead knight in the forest. At that point, the young man strips the knight of his armor, dons it himself, and rides off to seek King Arthur's court, the existence of which he is inexplicably aware of despite his sheltered upbringing. Arthur is impressed by the young man's beauty and bearing and consents to make him a knight, calling him *Libeaus Desconus*, the fair unknown. Gawain instructs him in the matter of arms.

Shortly thereafter, Libeaus Desconus asks to be given the next adventure and the typical sequence unfolds. The maiden Elene and her attendant dwarf arrive to ask for succor, Libeaus Desconus requests and is granted the adventure, and Elene complains to Arthur that she has been cheated. "Lord King, now are thy fame and thy manhood dishonoured when thou sendest a child, wild and witless, to deal mighty strokes, and yet hast valiant knights, Lancelot, Perceval, and Gawain, well proved in many a tournament!" (*Sir Cleges/Sir Libeaus Desconus* 25). Each new challenge is met and vanquished by the young knight, and eventually the maiden's mockery turns to praise as the dead giants and defeated knights begin to accumulate. Youth has proven itself. It is not always superior to age, but it is certainly not found lacking.

At times, the unwillingness of the old to acknowledge the power of the new is a factor in the former's downfall. Jamis, one of the tribe of fierce fighters known as Fremen in Frank Herbert's novel *Dune*, challenges fifteen-year-old Paul Atreides to a knife fight to the death. Jamis is overconfident because he considers Paul a mere child even though Paul has already injured and disarmed him using a version of what could be called marital arts. Jamis believes Paul was only able to overpower him by a fluke and intends to prove it. He cannot comprehend that the boy has been trained since he was a babe to be a fighter, and because he cannot accept that which is outside of his experience, Jamis dies.

Stilgar, the leader of the group of Fremen who accepted Paul into their midst, also finds himself in a position where he must confront Paul or lose his own right to lead his people. Stilgar, however, unlike Jamis, is capable of accepting change and seeing the value in the new, and as a result their challenge ends with both of them alive and tradition having been modified.

> "You think it's time I called out Stilgar and changed the leadership of the troops!" Before they could respond, Paul hurled his voice at them in anger: "Do you think the Lisan al-Gaib is that stupid?"

There was stunned silence.

[...]

"It's the way!" someone shouted.

Paul spoke dryly, probing the emotional undercurrents. "Ways change" [426].

Paul leads the people to see that killing off a strong leader in time of need would be like "smash[ing] your knife before a battle" (427). He reminds them that instead of fighting each other, they should be turning their knives against the real enemy, the Harkonnens.

Arrakis is Paul's ducal fief by Imperial fiat, but he stresses that he wants the Fremen to help him govern because he respects their wisdom and strength. To join the two cultures, Paul has Stilgar pledge fealty using the same rite that Paul's father had used with his men. Stilgar's position and power within the tribe are not changed; what has altered is his position in relation to the power structure of the entire planet. "'Stilgar leads this tribe,' Paul said. 'Let no man mistake that. He commands with my voice. What he tells you, it is as though I told you'" (429). The young man is the voice of the future. Those who can adapt, survive; those who cling mindlessly to the old ways, do not.

A further development of the fusion of opposites in this archetype is the portrayal of the child as hermaphroditic, combining the most desirable qualities of maleness and femaleness into a person who is whole in ways that individuals of either sex cannot be. The entire culture in LeGuin's *The Left Hand of Darkness* has evolved into a state of hermaphroditism, and the hermaphroditic beings consider the man who comes to visit their planet to be primitive because of his single-sexed nature even though the civilization of the visitor's world is obviously more technologically advanced. Jung would probably side with the Gethenians since, as noted in Chapter 5, in the Jungian scheme of things true maturity cannot be reached until a harmonious balance between the male and female sides of the psyche has been achieved.

Ender, of *Ender's Game*, is considered Earth's best chance for salvation. His sister was rejected because she was "too pacific, too conciliatory, and, above all, too empathic," all feminine traits and all desired, but not to the degree exhibited in the sister (250). The brother is unacceptable because he has an overabundance of the male qualities of aggression and dominance; of the brother one of the searchers remarked, "[he] has the soul of a jackal" (250). In Ender, these male and female qualities achieve balance; he can kill, but he does not enjoy killing; he can understand other cultures, but he does not lose his identification with his own.

Paul Atriedes is likewise seen as a savior partially because of his ability to integrate the male and female sides of himself. He is the prophesied Kwisatz Haderach; the only man who can take the Truthsayer drug and live. When a woman takes the drug, she can reach into her mind and retrieve memories of "many avenues of the past . . but only feminine avenues" (13). The Kwisatz Haderach will be able to take the drug and not only survive, but "find in the gift of the drug his inward eye. He will look where we cannot — into both feminine and masculine pasts" (13). Note that the male will be able to access not only the male memories that have been unavailable to the women but also the female memories. This merging of the masculine and feminine is not simply emblematic of the healing of the rift in the world, at times it is the agent required to heal an actual breach.

Robert Jordan's Rand al'Thor, like Paul Atreides, is the one foretold, the man who can use the power that had historically been the province of the women and not just survive but ensure the survival of his world. Paramount among the handful of pivotal figures in Jordan's Wheel of Time Series, Rand is the Dragon Reborn, the only man who can safely channel *saidin*, the male half of the True Source, "the driving force of the universe" (*Dragon Reborn* 594). Other men who attempt to channel *saidin* are driven insane or die because *saidin* was tainted with evil when the world was "broken" during the last catastrophic battle between good and evil. Both halves of the True Source, male and female, are needed to affect any lasting worldwide change.

In order to facilitate the combining of male and female power and allow for a united front against the evil that threatens to overwhelm their world, Rand agrees to take part in a ritual that is supposed to rid *saidin* of the taint. As part of the ritual, Rand must surrender himself to the female half of the True Source, *saidar*.

> Alongside the turmoil of *saidin*, *saidar* was a tranquil river flowing smoothly. [...]
> That was the first difficulty, to fight *saidin* while surrendering to *saidar*. The first difficulty, and the first key to what he had to do. The male and female halves of the True Source were alike and unalike, attracting and repelling, fighting against each other even as they worked together to drive the Wheel of Time [*Winter's Heart* 636–7].

So, too, the child hero must reconcile the male and female halves of the psyche to create a unified personality able to face the future.

Youth has always been the hope of the future. Basing a work on a positive image of the young of necessity implies hope. The young will inherit the world when the old have died out. If the young are perceived as being intelligent, strong, and capable, then the world will continue. If the young are fearful, confused, and weak, the future is uncertain. In medieval romances, the newly knighted youth nearly always achieved his goals: renown, the fair lady, and treasure in the form of property, jewels, or gold. This symbolized the continuation of the society into the next generation. Underscoring this were the genetic ties between many of the best of the new generation and the best of the old generation — Gawain and Lancelot both fathered sons who equaled or exceeded their fathers' abilities.

The negative side of this literary medieval youth is exemplified by Arthur's kingdom-usurping son Mordred. It is significant to note that all of the three sons just mentioned are illegitimate. This has no bearing on their prowess as knights or their virtue as Christians. Galahad is a bastard, but he achieves the Grail. The flaw in Mordred is not his bastardy, nor Arthur's failure to acknowledge him, as the other two are not acknowledged either. Mordred's failure is his inability to see beyond the present. He wants power for power's sake. He is not interested in ideals or virtues or God. He wants as much power as he can bribe, extort, or seize by force, and he wants it now. This is how he was taught to see the world by his mother, the evil enchantress Morgawse (or in other versions Morgan le Fay). He has allowed himself to be limited by the negative aspect of his society's archetypes, rejecting the positive and thereby becoming one-dimensional and losing his role as a youthful mediator. Galahad, on the other hand, acknowledges the sinful nature of mankind, but chooses not to give in to the sinful side of himself.

Beau fis, or Libeaus Desconus, is willing to endure the scorn of the lady he serves until such time as he is able to prove by deeds of arms that he is worthy of her respect. Mordred wants respect without having to prove he deserves it. Mordred is restricted by the limitations of the present. Like Jamis in *Dune*, Mordred wants to play by the old rules even though the world has changed. It works for a little while, but in the end, it brings about his death and the downfall of Camelot and all of Arthur's plans. Similarly, if Jamis and the men like him had gained control of the Fremen, *Dune* might also have ended in destruction and the downfall of a civilization.

The child archetype pervades science fiction and fantasy. Disch's disparaging remarks notwithstanding, the presence of the child should be seen as a positive element of these two genres. Like the worlds they inhabit or foretell, the children and adolescents who dominate many of these novels hold forth a promise of not only a world to come, which itself is sometimes in question in these days of nuclear weaponry, but a better world. It may or may not arrive, and it may or may not be as the story foretells. These things are immaterial. Like Ender passing a world down to the offspring of the queen of the buggers, what matters is the belief that there will be a world for us to pass down to our children.

11

The Voice of Experience:
The Wise Old Man

At the other end of the spectrum from the archetypal image of the child, but equally important in terms of ensuring a future worth realizing, is the archetype of wisdom personified in the wise old man. This person may be cast in a variety of forms. Medieval romances often portray the wise old man as a wizard, such as Merlin, but he appears in a variety of other guises as well, as a look at *Havelok* and *King Horn* will show. Since fantasy novels tend to include magic in the societies they depict, the wise old men in works like Williams' *The Dragonbone Chair*, Tolkien's The Lord of the Rings, and White's *The Once and Future King* are usually wizards or magic users of some kind. Science fiction opens the category up to include not only human scholars like Faber in Bradbury's *Fahrenheit 451* but also non-human sources of wisdom like the CD-ROM personality Dixie Flatline in Gibson's *Neuromancer*.

Jung refers to the wise old man as "an ambiguous elfin character" who can be "good incarnate" or "an aspect of evil" (*Archetypes* 227). While he is usually a doer of good who helps the hero of the romance, he can also be an agent of evil — Merlin and Gandalf on one hand and Rumpelstilskin and Saruman on the other. In either form, the wise old man is symbolic of the spirit, which in Jungian terms is that which is not of matter and not of nature but which is a thing's essence (208–9). Spirit, then, is like Plato's perfect form, that which a thing *is* when stripped of all of its physical attributes. The wise old man is associated with knowledge and "... goes back in direct line to the figure of the medicine man in primitive society. He is, like the anima, an immortal daemon that pierces the chaotic darknesses of brute life with the light of meaning. He is the enlightener, the master and teacher..." (36–7).

While modern man has rationalized and internalized the "spirit" or *daemon* the wise old man represents, originally that spirit "came upon man from without," providing information or aid at a crucial point when the hero had reached an impasse which he appeared to be unable to surmount using the skills he had acquired up to then (Jung, *Archetypes* 252). The child, too, is the source of answers in the time of confusion and indecision, but the child is symbolic of creative solutions arrived at intuitively. The wise old man symbolizes meaning derived from reason; the hero has to take all of the information he has learned up to the point of the impasse, process it, and formulate a meaning for it. In most forms of romance, the wise old man is a character separate from the hero—a teacher, a mentor — but psychologically he is the hero's own higher cognitive powers, the ability to make sense of the world around him. Often the wise old man in the story does not supply the hero with direct answers but merely points him in the direction that will lead to the answers if the hero is clever enough.

Arthur learns a great deal from Merlin in T. H. White's *The Once and Future King*, a lighthearted fantasy based on Malory's *Le Morte D'Arthur*. This is done by turning Arthur, or Wart as he is affectionately called, into various other living things so he can learn about life by seeing it from a variety of perspectives, including those of a bird, a fish, and an ant. Only in rare instances, like the first time Wart is changed, does Merlin join the boy. Merlin prefers to send Wart off on his own to see how he manages; the wizard believes that "Education is experience, and the essence of experience is self-reliance" (46). Merlin provides the opportunities for Wart to gain the information he will need as Arthur, ruler of Britain, but it is up to Wart to winnow out the valuable information from the useless.

The appearance of the wise old man is usually linked to a specific character or group, not to the general public. When Wart asks Merlin why his foster brother Kay cannot be turned into something and join Wart in a lesson, Merlin replies, "I cannot change Kay into things. The power was not deputed to me when I was sent. Why this was so, neither you nor I am able to say, but such remains the fact" (90). The wisdom he embodies is to be given only to the designated recipient.

The wise old man typically does not prophesy on demand, but only in time of need. This is made clear in Geoffrey of Monmouth's *The History of the Kings of Britain* when Aurelius Ambrosius orders Merlin, yet another incarnation of this best known of the wise old man figures, to prophesy just so people will hear marvels.

> "Mysteries of that sort cannot be revealed," answered Merlin, "except where there is the most urgent need for them. If I were to utter them as an entertainment, or where there was no need at all, then the spirit which controls me would forsake me in the moment of need" [196].

Frequently, the wise old man appears in the medieval romance in the form of a holy man, a dwarf, or an older knight who appears at a crucial juncture to supply needed advice. The mysterious knight in the early English romance, *Sir Amadas*, is one such example. Sir Amadas has given away his money and goods to help others. After he has given away the last of his money to a widow who needs the funds to bury her husband, Amadas finds himself shunned by the others in his class because he is now impoverished. He laments his former generous ways because he thinks ". . . folk set no store by a man that hath little goods" (Rickert 57). But just as Amadas is questioning his own values, a mysterious knight appears and admonishes him, "A man that gives of a kind heart alike to good and evil, will come out somehow" (59). So Amadas continues onward and stops regretting his charitable ways.

When Amadas later wins lands and a lady and the couple has a child, he is willing to sacrifice all to repay the mysterious knight who aided him. The knight turns out to be the ghost of the man Amadas gave the widow his last funds to bury, however, so Amadas has, in effect, already prepaid his debt (65–6). The knight was simply bringing to light what Sir Amadas should have known all along—"Ye should not lament so, for God may make a man to fall and rise again; His help is aye near!" (58). Amadas had the information needed to understand and accept his changes in fortune; the knight merely reminded him to use it.

At times, the wise old man assumes a form of deathlessness akin to the Christian analogue of God the Father. This is not to say that the wise old man is actually an immortal, although this is sometimes true, but rather to argue that the knowledge he passes on is sufficiently important that a means has been devised for it to survive from generation to generation. Morgenes and Simon in Williams' *The Dragonbone Chair* and Faber and Montag in *Fahrenheit 451* have books. The Merlin of *The Once and Future King* is living life backwards—youthening as it were—so he can tell Arthur the future because it is his own past. The Merlin of Marion Zimmer Bradley's *The Mists of Avalon* is a title held by a succession of men who hand down their knowledge one to the other so nothing is lost. Dixie Flatline, in Gibson's *Neuromancer*, is a person reduced to code on a CD-ROM. None of these wise old men are immortal in the sense that gods are immortal, but their knowledge remains within the communities of which they are a part.

Sometimes the wise old men come in pairs, good and evil, balancing each other. One such pair is comprised of King Godard of Denmark and Grim the fisherman in the Middle English romance *Havelok*. Godard has been entrusted with the care of Havelok and his two sisters, the children of the late king of Denmark. Godard has other plans, however, that do not include sharing Denmark with any royal heirs. To that end Godard "put them in a castle where they wept bitterly for hunger and cold. When he had presently brought all the land into his power he planned against them a very great treachery" (*Three M.E.R.* 56). Godard kills the sisters and plans to kill Havelok, but he finds he cannot kill the boy himself so he gives Havelok to one of his fisherman, Grim, and orders him to drown the child during the night.

Grim has every intention of following Godard's orders until he and his wife discover who the boy really is. Light shining from his mouth and "a king's mark, very bright and fair" give away Havelok's identity, and rather than murder his true king, Grim takes Havelok and his family and flees to England (59). There he does the best he can for the child until he is an adult and able to find his own way in the world. Although Grim has died by the time Havelok assumes the rulership of Denmark and England (gained through marriage), Havelok rewards Grim's children for the old man's help. In this case the old man did not dispense knowledge to the hero, he kept knowledge to himself that protected the hero until the hero could defend himself. Godard, on the other hand, taught by negative example what a good ruler should do. Havelok makes sure that Ubbe, his friend and the man set up to rule over Denmark while Havelok is ruling England, will be nothing like Godard and "should so rule Denmark that no complaint should come to him [Havelok]" (89).

At times the same person can be both the good and bad wise old man at different points in the tale. At the beginning of the Middle English romance, *King Horn*, King Ailmar of Westernesse is the good wise old man. He provides a refuge for Horn and the twelve companions with whom he has been set adrift by the Saracens who killed Horn's father and captured his homeland. King Ailmar is particularly taken by Horn and asks his steward to make sure that, in addition to the instruction in courtly behavior that all of the boys would be receiving, Horn be taught harp and song (*Three M.E.R.* 21–22). Ailmar continues to dote on the boy and when it comes time for the young man to be knighted, the king acquiesces readily, saying, "'Greatly hath Horn pleased me, and I will dub him and afterward he shall be my darling. He himself shall knight his twelve comrades'" (27). To further endear himself to the king, Horn slays an entire shipload of Saracens who have landed on Ailmar's shores intending to conquer his kingdom.

The very next day after Horn has slain the Saracens, a jealous companion of his pours lies about Horn into Ailmar's ears. Ailmar discovers Horn with Rymanhild, the king's own daughter, and banishes Horn without even asking him to explain himself. "'Away, thou vile thief!' he cried, 'never more shalt thou be dear to me! Go out from my hall or with my sword I shall smite thee'" (31–32). Ailmar has become the evil old man and the role of good old man shifts to the King of Ireland into whose service Horn is accepted. When Horn refuses the King of Ireland's daughter's hand in marriage on the grounds that he, Horn, is already betrothed, the king is not only gracious about the refusal but goes so far as to provide the soldiers needed to help Horn rescue his beloved Rymanhild.

In each case the king provides aid to Horn when he is exiled, but Ailmar fails to trust Horn and listens to lies and slander that contradict his own experience. The King of Ireland, who has less reason to support Horn because he has known him a shorter time and who would stand to benefit by *not* helping Horn, provides the help Horn needs. He remains consistent in his role as benefactor, whereas Ailmar moves between the light and dark manifestations of the archetype.

We find the wise old man in the science fiction novel and fantasy novel, too, often as the source of pivotal information. Professor Faber fills this role in *Fahrenheit 451*. When Montag goes to the man and asks Faber to help him learn to understand what he is reading because he feels the lack in his world may come from the loss of books, Faber explains that it is not the books but the thoughts captured within the books that matter.

"Books were only one type of receptacle where we stored a lot of things we were afraid we might forget. There is nothing magical in them at all. The magic is only in what books say, how they stitched the patches of the universe together into one garment for us" [82–3].

Faber does not tell Montag the answer to what is wrong with their world. He tells him to think for himself and allows Montag to discover that simply by refusing to accept their society's power over them humans have the means to free themselves from the trap they have created.

Similarly, Ducem Barr, whose father Onum Barr was one of the last people in The Empire to encounter a member of the First Foundation in person in Asimov's *Foundation and Empire*, is sought out by a young Bel Riose. Riose, a warrior eager to fight the enemies of The Empire and make a name for himself, is seeking information about the magicians believed to inhabit the space just beyond the edge of the empire. Barr provides what factual evidence he has, and more importantly, explains what he has pieced together for himself over forty years concerning Hari Seldon and the Foundation (16–9).

Riose is skeptical and ignores Barr's implied warning about the power of the Foundation, but the wise old man has spoken truth. It is the fault of the seeker that he does not recognize it. Meaning has been provided for Riose, but since it is not the meaning he wants the information to yield, he chooses to disregard most of the old man's words. The wise old man can only guide, not force. As Barr himself says to Riose: "'You have demanded my knowledge of me and threatened its extortion by force. If you choose to meet it with skepticism, what is that to me?'" (17).

Even in the grim, darker science fiction world of cyberpunk, the wise old man surfaces; he may look a bit different, but he is there. In William Gibson's *Neuromancer*, McCoy Pauley, also known as Dixie Flatline, is a ROM construct, a person preserved as computer code. He is also the archetypal image of the wise old man. His knowledge is so essential to the project that Case, the main character and ace hacker, has been hired to do, that the people Case is working for stage an elaborate diversion in order to steal Dixie's construct from a major corporation. Pauley is called Flatline because his EEG went flat when he tried to crack the security on an Artificial Intelligence's programming. Since this is precisely what Case has been hired to do, although he did not know it when he was hired, Flatline's advice is invaluable to Case, both as to what to try and what not to try (114–5). Without the dead man's knowledge and sometimes his aid in negotiating computer code, Case cannot succeed.

The wise old man of most fantasy novels is one of the genre's stereotypes — the wizard. Fantasy is rife with wizards. Gandalf and Saruman in The Lord of the Rings, Merlin in *The Once and Future King* and others, Morgenes in Tad Williams' Memory, Sorrow & Thorn trilogy, Silvercloak in the Fionavar Tapestry: in each of these novels there is a wizard or magic user who steers the hero in the right direction.

The mage may be presented initially as someone ordinary, but his true character and role will not remain hidden. *The Summer Tree*, the first book of Kay's Fionavar Tapestry, introduces the reader and the characters in the book to a man known as Lorenzo Marcus, lecturer on Celtic lore. In a matter of pages, a few hours in the time table of the novel, Marcus is revealed to be a mage named Silvercloak who has come from an alternate world called Paras Derval ostensibly to recruit five humans to participate in a celebration, but actually because Silvercloak has had a premonition that the young college students will be needed in some way in his world. He is a figure of mystery leading them to possible danger without telling them the whole story, but he is also a man of power whose very presence protects the young people from an evil creature who has slipped through during the mage's transit between worlds, and he is a healer whose skills can cure the wound inflicted on his companion dwarf by the evil creature's bite.

Since fantasy is about worlds whose rules differ from ours it makes sense that one role of the wise old man in fantasy is to teach the inhabitants of the world how to manipulate their world and to reveal to the reader how the world operates. One such character is Morgenes in *The Dragonbone Chair*. Morgenes' apprentice Simon is complaining about having to read and write when he wants to learn magic instead. Morgenes tries to explain to Simon the importance of reading and in so doing tells the reader something of the world in which the story is taking place.

> "Books," Morgenes said grandly, leaning back on his precarious stool, " — books *are* magic. That is the simple answer. And books are traps as well."
>
> "Magic? Traps?"
>
> "Books are a form of magic — " the doctor lifted the volume he had just laid on the stack, "because they span time and distance more surely than any spell or charm."

[...]

"A piece of writing *is* a trap," he said cheerily, "and the best kind. A book, you see, is the only kind of trap that keeps its captive — which is knowledge — alive forever. The more books you have," the doctor waved an all-encompassing hand about the room, "the more traps, then the better chance of capturing some particular, elusive, shining beast — one that might otherwise die unseen" [78].

Both Simon and the reader are being told that this is a world that values information. It may also be a world that relies on swordplay and magic, but knowledge gained from books is so powerful that Morgenes' primary goal in instructing Simon is to teach him to read so the boy can have access to that knowledge.

Simon does not see this connection. To him magic means spells and incantations and hocus-pocus. He cites the actions of the other magic user in the story as an example of what he believes magic to be. Morgenes' reply lets Simon and the reader know the difference between the types of magic the two practice and why Pyrates, Morgenes' foil, is evil.

"I spoke to you of traps, of searching for knowledge as though hunting an elusive creature. Well, where I and other knowledge-seekers go out to our traps to see what bright beast we may have been lucky enough to capture, Pyrates throws open his door at night and waits to see what comes in. [...] The problem with Pyrates' approach," he continued, "is that if you do not like the beast that comes to call, it is hard — very, *very* hard — to get the door closed again" [80].

Here we have both faces of the wise old man, the good and the evil, and instruction to the hero as to which to follow. It is instruction only, however. Simon must choose for himself.

Affiliated with the wise old man is the figure of the trickster. Sometimes this is the evil aspect of the wise old man. This might seem contradictory, since the trickster is usually considered very primitive, in Jung's words, "... an archetypal psychic structure of extreme antiquity. In his clearest manifestations he is a faithful reflection of an absolutely undifferentiated human consciousness, corresponding to a psyche that has hardly left the animal level" (*Archetypes* 260). Yet, it is that very primitive nature that makes the trickster the companion or alter ego of the wise old man. Because man has moved away from his primitive nature toward his intellectual, reasoning nature, he needs something to remind him of that primitive side so he does not revert to it. That something is the trickster. "It holds the earlier low intellectual and moral level before the eyes of the more highly developed individual, so that he shall not forget how things looked yesterday" (267).

The very controlled, ultra-civilized city world of Clarke's *The City and the Stars* has a figure called Khedron the Jester programmed into the city plan as a means to provide an element of chance, disruption, and misrule designed to keep the society from stagnating. Khedron also serves as a reminder of how unpredictable life was before the City was built and the new society was established. By providing the figure of the jester, the city anticipates and forestalls rebellion against the orderliness of its world. All the malcontent has to do is look at the havoc wreaked by the jester when he is set loose, and he can see how much nicer the neat orderly world is in comparison.

The wise old man is many things— teacher, mentor, aid in times of indecision, spirit, intellect, reason. The archetypal images reflect an archetype that encompasses that which we deem significant knowledge and the means to convey that knowledge to others. The wise old man provides a balance for the image of the child. Whenever the hero reaches an impasse, he has to make a choice. He must decide if this is a situation where he can think through the information he has gained and make an informed decision based on the accumulated knowledge of his reason or if it is a situation where he needs to seek to find a new, intuitive solution to the problem. The author may sway the hero's decision, however, by including an image of either the archetype of the child or the wise old man in the story at the crucial juncture. Both are acceptable ways of solving dilemmas and their respective value is evident in the fact that, often, both archetypal images appear in the same story, wisdom balancing intuition, age balancing youth, new ideas springing forth to eventually be added to the accumulated knowledge to be passed down through the generations. In Jung's words, "Graybeard and boy belong together" (*Archetypes* 215).

The wise old man's presence at the right moment in the story is essential. This can be ascertained from the description of when the wise old man is apt to appear. "The archetype of spirit in the shape of a man, hobgoblin, or animal always appears in a situation where insight, under-standing, good advice, determination, planning, etc., are needed but cannot be mustered on own's own resources" (216). Put another way, "The old man always appears when the hero is in a hopeless and desperate situation from which only profound reflection or a lucky idea ...

can extricate him" (217–8). The wise old man steps in and provides the wisdom, the aid, the magical object, the secret information that the hero needs to succeed at the moment. Sometimes the situation for which the wise old man has prepared the hero does not occur until the future, when in a moment of crisis the importance of what the old man has provided becomes apparent.

As important as the old man's arrival is his eventual absence from the story. For the hero to be come truly successful, he must someday be able to confront the world without the wise old man. The knowledge and patterns of inquiry the old man provided should give the hero the ability to reason out a solution for himself. At some point in many of these stories, the hero turns to the wise old man only to discover that he is not there and the hero has to solve his own problems. Like any good teacher, the wise old man's goal should be to make himself obsolete. Occasionally, the old man will surface later in the tale, after the hero has proven that he can think for himself, to acknowledge the hero's accomplishments, to resume the role of advisor, or to provide the next level of instruction, but just as often, the wise old man remains at a distance, recognizing that he is no longer needed.

Merlin, in many of his literary incarnations, is at Arthur's side during his youth and early years as king but then leaves, obliging the king to make his own decisions. In some versions, Merlin leaves to pursue other interests; in others he is trapped in the crystal cave or some other living tomb by Nimue, the woman to whom he taught magic and with whom he fell in love. Malory's *Le Morte D'Arthur*, follows the Nimue tale. In it, Merlin becomes enamored of Nimue, who is one of the damsels of the lake. She gets Merlin to teach her his crafts of enchantment and eventually Nimue uses the knowledge to trap him under a rock. Merlin, knowing what will befall him, provides what last minute advice he can for Arthur.

> [...] and so he told the king many things that should befall, but always he warned the king to keep well his sword and the scabbard, for he told him how the sword and the scabbard should be stolen by a woman from him that he most trusted. Also he told King Arthur that he should miss him, — Yet had ye lever than all your lands to have me again. Ah, said the king, since ye know of your adventure, purvey for it, and put away by your crafts that misadventure. Nay, said Merlin, it will not be; so he departed from the king [Caxton 57–8].

Whatever the stated cause for Merlin's departure, the underlying cause is the need to let the hero stand on his own. Arthur's authority among his fellow kings would be undermined if they believed his leadership was supported by the crutch of Merlin's magic. The other kings might decide that if they took away Merlin, Arthur would fall. To solidify his position, Arthur must take what he has learned from the old man and show that he himself has the ability to apply knowledge and judgment.

In some stories the wise old man's departure is precipitous, often he is killed or dies protecting the hero, and the hero has not learned everything he needed to know. This is part of the story — the hero having to discover the missing information the wise old man might have provided. Gandalf, from The Lord of the Rings, is one example. When Gandalf falls into the chasm while fighting the Balrog in Moria, the companions lose his guidance and aid. This is a serious matter for all of them, but especially for Frodo, the ringbearer, and his good friend Sam Gamgee. The other companions rejoin Gandalf later in the story, and he is able to help them fight the various forces of evil that have been loosed in the multi-fronted conflict between good and evil.

Frodo and Sam, however, have split off from the larger group before Gandalf has returned to it, and so they must continue on their way doing the best they can with what they have been taught up to the point when Gandalf disappeared. Theirs, of course, is the primary quest. If they fail, little that the others have done will be of any consequence. Therefore, once again, it is the hero who must take the wisdom imparted by the wise old man while he was present and apply the lessons once he is absent. If the pupil has not learned well, the world may suffer.

Gandalf's are the words Frodo quotes to Faramir, Captain of the soldiers of Gondor, when Faramir asks whether or not he should allow Gollum to live.

> "The creature is wretched and hungry," said Frodo, "and unaware of his danger. And Gandalf, your Mithrandir, he would have bidden you not to slay him for that reason, and for others. He forbade the Elves to do so. I do not know clearly why, and of what I guess I cannot speak openly out here. But this creature is in some way bound up with my errand" [Two Towers 373–4].

It would have been a simple thing for Frodo to rid himself of an unwanted encumbrance at this point. All he had to do was tell the Captain to proceed, and Gollum would have been captive or dead.

Fortunately, Gandalf's pupil was attentive. Frodo is unsure why Gollum must be allowed his life and freedom, but he knows that Gandalf granted it and he will do no less. Since Gollum, not Frodo, is the one who actually returns the Ring of Power to the fires of Mount Doom and keeps the evil Dark Lord from obtaining it and gaining complete control over Middle-earth, it is well that Frodo stays Faramir's hand.

Frodo has had the benefit of additional tutors who fit the wise old man archetype as well — the Elves. Shortly after Gandalf is lost in Moria, the companions arrive at the Elven land of Lothlórien. There Galadriel, the lady of Lórien, tests the constancy of their hearts, and Celeborn, the lord of Lórien, provides them with boats and information regarding the land they will be entering. Together the Lord and Lady give gifts to all of the companions, some practical gifts such as bows and scabbards, some magical gifts such as earth that will bring rich growth wherever it is scattered. To Frodo, the story's hero, the elves give light: literal light, "the light of Eärendil's star, set amid the waters of my fountain. It will shine still brighter when night is about you," and metaphorical light, the knowledge the elves have imparted to Frodo during his stay in Lothlórien (*Fellowship* 488).

In *Neuromancer*, the CD-Rom personality, Dixie Flatline, stays with Case until almost the very end, but even he exits before the final hour and forces the hero to prove that he has achieved self-awareness and self-reliance. Dixie had asked Case to erase him from the CD when the job was over. Just before the end of the job, Case learns that Dixie has gotten his wish and has been erased. This means that Case must make the final run at cracking the security on the Artificial Intelligence by himself. The words of others, the skills he has learned from them, his emotions, and his own abilities are all Case has to rely on, and they are enough. "In the instant before he drove Kuang's sting through the base of the first tower, he attained a level of proficiency exceeding anything he'd known or imagined. Beyond ego, beyond personality, beyond awareness, he moved, Kuang moving with him, evading his attackers with an ancient dance..." (262).

The wise old man makes his appearance, dispenses knowledge and aid, and disappears. The hero may avail himself of the wise old man's assistance multiple times in one story. At some point, however, the wise old man, like the father figure with whom he is often associated, must step back and let the hero stand on his own. It is the success or failure of the hero after the departure of the helper that really determines the hero's worth, and the world needs the hero to be successful. He is the one who gathers the accumulated wisdom of those who came before him and uses it to forge a more promising future for those who will follow.

12

Cutting the Apron Strings:
The Great Mother

As the preceding chapters have demonstrated, the wise old man represents accumulated wisdom and the father figure, and the youth represents innovation and a melding of the male and female parts of the self. No mention has been made yet of the adult female, but that figure is crucial to the development of the self and to many of the romance tales. The great mother is one of the principal archetypes; she is both the figure who provides the support necessary to break away from one's own limitations and strike out on the adventure that will help form the self and, simultaneously, the deadly enemy against whom the hero must battle for that selfhood. The female plays many roles in the development of both story and psyche: she is the anima or feminine side which the hero must learn to accept in order to achieve a healthy sense of wholeness; she is the temptress leading him from the path; she is the goddess guiding him through the mazes of maturation; she is the figure standing behind him cheering him on to victory; and she is the suffocating presence which keeps him from growing up.

The mother can be the source of life or the terrible mother, the source of stagnation and even death. The terrible mother brings death and destruction, war and flood and famine; for her "... blood is dew and rain for the earth, which must drink blood in order to be fruitful" (Neumann 74). In some cases, the same figure may represent the negative aspect of the mother archetype to one individual and the positive aspect to another. This is can be seen in fairy tales such as *Cinderella*. In one version of the tale, Cinderella is aided by the spirit of her dead mother, who makes her beautiful enough to eclipse the attractions of her selfish, greedy half-sisters (and all the other young women at the ball). At the end of that same story, however, when the selfish sisters have their eyes pecked out by the birds which dwell in the hazel tree growing from Cinderella's mother's grave, the birds are presumably acting on orders from the dead mother's spirit.

As was mentioned in the chapter on the youth, each man has elements of the feminine in him; these constitute the anima, which must be accepted and incorporated into himself in order to reach self-awareness. For women, there is a corresponding male side, the animus, which must be similarly addressed. Both men and women must break away from the mother before they can become unique, self-reliant individuals. The archetype of the great mother and the role of the anima are prevalent in and essential to medieval romance, science fiction, and fantasy. The hero must leave the nurturing shelter of home to find his selfhood and make a name. Often a terrible monster must be slain before the hero can win his reward or move closer to his ultimate goal. The great mother must lay the groundwork for growth and later autonomy, and the terrible mother must be defeated and forced to relinquish her hold.

In the medieval period, the system of courtly love provided a convenient societally-embedded structure for the expression of the anima. As Jungian psychologist von-Franz notes in her essay "The Process of Individuation," the anima was physically manifested in the woman the knight chose as his lady, the one for whom he did his knightly deeds and to whom he dedicated his victories. Who the knight chose as his lady could be quite important as not all anima figures are positive. If he chose the wrong woman, he might find himself at odds with his feminine side rather than in sync with it. Later, the focus shifted from the individual woman to the more symbolic and encompassing worship of the Virgin Mary (196). Placing the Virgin in the anima role suggests an attempt on the part of the Church or of society to ensure that each knight would cultivate the positive aspect of the anima rather than the negative.

There were risks involved with this courtly love system. Sometimes, the woman of the knight's choice was unavailable, such as Lancelot's great love Guinevere, King Arthur's wife. In this case, there was no winning solution. While Lancelot did great deeds in the name of Guinevere, he was never able to free himself from the negative aspects of his anima. When he did try, he went mad for a time. He then attempted to live with another woman, Dame Elaine — who loved him, but whom he did not love and hence would not incorporate into his image of self. From this union came Galahad, the perfect knight, but Lancelot himself would not turn away from Guinevere and give himself over to Elaine's guidance. Hence, he ended up barred from his life's goal, attainment of the Grail.

Guinevere is, in some ways, a negative manifestation of the anima for Arthur as well because his inability to take decisive action in respect to her — to either possess her entirely, without sharing her physically or emotionally with Lancelot, or put her aside because she is both barren and unfaithful — is what ultimately tears Camelot apart and leads to the downfall of the kingdom. Arthur has been helpless to prevent this fate, but foresees it as soon as word reaches him that Lancelot and Guinevere were caught together and Lancelot has escaped. "Alas me sore repenteth, said the king, that ever Sir Lancelot should be against me. Now I am sure the noble fellowship of the Round Table is broken for ever, for with him will many a noble knight hold; and now it is fallen so, said the king, that I may not with my worship, but the queen must suffer the death" (Malory, Caxton, 500). Arthur must banish one of his best knights and condemn his queen to death because he cannot control his own feminine aspect and incorporate it into his psyche. Arthur's focus is on his male side, to the detriment of his female side: "my heart was never so heavy as it is now, and much more am I sorrier for my good knights' loss than for the loss of my fair queen; for queens I might have enow, but such a fellowship of good knights shall never be together in no company" (500).

These characters present mixed portrayals of the anima. Under the right circumstances, Guinevere could be a positive female character and help guide either Arthur or Lancelot to a state of inner unity. Her failure to do so for either is largely a situational one rather than one attributable to any inherent evil on her part. Morgan le Fay, on the other hand, chooses to guide men down the path to destruction and seems to delight in doing so. Even her lovers are disposable tools in her personal quest for female power at the cost of male power. She is the castrating destroyer. She uses her husband to get the sons she needs to do the physical tasks she wants accomplished. She uses Arthur to create a semi-legitimate heir to the throne, and then she molds that son, Mor-dred, into her own creature — one she will never allow to have full auton-omy. Later she uses Accolon, her lover, to try to remove Arthur from power. Her tools are sex, skill with words, beauty, and a clear sense that what she wants is right, no matter what the rest of the world thinks. No man can stand against her will; at times she ensorcels men for extended periods just for the "sport" of it, as when she and three other queens capture and imprison Lancelot in hopes of making him choose one of them to be his paramour. She, as terrible mother, does not triumph, but she is never fully defeated either. She is a reminder that, even if a man does not like his feminine side, he needs to accept and regulate it or he may find it controlling him. Harmony and hope for the future come from balance within the psyche and society, not suppression and denial.

Gawain, like Arthur and Lancelot, is confronted by his anima, but he fares better in managing it. When Sir Bertilak's wife tries to seduce Gawain in *Sir Gawain and the Green Knight*, he does not reject her out-right. He understands that a balance must be maintained between his courteous, social, feminine side and his independent, prideful, male side. He demurs when she praises him, turns praise back on her, asks for nothing, and only agrees to a kiss because she makes it clear she will consider it a discourteous act for him to refuse. As the poet assures us, "he fenced with her featly, ever flawless in manner" (Tolkien 58). Gawain is tested twice more. On the second day, he continues the polite fencing of the first day, even though the lady has become subtly more insistent. She reminds him that he could take what she offers by force if he wished, but he counters that a gift must be freely given, a reply which both assures the lady that he will not force her and reminds her gently that if he does not willingly take up the offer of her favors and proffer his love in return that she should not force the issue either.

The third day is the most difficult. Very little time remains before Gawain has to face the Green Knight and the likelihood of his own death. While Gawain has managed to keep his equilibrium thus far, on the third day, the lady pushes even harder for Gawain to have sex with her. The lady may be offering him his last chance for lovemaking before death, his last chance to indulge himself in the life force of the great mother. Whether or not the lady of the castle is a positive or negative image becomes a bit unclear at this point, and the author interjects an addi-tional expression of the anima to make the position of the host's wife evident. The lady is relegated to the negative side when she is set in opposition to the Virgin Mary, a positive image of the anima, who is called upon to help guard Gawain from falling into sexual temptation and a betrayal of his host.

> "They spoke then speeches good,
> much pleasure was in that play;
> great peril between them stood,
> unless Mary for her knight should pray" [73].

Gawain is offered the opportunity to extricate himself from his awkward position by asserting he has another lady and therefore is not available to be the knightly lover of the host's wife, but he chooses not to prevaricate. Unlike Arthur, he refuses to pretend. Difficult as he finds it to refuse the lady, he tells her no; it is a polite no, but it is, nonetheless, a no. The only thing he does not refuse from her is the green girdle which she claims will save his life when he confronts the Green Knight. Gawain does acknowledge his feminine side, but he picks and chooses what he will take from it. When he realizes that taking the girdle was wrong, he accepts his error, acknowledges his human frailty, and learns from his mistake, keeping his psyche intact and, perhaps, achieving a higher level of maturity at the same time.

Fantasy novels are also filled with representations of the great mother archetype. In works such as the Lord of the Rings, the females are almost exclusively good mother characters. The one woman who rejects this societally approved role, Lady Éowyn of the Riders of Rohan, has to take on the semblance of a man for the duration of her rebellion. In the end, however, her stint as a warrior simply causes her to end up in the correct place at the correct time to assume her feminine role of wife. She is wounded when fighting as a warrior of Rohan in the Battle of the Pelennor Fields, and while in the House of Healing forms a relationship with Faramir, the steward of the city she has helped defend. The two serve to draw each other out of the depression into which each has fallen, and over time a love blossoms between them. When Faramir finally declares his love and asks Éowyn to marry him, she hesitates but in the end accepts, turning from her warlike persona back to a more feminine persona: "I will be shieldmaiden no longer, nor vie with the great Riders, nor take joy only in the songs of slaying. I will be a healer, and love all things that grow and are not barren" (Tolkien, *Return* 300). While an argument could be made for her time as a warrior being a face of the terrible mother, her society's perception of the warrior role as a strictly male one, and her need to disguise herself as a male in order to be allowed to fight, suggests that she is not acting within the realm of the female in this story.

The Lord of the Rings' other female characters tend to be nurturers. Among the nurturers are the fairy nobility: Arwen Evenstar, daughter of Lord Elrond of Rivendell and the intended of Aragorn, heir to the kingship of Gondor, and Lady Galadriel of Lórien, who gifts the fellowship with royal emblems, metal and woodcrafts, strands of her hair, rich loam and unquenchable light. Other images of the mother are more homey figures, such as the hobbit Rose Cotton, whom Sam Gamgee marries upon his return to the Shire. She objected to Sam's adventure, but said nothing to dissuade him from going. Instead, she waited patiently for him to marry her when he returned from his journey. Even the Entwives, the absent spouses of the Ents, are seen as symbols of the home and domestication; they are the tenders of crops, the growers of gardens, the teachers of the cultivation arts. The only real example of a terrible mother in this work is Shelob, the gross, spiderlike creature who poisons Frodo with her bite and plans to drag him off to her lair as a meal. She is, quite literally, a devourer, who binds Frodo and keeps him from fulfilling his quest. She is ultimately defeated by Sam, the devoted friend, who steps in and frees his companion when Frodo has been immobilized by the actions of the terrible mother.

Better examples of complex mother archetypes can be found in Robert Jordan's *Eye of the World*. In this book, there is a sisterhood of women called Aes Sedai who can wield *saidar*, the life force of the universe. Because of their power, they are feared, but because they use their powers constructively, they are also respected in most areas of their world. Moiraine, an Aes Sedai of the Blue Ajah, is the woman who has come to rescue and guide the three young men whose fates are central to the story. She is a typical example of the mother archetype, right down to her taking charge of these young innocents so they do not get themselves killed. "You are all eager to run off to Illian and forget about Trollocs, and Halfmen, and Draghkar? [...] The Dark One is after you three, one or all, and if I let you go running off wherever you want to go, he will take you" (151). She is not a simple nurturer figure though, as the rest of her speech to the three reveals: "Whatever the Dark One wants, I oppose, so hear this and know it true. Before I let the Dark One have you, I will destroy you myself" (151). She is both sides of the mother in one person, the protector and the punisher, but what she is not is an embodiment of evil. As she explains to Egwene, a young woman who seeks to become Aes Sedai, "The Aes Sedai you will find in Tar Valon are human, no different from any other women except for the ability that sets us apart. They are brave and cowardly, strong and weak, kind and cruel, warm-hearted and cold" (153). Evil women do exist among the Aes Sedai — the Black Ajah — a group of women who pervert power to accomplish negative ends. They are renegades, however, and even their fellow Aes Sedai would not hesitate to destroy them if the Black Ajah members' identities were known.

Many of women in the Wheel of Time series of which *Eye of the World* is a part are examples of this complex nature of the mother. The Wisdom of the small town from which the main characters come is in charge of healing and she and the larger Women's Circle control a portion of the town's governance. The Wise Women of the Aiel provide healing and guidance and add the ability to walk the world of dreams as well. At times they not only walk the dream world but shape events there which affect the waking world. Their power is evident by the respect with which they are held in their own culture.

As the title of this chapter suggests, one of the important aspects of the mother archetype is the separation of the hero from the control of the mother. Individuals must undergo this separation in order to become independent adults with differentiated identities capable of achieving wholeness in the course of time. This process is exemplified in literature by the hero breaking from the control of the guiding female in his life and striking out on his own. Several books in the series after Moraine's assertion in the *Eye of the World* that Rand al'Thor and his friends need her protection, Rand strikes out on his own to try to win his way through a daunting maze of dangers to defeat his enemies and gain control of his own destiny. He slips away in the middle of the night, leaving a note explaining that he wants to face the Dark One alone and stop endangering his friends. Not surprisingly, Moraine's response is that of a mother whose willful child has failed to see that she can protect him better than he can protect himself. "This may well be what the Pattern has chosen, yet I did not mean for him to go off alone. For all his power, he is defenseless as babe in many ways and as ignorant of the world" (Jordan, *Dragon*, 55).

Her concerns are not unfounded, but Rand manages not only to survive, but to achieve the next magical artifact needed to confirm his position in the story and help him defeat the powers of darkness by which Moraine fears he will be overwhelmed. She has had to let him carve out his own path in the world, even though she feels she could show him a simpler or safer path. Each of us must take that step away from the guiding female presence or we will never have a chance to attain selfhood. So, too, society must trust that it has prepared each generation to face the challenges that will come to it and to triumph, ensuring that there will be another generation to follow, a generation which might even outdo its predecessor and move mankind a step closer to human perfection.

Science fiction has often been criticized for its lack of strong female characters. While fantasy, although not Tolkien's fantasy, is inhabited by many strong-minded and independent women — heroines, good mothers, and evil mothers alike — much of science fiction, especially that written early in the twentieth century, has few female characters or has female characters whose only role is either to spur the hero on to save the world or get in his way so he has to overcome the obstacle of a clueless, unscientific woman en route to saving the world. This stereotype is lampooned in Sharyn McCrumb's *Bimbos of the Death Sun*, a book about a serious science fiction author who is obliged to give a racy title to his work and put a scantily-clad, buxom woman on the cover to ensure sales.

Often anthologized stories from the 1930s and 1940s, the Golden Age of science fiction, include Lester Del Rey's "Helen O'Loy," about two men who create the perfect woman — a robot, of course, and Theodore Sturgeon's "Microcosmic God," about a man who creates a new life form (a nice example of man usurping the female procreative role and eliminating the need for women altogether) and who, after a number of less than desirable interactions with society at large, spends the last years of his life holed up on an island under an impenetrable shield with his new creations and one male scientist buddy.

In a number of these stories, the great mother has been robbed of her power, subjugated by the world of science and men. The clearest example of this may be Tom Godwin's 1954 story "The Cold Equations" in which a spaceship pilot has to jettison a female stowaway because she is endangering the ship's mission, which is to bring serum to help six men who will die without it. She has walked into the situation innocently, wanting only to visit her brother, and ignorantly, having no understanding of the operation of the mini-shuttle on which she has stowed away. If she does not step out into space and die, she and the pilot will both die due to overload on the ship's resources. Then the six men waiting for the serum will die because the medicine will never reach them. The female must be sacrificed for the preservation of the male society. She can kill herself or she can kill them all but either way she must die.

Later science fiction has expanded the representation of women. Some of this was, no doubt, due to the increase in the number of female authors writing science fiction. Authors such as Ursula LeGuin, Andre Norton, Marion Zimmer Bradley, Anne McCaffrey, Octavia Butler, and Suzette Elgin have added many new aspects to the role women characters play in science fiction. Powerful women set out on their own quests, sometimes guided by a wise old woman in place of the wise old man. Women in auxiliary roles have moved from their traditional helpless female stereotypes to a more realistic range of human types. (To be fair, male roles in science fiction have also become more varied over the years as well.) In a series by McCaffrey which begins with the novel *Powers That Be*, one of the main characters is a sentient planet, Petaybee, which is clearly female and carries overtones of ancient mythological figures such as Gaia, the Greek Earth mother. Appropriately, Petaybee turns out to be one of the great mothers of the story, guiding and aiding the settlers.

The great mother archetype can be seen in Octavia Butler's *Dawn* as well. Here the future of mankind is assured, but only if humans blend their genetic material with aliens. This is one of the futures some science fiction writers foresee, and whether or not this is a future which a given reader sees as indicative of hope depends a great deal on how xenophobic the reader is. Is hope for mankind to be confined to mankind as it now exists, or does it extend to mankind as it could become? The Biblical version of mankind's future holds out transformed, resurrected humans, reembodied after death and purged of all inclination toward sinfulness, as the image of mankind's destiny. Various other cultures offer reincarnation of the human soul in a plethora of forms—many of which are not human—as a means for mankind to learn and improve. Perhaps, then, there is room for a science fiction version of mankind's future in which the best human qualities are preserved and blended with the best qualities of another species.

The possibility of such a transformation of the human species is one of the main issues addressed in Butler's book. Those humans who cannot adjust to the blending of human and Oankali weed themselves out of the gene pool by either committing suicide or retreating into mental illness. Among those who can adapt, certain individuals are trained to be mothers of the new race; Lilith Iyapo is one of these mothers. First, she is brought into an Oankali family; then, she is genetically altered to make learning and understanding the aliens' culture easier and procreation with an Oankali possible; and, finally, she is put in charge of a group of humans who need to be awakened from the hibernation state in which the aliens have stored them and taught how to adapt to their new situation. Since these humans are being kept alive in pods full of fluid, Lilith must perform a birthing ritual with each as she pulls the pod open and extracts the naked person from within it.

While the "newborns" are fully developed adults, they are infants in their understanding of the world in which they find themselves. It is Lilith's job to teach them to survive and, ultimately, to let them go and see if she has succeeded in imparting the necessary skills. "'I think these are our final tests,' she said. 'People leave camp when they feel ready. They live as best they can. If they can sustain themselves here, they can sustain themselves on Earth'" (214). She is not allowed to join her "children" when they are returned to Earth to establish a new civilization there. They are on their own. Although they do not believe the things she has told them, she has told them the truth. Like children leaving home to create their own lives though, they will have to test her information against experience before they accept it.

Lilith has been chosen to be the great mother not only to the humans, however, but also to the new generation of mixed human/ Oankali. Her Oankali ooloi — arguably a hermaphroditic version of the great mother, as contradictory as that sounds — has mixed the necessary genetic materials from Lilith, her partner Joseph, and Dichaan and Aja-has, her male and female Oankali family components, and created two children: one being borne by Lilith and the other being borne by Aja-has. Against her will, Lilith has become the mother of a new form of human. She hates the idea, but she is not quite willing to let the child die. Instead, she channels her anger, frustration, and energy into teaching the future "awakenings" of purebred humans to rebel and reject the Oankali, a symbolic but sterile gesture since Oankali only send to Earth humans whose genetic make-up has been altered to render conception impossible without the intervention of an ooloi. Human survival has been insured, but only if the humans include the aliens in that future. For some, Lilith included, this is an unacceptable option. She expects the released humans choose to die out rather than comply: "You won't get many back anyway. Some will think the human species deserves at least a clean death" (245). Yet, in spite of her words, she continues to live, and to teach, and to bear an Oankali/human hybrid child.

There is another approach to the concept of the female which appears in many works of romance, science fiction, and fantasy, and that is the tripartite goddess of which the mother is an integral part. A number of ancient religions, including some Celtic, pre-Christian forms, encompassed this concept of the female in which the goddess has three faces: the maiden, the mother, and the crone.

The mother has been discussed in some detail above, but in this trinity she has the special role of procreation which the other two aspects of the goddess do not encompass. She is fertility; she is sexuality; she is that which tempts man from his intellectual pursuits. She is also the nurturer and guide discussed above, but here we see more clearly the face of the feminine which so often appeared in those older works of science fiction. Perhaps this was related to the age of the target audience, the early adolescent male, who was caught between the influence of his mother, whom he wanted to escape but without whom he was not quite ready to survive, and the temptation of the females of his own age, whom he wanted to attract and impress but was not yet sure enough of his own sexuality to do so successfully. A goodly percentage of the female characters in the science fiction of the beginning of the twentieth century seem to fall rather neatly into these categories—the protective mother and the sexy dish.

The maiden adds a new element to the picture. She is like the youth discussed in Chapter 10. She is innocence and intuition and innovation. She is the spark of a new idea when old ways do not suffice. She is also sexual potential. Individuals, young and old, sometimes refrained from sexual involvement in order to harness the power of virginity. In the story of Galahad, part of his strength comes from the fact that he has never had sexual contact with another human being. Lancelot, too, is capable of great feats of healing prior to his involvement with Guinevere. The expenditure of sexual energy, however, is often equated with the loss of purity or the life force and, hence, of spiritual or magical ability. Even when the powers are not lost, they are often weakened or altered in some way. Merlin's sexual desire for Nimue, even in versions of the story where that desire remains unconsummated, renders him vulnerable to her magics and allows her to trap him, living, under a rock. In some stories, the character will not reach his or her magical potential until he or she reaches an age of sexual maturity. In Jordan's series, for instance, the Aes Sedai typically wait until a girl has passed puberty to begin training her in the use of her gifts, and men who can channel *saidin* do not usually exhibit the ability until after they reach sexual maturity.

In other stories, powers alter as the level of physical maturity changes. Only the Virgin can be sent to be the consort of the Horned God, and that virginity is an offering to the god. Once it has been offered, the woman moves to the role of the mother whether she conceives a child or not, since virginity is a gift that can only be offered once. This is the role Morgaine assumes in Bradley's *The Mists of Avalon*. All the powers associated with virginity and with motherhood are latent in the figure of the maiden. She has the potential to remain virgin and harness the powers only available to virgins, a destiny much more common for women than it is for men. She also has the potential to become a mother and harness the procreative powers to which males to not have access. In either role, she has the power to influence the males around her and help shape the future of her world.

At the opposite end of the life cycle, the crone is waiting, a symbol of loss of fertility (or barrenness) in women and in the land. Guinevere, for example, may have been a young woman in the Arthurian tales, but her inability to bear children and ensure the lineage of her lord is more in line with the role of the crone. Guinevere will never bear children, and her sterility has devastating implications for Britain. The good work Arthur has done will all be swept away when he dies because he has no legitimate heir of his body to raise to take his place. In addition, the crisis which develops from Arthur ignoring Guinevere and Lancelot's relationship might never have occurred if Guinevere was not barren because Arthur would have had to address the adultery problem at a much early point in the story. He would have been obliged to because he needed to be sure that the children who were inheriting his kingdom were really his children.

A more traditional example of this aspect of the crone may be Morgan le Fay in *Sir Gawain and the Green Knight*. In this work, Morgan le Fay is disguised as an ancient "held in high honour by all men around her" (Tolkien, 48). She appears old and ugly with black eyebrows, bleary eyes, hideous lips, "bulging buttocks," "short body and thick waist" (48), and her intent is as ugly as her semblance. She hopes to bring death and dishonor to Arthur's court either by shaming the men who are afraid to accept the knight's challenge or by horrifying the ladies. As Sir Bertilak explains to Gawain,

> "She put this magic on me to deprive you of your wits,
> in hope Guinevere to hurt, that she in horror might die
> aghast at that glamoury that gruesomely spake
> with its head in its hand before the high table" [95].

Despite the negative elements associated with the crone, she could also be the female analog to the wise old man archetype. She is the repository of wisdom, the source of information about how the culture has handled various challenges in the past. This was seen already in Chapter 9 with the example of the Reverend Mother in Herbert's *Dune.* In the same book there are also the Bene Gesserit, a line of women stretching back into ancient days who have seeded worlds across the galaxy with prophecies so that each will be receptive to the Bene Gesserit influence and each may be the fertile ground from which springs the prophesied individual who will put their plans for the universe into motion. Unfortunately, a little human love and disobedience short-circuits their plans and the man they had hoped to create through selective breeding, place in a position of power, and manipulate to their own ends is born and raised outside their influence. Paul, the man in question, taunts them with their failure, "'Observe her, comrades! This is a Bene Gesserit Reverend Mother, patient in a patient cause. She could wait with her sisters— ninety generations for the proper combination of genes and environment to produce the one person their schemes required. [...] Here I stand... but... I... will... never... do... her... bidding!'" (477). In spite of his rebellious words, he is quite aware of the knowledge and influence these women represent, and he marries the Bene Gesserit-trained daughter of the Emperor in order to combine the various strains of power in his world.

Whether express or implied, the image of the woman as mother recurs in these three types of literature. Inherent in the mother is hope. The very nature of a mother's existence is based on the concept of regeneration, of creating a new generation to face the world. Were there no hope, maidens would refuse to step into the mother role. Why bring a child into a world with no future? Surrounding the maidens and mothers are the living reminders of what happens to the world when hope is gone; life diminishes until it becomes like the crone, a wisp of what it used to be, sterile, headed for death. The crone, however, can be more than an exemplum of sterility of the body; she can also be a reminder of the fertility of the mind, a power which is needed for each generation to survive. She, and her counterpart the wise old man, share their experience with each new generation, providing both guidance and a tradition against which to rebel to create a new tradition.

The terrible mother forces the hero to stand up and test his mettle. She lets him learn his strength and keeps him from becoming complacent. If the hero is not strong enough for his task, she kills him and makes way for the next contender. Terrible mothers in literature help remind society that it too needs to avoid hiding behind tradition, that even cultures need to step away from the "mothers" who bore them and try new ways of interacting with the world around them. Terrible mothers can help keep civilizations from becoming like the Empire in Asimov's Foundation series, which has fallen into stagnation and become so comfortable that it has forgotten how to be creative and productive, or like the world of *Fahrenheit 451°*, which is peopled with characters so fearful that inaction in the only action most of them are willing to risk taking.

Hope is born with each new child. Together, the great mother and the terrible mother create life, nurture it, and urge that new life out into the world to keep the life cycle going. In medieval romance, fantasy, and science fiction, the images of the mother archetypes may help keep society from collapsing or cause that collapse, make people reassess their worlds or their places in their worlds, or foreground the need for either tradition or change. In any case, they keep the imperative for regeneration before the eyes of the reader and provide reassurance that as long as there are mother figures there will be hope for a future.

13

Phoenix from the Ashes: The Transformation

The goal of the psyche in integrating the contents of the collective unconscious into the realm of the conscious mind is to effect a transformation, which ideally results in individuation. The person who has successfully grappled with and subdued his shadow and acknowledged and come to terms with his anima (or in the woman's case animus) is a person who has earned the right to call his soul his own. In the modern world, this struggle tends to take place internally. In both medieval and modern literature, however, the struggle is usually projected out onto the surrounding world.

In works like Malory's *Le Morte D'Arthur*, Andre Norton's *Year of the Unicorn*, and Theodore Sturgeon's *More Than Human*, the struggle for selfhood becomes a fight for survival in a world filled with hostile forces and unexpected assistance. Neither the forces of evil nor the forces of good are required to present themselves openly as such; one of the tests of personality and of the literary hero is to determine which things are really as they seem and which are counterfeits. The transformation that follows the passing of these tests of moral discrimination entails acceptance of the self in all its facets and leads to the creation of a whole, unified person who, in most cases, is stronger or in some way better than the person he or she had been before.

One example of transformation in medieval romance can be found in the story of Arthur's fight with Accolon. All of the key elements are here for the transformative event: the evil female part of the self balanced by the good female side of the self, the reconciliation of the evil and good sides of humankind, the fight for control, the magical aid. In this adventure, Arthur seeks to free himself and others from prison by fighting on the side of Sir Damas, a man he knows to be a false knight. He chooses to do this because if he is victorious, twenty good knights who are being held in prison will be freed and because he would rather die fighting than rot in a dungeon. He accepts the fight on the behalf of his shadow self, but he does not concede its superiority or the rightness of its position.

A critical step in transformation is sorting out the true from the false, the real from the illusion. Arthur has awakened in prison and is without his armor or arms. He is furnished with what he is told are his own sword and scabbard but are actually copies. Excalibur, Arthur's magical sword, has been stolen from the king through the wiles of Morgan le Fay and delivered into the hands of Accolon, Morgan le Fay's lover and the man against whom Arthur will be fighting. As Arthur fights he gradually realizes that the sword he holds is not Excalibur though it has the semblance of that sword. He suspects that the sword Accolon wields is, in fact, his own.

> When Arthur beheld the ground so sore be-bled he was dismayed, and then he deemed treason that his sword was changed; for his sword bit not steel as it was wont to do, therefore he dreaded him sore to be dead, for ever him seemed that the sword in Accolon's hand was Excalibur, for at every stroke that Accolon struck he drew blood on Arthur [Caxton 64].

After he has become aware of the deception, Arthur's false blade breaks at the hilt, and Nimue, here identified with the lady of the lake, intervenes and makes Excalibur fall from Accolon's hand. Arthur leaps to grasp it and recognizes it immediately as his own sword. "And therewithal Sir Arthur lightly leapt to it, and gat it in his hand, and forthwithal he knew that it was his sword Excalibur, and said, Thou hast been from me all too long, and much damage hast thou done me... (65).

As it turns out, the entire fight is a treasonous enchantment wrought by Arthur's sister Morgan le Fay in an attempt to bring about the king's downfall. Had he not fought, he would have remained imprisoned and Accolon could have returned to Camelot with some story of how a dying

Arthur had given him Excalibur. A similar story would have sufficed had Accolon won the fight between the two of them. Only by recognizing Excalibur, the magical aid that had been given to him earlier in his life, and seizing the opportunity to reclaim it when the right moment came was Arthur able to overcome the evil female against whom man must inevitably struggle. This conflict was balanced to a degree through the assistance of the good female who allowed Arthur to reclaim what he had lost. Ironically, the female who is aiding Arthur was the evil female for Merlin, the one who trapped him under the rock. This duality serves as a reminder that every archetype is expressed in both good and evil images.

Arthur has seen through the illusions cast before him and determined which characters in his fight are on his side and which are not. He has been duped for a while, but clear sight has returned, clear enough that he is able to see that Accolon, too, has been deceived and to forgive the man and show him mercy. Accolon dies of the wounds received in the fight, and the king sends his dead body to Morgan le Fay to emphasize that she has lost, both the advantage and her lover.

Arthur has passed several tests in this short section of *Le Morte D'Arthur*. He has recognized that it is necessary to side with the enemy occasionally, if doing so will bring about the greater good. He has seen through deception to truth. The evil female has sought his downfall, and he has worked free of her wiles while remaining sufficiently unbiased against her sex to accept Nimue's aid. At the end, he has shown he can be merciful and just. Arthur ends up being less vulnerable to trickery and more aware of his own capabilities as a knight and as a ruler.

Many fantasy books pick up this theme of transformation of the self. Several authors, Andre Norton and Ursula Le Guin, to name two of the best known, often make the search for and subsequent transformation of self the point of the story. The theme of transformation is central to *Year of the Unicorn*, the third of Norton's Witch World novels. The main female character, Gillan, is a fosterling in a society that has no place for her. Her story parallels closely the experience of self-integration and transformation and so will be considered in depth. As a child, she had been seized as a prize in battle, but her captors had themselves been seized, and so she found herself growing up in a world to which she had no connection, and no knowledge of any other world to which she could return. She is, right from the start, a lost soul.

Recognizing that she has to make a future of her own design, she opts to trade places with a woman who has been promised as one of a group of brides bartered for military support from the men known as the Were-Riders. One of Gillan's first tests, like Arthur's, is to separate reality from illusion. The brides are taken to a meeting place where richly embroidered cloaks draw each young woman off into the mists to meet the cloaks' individual owners. Gillan, alone among all the young women, sees the real cloaks through the glamour that has been cast upon them.

> the beauty of the stitchery and gem was a shimmer above darker color, where there were still designs, but these oddly like lines of runes for which I could summon no meaning, and all were alike in that they had the ashen hue of the earth on which they lay.
>   The longer I looked and willed, so more did the enchantment fade and dim. Glancing to the left and right at the rest of my companions I saw that with them this was not so, that they saw only the surface and not that which lay beneath [*Year* 57].

Gillan is drawn to one of the cloaks, even though she can see that it is of gray and brown cloth and fur, not tapestry and jewels. She makes an informed choice based on what is really offered; the others make their decisions based on magic, illusion, and unfounded promises.

Gillan's ability to see things on two levels is part of her inheritance from her unremembered Estcarpian parents. It is a trait both unexpected and unwanted by all of the Were-Riders save the half-blood, Herrel, whose cloak she selected. She tries to keep her ability secret, but the society she has joined is heavily invested in maintaining an illusion that they are something other than what she knows them to be, and they are threatened by Gillan's clear-sightedness. The men, in particular, try to overcome her threatening, female, Witch abilities. Time after time, the Were-Riders try to catch her in a web of illusion and force her to remain there. First, they try to trap her soul in the dream world as she sleeps, an illusion that will take the place of reality if she is unable to extricate herself. She wills herself back into her body, but their assault continues. The next attempt on her selfhood comes when Halse, a Were-Rider who did not win a bride and feels Herrel does not merit one, plots to reveal to Gillan that Herrel is both man and mountain cat, it being the nature of the Were-Riders to assume beast-form when they fight. Gillan is terrified at first, but her true sight allows her to see the man and ignore the cat. "For an instant only did I see fur on his shoulders, a mountain cat's muzzle in place of his face? But I willed to see a man, and there-after I did" (80). Unfortunately, Gillan's inability to accept the animal side of her husband impedes her own transformation and allows the Were-riders to divide her against herself.

Gillan's initial, conditional acceptance of her husband crumbles under the Were-riders continued assault on her mind. The magic being used against her makes her unsure of her husband's loyalty, so she pushes him away emotionally and physically. This distance proves to be both her undoing and her salvation. Had she joined physically with Herrel and consummated their marriage, Herrel would have been able to shield her from the magic of the other Were-Riders and the machinations of Halse. His protection would have saved her from her enemies, but it would not have allowed her to come to terms with her own abilities and shortcomings.

She needs to integrate herself, not have someone do it for her; unless she does it herself, it is not a genuine or lasting transformation. Gillan's lack of a physical bond with her husband allows the other Were-riders access to her mind, but her virginity also provides her with the power she needs to break free of their control using the Witch powers inherited from her parents. Her hesitation in accepting her husband's dual nature, and by extension her own, makes her psyche vulnerable to the machinations of others and results in her having to surmount numerous obstacles before achieving selfhood again, but the struggle against and ultimate victory over the hostile male element allows Gillan to find the inner strength to achieve selfhood in the end.

Were-Riders attack her mind and split her into two selves, a socially acceptable compliant one who is taken with the Were-Riders when they enter their hidden land and an unacceptable noncompliant one who is left behind to die. Like the human psyche that is torn between a socially acceptable facade and the real self hidden behind it, Gillan must rejoin the two parts of her being to survive. The difference is that she must literally rejoin the two halves, or she will lose her real Self to an artificial Self created from the parts of her character that the Were-Riders found acceptable.

Not surprisingly, augmenting the strength of one Self saps the strength of the other Self. The Riders keep pouring the force of their magic into the false Gillan, and they accelerate the process once they realize that the real Gillan has not died in the wilderness where they left her and is, in fact, in pursuit of them and her other Self. Gillan, then, is not only battling to find a self that is held by hostile forces, but also fighting to keep from having her life energies drained to feed the simulacrum and allow it to usurp her place. She is aided in her fight by rediscovering her husband and realizing that he has been betrayed as well and had never participated in the efforts to eradicate her personality; he had always been on her side. He has moved from offering to be her protector, which makes hers a passive, inferior role, to offering to be her partner, an active, equal role.

Herrel and Gillan decide to take the offensive and force a confrontation with the other Were-Riders. Their combined efforts allow Herrel to fight Halse and defeat him, winning back control of Gillan's other Self. Unfortunately, Gillan has severed the connection to that other Self by overusing her witch powers to protect Herrel from malicious magic during the battle. She has, literally, lost her Self, the half which had been stolen from her by the Were-Riders. Both selves will die if they are not rejoined One can survive fragmentation of the self and loss of facets of the self, but if the life spirit flees, the body will follow soon after.

The search and the battle in the illusional world read like a fantasy version of the Jungian process of integration and transformation. Although her mission was clear before she entered the illusion world, once she arrives there, Gillan retains only a vague sense of a need to search for something.

> There was—there was something I must find. It was not a tree, nor anchorage. But I must find it—yes, yes. I must find it! A raging need for that filled me, as if I had drunk it out of a cup—was fever in me.
>   What did I seek, and where? Please, I must know—I *must* find out!
>   I—I must find Gillan. And who was Gillan? [*Year* 238]

Like most people, she is not sure of what comprises self; she knows she must look for it but she is unsure what it is she is seeking.

Before she can find her goal she must confront her fears, as must we all. She runs through the woods calling for Gillan, beset by unnamed spectres, poisonous vegetation, evil insect life, and other corrupted forms of the things she had known in the waking world. After a long period of silence, during which Gillan refuses to give up hope, an answer comes to her calls. She is appalled to discover that the source of the reply, which she thinks is the Gillan she was seeking, is a particularly loathsome bird, "a small horror of loose, leathery skin, naked wattled head, a head three-quarters rapacious beak" (242). She runs away from it, but it follows her and keeps circling her and diving at her, even walking between her feet once, trying to trip her and demanding her attention.

Finally, the bird's persistence forces Gillan to reassess it and herself. Unpleasant as parts of ourselves may be, sometimes they are the parts with the answers. She rejected the bird because she could not accept it as Gillan, but who was Gillan? As she ponders this question, an important revelation occurs.

> Gillan — who was Gillan? Why — *I* was Gillan! I halted in the sea of grass. I hunted Gillan, yet also was I Gillan. How could that be? Memory, very faint and far away, stirred. Once there had been one Gillan, and then two. Now I must search for the second, that two might be one again. The bird named me Gillan and Gillan I was [244].

She has learned who she is and whom she has come to seek. She has also accepted the bird as a guide. Guide her it does, like a wise old man figure, until she reaches a path that leads unerringly to where she needs to go, and then its knowledge is no longer needed, so it flies off.

What Gillan finds at the end of her search, however, is not one self but hundreds, reflected back from mirroring walls. She must determine which one is the Gillan created by the Were-Riders magic and which are but shadows. Frustrated she seizes upon one, but another voice in the valley assures her it is not the right Gillan. Herrel, in a guise fitting the illusion world, has come to aid her. He cannot tell her which is the true Gillan, but he can provide support and confidence. He serves as another guide or mentor reminding her that she already has the means, through the use of her Witch powers, to select the right Gillan from all of the imposters.

She finds the right Gillan, but that Gillan's body is dead, and the living Gillan realizes she does not know how to join with it to make the two one and alive again. She cries out for aid and an answer comes, "Death and life — they were the opposite in this world, Gillan had died here afore time, to give birth to Gillan — this Gillan in whom I now dwelt. Therefore, this Gillan must die so that that other could live again" (254). She seeks and finds Herrel, who fails to understand what she is asking of him, but ends up doing what she needs done. In his grief and confusion, he strikes out and kills one Gillan, allowing the other Gillan to live again.

She had to die to live, as parts of our personalities and spirits must give way so that other parts can flourish. Fears haunted her, and she overcame them. Weakness threatened to keep her from success, but friends and strangers lent strength and wisdom that allowed her to find her path and continue onward. Gillan's goal was to combine the divided Gillans into one united Gillan and resume the life she was leading before the magic sundered them. But the Gillan who returns from the quest for self in the illusionary world is a different Gillan than the one who went there. She has changed, transformed, and become stronger. She has learned to accept all of the parts of her personality, even the ones she does not like.

> Who is Gillan? No, rather what is Gillan? She is this and this, and she is also that. Some parts of her could I welcome, others would I shun if I could. For this was a measuring and an inner seeing of Gillan such as I had never known and it made me writhe for a nakedness beyond all stripping I have believed could exist. Almost did I wish to forego the awakening of that Gillan who had such small meannesses, such ill within her.
>
> Who is Gillan? I am Gillan, in this way was I fashioned, by nature, by the will of others, by my own desires. And with this Gillan am I united for good or ill, therefore I must pick up the burden of being Gillan and — awake! [274].

And, in accepting herself she has also found a true acceptance of Herrel in all of his forms— man, mountain cat, husband, friend, ally.

At the end of the book, the couple realize they no longer belong in the society within which they have found themselves. Herrel says as much to the keeper of the gate who challenges their right to leave the city. "'I do not know now what I am, for we have been a journey [sic] like to change any living thing. But of these towers I am not, nor is Gillan. So we shall go to seek that which we are —for that we must learn'" (280). They have realized one of the truths Jung stressed in his writing: the finding of self is a continuous, not a onetime, process. "The condition of complete, fully developed authenticity toward which an individual life moves, unevenly, increasingly slowly and deliberately with age, and without ever reaching it, is the *Self*" (Cohen 27).

While Norton begins with a self that is unified and allows the reader to experience the transformative process by magically splintering that self and then showing the self's reunification, in the science fiction novel *More Than Human*, Theodore Sturgeon begins with five separate beings who are trying to find a way to unite into one being. Early in the story, Lone, the "idiot" who is the center of the original grouping, demands to know who he is. Baby, the idiot savant of the group, tries to explain the group's unique construction through Janie, who does their speaking: "He says he is a figure-outer brain and I am a body and the twins are arms and legs and you are the head. He says the 'I' is all of us" (82).

This explanation satisfies Lone temporarily, but he later realizes that there is no "name" for the type of being the group has created. For Lone and the others the question is not whether they can integrate into a single, individuated self, but what they have become when they do. The group can achieve self, but not self-awareness.

Lone is able to absorb information directly from the mind of Alicia Kew, a woman he has met, yet even though he has her read extensively on telekinesis, teleportation, telepathy, clairvoyance, and gestalt and later "on evolution, on social and cultural organization, on mythology, and ever so much on symbiosis" (136), no answer surfaces. Frustrated by the gaps in the material supplied him, Lone finally describes the group to Alicia and asks her if there are books on such things. She grasps that he is describing a "gestalt life-form," but cannot aid him in his search for evidence about whether such a thing has ever existed. She is skeptical about the possibility of a gestalt entity existing, but he assures her that it not only can but does: "It does. A part that fetches, a part that figures, a part that finds out, and a part that talks" (137). He is forced to discuss the entity by naming its parts because it has no other name. As Lone understands it, "*'Name' is the single thing which is me and what I have done and been and learned*" [author's italics] (32). Name, that which encompasses all that we are, is exactly what Lone is searching for but cannot find.

Lone is killed in an accident, and the entity slowly begins to break apart. The self is fragmenting and losing what identity it had. The children go to live with Alicia Kew, who treats them well, but makes the mistake of trying to separate them, delegating the twins to the servants' quarters because they are black and placing Baby in an institution. The group resists these overt efforts to divide them up but they begin to lose their group identity in a subtler, more long term way as they begin conform to the society around them. Gerry can feel the Gestalt faltering and fading:

> "We all woke up at the same time. We all did what someone else wanted. We lived through a day someone else's way, thinking someone else's thoughts, saying other people's words. Janie painted someone else's pictures, Baby didn't talk to anyone, and we were all happy with it" [127].

The danger of disintegration is particularly onerous to Gerry because he has come to realize that he is the replacement for Lone, "the one kind of person who can pull 'em all together, like a brain pulls together the parts that press and pull and feel heat and walk and think and all the other things" (138). Alicia was the rule maker, the dispenser of social values, and she threatened the Gestalt by imposing her own personality on the component members. Eventually, Gerry kills Alicia to prevent the group entity's demise. Gerry explains his actions when he later seeks the help of a psychotherapist:

> "My *gestalt* organism was at the point of death from that security. I figured she had to be killed or it —*I*— would be. Oh, the parts would live on: two little coloured girls with a speech impediment, one intro-spective girl with an artistic bent, one mongoloid idiot, and me — ninety per cent short-circuited potentials and ten percent juvenile delinquent. [...] It was self preservation for the *gestalt*" [147].

As the head, it was Gerry's responsibility to make sure the entire organism kept functioning.

The characters in the book draw an analogy between their roles and parts of the body; a similar analogy can be made to the mind as well, especially since all of their talents are mental talents. All of the children are parts of the personality, but they cannot be a person until each has been considered, accepted, and given a place in the schema of the individual. This is where the analogy breaks down in this example and in the characters' lives as well. There is a general pattern governing personality, whether or not the individual can find his or her personal version of it. As Lone discovered, however, there is no precedent for the type of being they were trying to create and therefore there is no clearly defined place for each of the sub-entities in their struggle to become one being.

During the attempt to become a whole being, Gerry, the head of the Gestalt body, becomes carried away with his own power. He allows the shadow side of the group entity's personality to dominate. At first this is manifested by Gerry excelling in school, then by his being able to control anyone through his own telepathic abilities, but finally he decides that since he can have anything he wants nothing is worth having. He stops doing anything at all and begins to regress. The result is a very powerful telepath with a child's morality, a petty, angry child. A piece is missing and the self cannot integrate. Truth has been distinguished from falseness, but there is no one in the group whose role it is to make decisions about good and bad, right and wrong. This lack is remedied by the addition of Hip, a man who allowed himself to be discredited as a soldier and a scientist and who went insane before he would renounce as true that which he knew he had seen the evidence to prove. As Janie describes it to Hip, he will be "The prissy one who can't forget the rules. The one with the insight called ethics who can change it to the habit called morals" (233). Hip prefers to see himself as "the still small voice," but he does accept the role (233).

Hip realizes that morals do not apply to the Gestalt being because morals are "Society's code for individual survival" (223). As far as Hip knows, there is no one else like the Gerry/Janie/Bonnie/Beanie/Baby aggregate and therefore they have no society. Ethics, on the other hand, are about "An individual's code for society's survival" (223). Since the Gestalt being wants to be part of a larger society of similar life-forms someday (it having been established that the entity is immortal even though individual parts will die off as Lone did), it needs to set down rules that will allow that future society, and itself, to survive and flourish.

It is up to Gerry to integrate the addition into the Gestalt being, not just admit that a code of ethics is a good idea. Hip can be admitted to the group only if Gerry, the self, is willing to allow restraints to be imposed upon his behavior. To switch to Freudian terms for a moment, Hip, the superego, must wait for Gerry, the ego, to decide whether it is going to cede some of its control.

Gerry does accept Hip and the ethos that Hip represents, and as soon as he does so, the Gestalt being is allowed to learn that it is not alone, that others of its kind do exist. Not until Gerry and the rest of the Gestalt being could see beyond themselves did the other Gestalt beings feel they were ready to be admitted into the greater Gestalt society. When the new Gestalt being asks whether it was "the ethic" that finally completed it, the others reply, "Ethic is too simple a term. But yes, yes ... multiplicity is our first characteristic; unity is our second. As your parts know they are parts of you, so must you know that we are parts of humanity" (234). The Gestalt being had to know itself, before it could know others.

Gestalt is Sturgeon's term for the entity he creates in his novel and it is an apt choice. Each of the characters in the novel is limited. Each represents some aspect of the powers of the mind, but none can function as effectively on his or her own as they can together. They are transformed through the experiences of loneliness and loss, union and acceptance, confronting and defeating the shadow side of "themself," and turning their vision outward to society and their role in it. They become something greater together after sharing all of the experiences they live through as Homo Gestalt.

Transformation is the goal of the psyche. The individual must take all the accumulated knowledge about the self, accept it, and forge a complete person from it. Neumann refers the experience back to the hero "... the hero is one who can call his soul his own because he has fought for it and won it" (379). Because the hero has done this, the reader is able to see that it can be done, that an individual can accept all of what he or she is, was, and can be and forge it into something more, something better. The reader can then make the leap from individual transformation to societal transformation. If one person can change, then society can change. If the individual can become better, more unified, more at peace within himself, then it should be possible for individuals to work together, like facets of the psyche, to accomplish this on a larger scale. This is the hope that these works hold out to society, the hope that in this state of unity the individual, or society as a whole, can move into a future of its own devising and that the resultant future can be a positive one.

14

A Light in the Darkness

The ascendancy of mimetic literature evident in the twentieth century does not stand as the societal standard for literature throughout the ages. Instead, romantic and realistic literature have tended to run in cycles as civilization surfeits itself on each one in turn and as societal needs vary. As one type of literature gains the preeminent place, the other submerges and surfaces in marginalized literature. At one point in history, folktale and myth were accepted forms of literature for adult consumption; now, they tend to be relegated to the children's section or are designated a field of study for scholars. Fairy tales have met with the same fate. Conversely, the mimetic prose of the Middle Ages tended to be solely the purview of the church, and the romantic prose was the property of the noble public at large.

What most modern readers are seeking from the medieval period is not physical reality, but archetypal reality. Even the most ardent twenty-first century reader of medieval romance or its derivative fantasies would most likely be appalled to be dropped unceremoniously into the real world anytime between the eleventh and fifteenth centuries. Hollywood glamorization notwithstanding, the medieval world was, for the most part, a harsh, unlovely place compared to the world of the late twentieth and early twenty-first centuries. Camelot itself would have been a cold drafty pile of rock or timber with dirty rushes strewn on the floor, its meals served with a minimum of utensils at long plank tables under which the dogs and the young scavenged for scraps. Over all would have lingered the pungent odor of too many unwashed bodies in too little space.

The protagonist in Connie Willis' fantasy novel, *Doomsday Book*, has exactly this sort of disorienting experience when she uses time travel to return to the 1300s to study the medieval period *in situ*. She errs in her calculations and arrives during the worst of the Black Plague. Modern medicine has rendered her body immune to the physical effects of the disease, but nothing can immunize her against the devastating psychological and emotional effects of the disease. She witnesses whole households that have been obliterated, leaving no one alive to bury the dead. She sees the dead unceremoniously tossed onto carts and trundled off to a mass grave and the dying abandoned by the living out of fear of contagion. The world she finds is not without its moments of beauty, but they are rare and precious because of the darkness of the setting which surrounds them.

The modern reader of medieval romance would be returning to a time in which every child began to take part in the work of the household as soon as he or she had the physical coordination to do so. Children of the lowest social classes were put to work as young as possible out of economic necessity. The children of the wealthy were not excluded from work either; sons were taken from their mothers at around age seven and sent out to other households with whom their families had or wanted to have alliances. The child's removal at this age kept him from being coddled by the mother, minimized the chances he would grow up "soft" due to preferential treatment in his own home, and fostered both political and social ties between the households. After a number of years as a page, a young man would advance to the position of squire and begin preparing in earnest for his life as a knight. If the son was headed for the Church rather than the battlefield, he would be sent to live with priests in order to learn his letters and the other skills needed for his profession.

Girls fared no better. Rich or poor, girls needed to learn to run a household. Whether they were learning needlework or how to pluck a fowl, girls received training designed to prepare them for the work they would be doing in the future. As soon as a girl was of breeding age, she was married off as advantageously for the family as possible. Childbearing was her lot, either to provide laborers or heirs. If she started young enough and produced enough children, the odds were that some would survive to adulthood. Gossamer gowns and burnished armor, majestic castles and gaily draped jousting fields look wonderful on the screen, but they capture only a small glimmer of a world where reality was much grimmer.

Knowing that this disparity exists does not seem to eradicate the longing that many readers feel when reading Malory's *Le Morte D'Arthur* or Chrétien de Troyes' Arthurian romances. There is something in the medieval world that calls to people. One of the things people may be seeking is a connection to the archetypes behind the archetypal images many of these legends present — the child-hero, the wise old man, the conflict of light and darkness, of good and evil, the cycle of death and rebirth.

Modern man has created an imbalance within himself and his society by seeking to replace the irrational with the rational rather than creating a harmony between the two. Humans are not purely rational beings, and when we create one-dimensional selves, our subconscious minds reach for the archetypes needed to restore a balance.

Jacobi describes the reactions of such humans in his book *Complex/Archetypes/ Symbol in the Psychology of C. G. Jung*:

> For too many individuals are cut off from the figurative language of their psyche, and these are precisely the highly civilized, the intellectuals. They are no longer capable of grasping anything more than the outward facade, the semiotic aspect of a symbol. They have a secret fear of the ultimately inexplicable element that attaches to every authentic living symbol and thus makes a full rational understanding of it impossible [87–8].

The inexplicable makes these people uncomfortable. People like the ones Jacobi describes are the ones who dismiss science fiction and fantasy literature because it could not be true on a literal level, and relegate the Arthurian romances to the children's section. They accept the world as it is because "that's how it is."

These are also the people who perceive the average science fiction reader to be an adolescent male even though surveys, such as the 1986 one cited in Bainbridge's *Dimensions of Science Fiction*, show that in actuality only 59 percent of science fiction readers are men and the mean reader age is 34. The readers of science fiction are more open to the archetypal images presented in their preferred reading material and perhaps that gives them an aura of childlikeness to those who see archetypes and the irrational side of human nature as belonging only to children, primitives, and followers of religions.

Science fiction has often been accused of being "shamelessly optimistic" (Clareson, *Understanding* 37) or "almost entirely hopeful" (Blish 54). This is less true today than it was in the first half of the twentieth century, or at least it is not as obvious, but science fiction does tend to be the genre writers turn to when they want to create a positive image of the world's future. This freedom, as Robert Hunt explains in his article "Visionary States and the Search for Transcendence in Science Fiction," arises from the fact that science fiction remains "one of the last unembarrassed genres; authors and readers are still eager to debate the meaning of reality and the mysteries of belief, and have no fear of censure from a powerful critical establishment" (65).

Religion, too, deals with "the mysteries of belief"; like science fiction it is more concerned with the future rather than the present. The similarities between these two modes of experience are the basis of Fredrick A. Kreuziger's *The Religion of Science Fiction*. Like this study, *The Religion of Science Fiction* argues that science fiction is a literature of hope. But, unlike this study, the argument does not extend to fantasy or medieval romance and is couched in strictly religious terms. Kreuziger designates science fiction as religion based on Peter Berger's definition of religion in *The Sacred Canopy*: "Religion implies that human order is projected into the totality of being. Put differently, religion is the audacious attempt to conceive of the entire universe as being humanly significant" (Berger 28); as Kreuziger observes, "the correlation with science fiction is obvious" (1). In particular, Kreuziger is considering science fiction of an apocalyptic nature; apocalyptic in this case signifies literature which provides "... hope in a time of crisis. It is a statement of faith and hope in the face of a world experienced as falling apart" (7).

Jung saw the world as trying to subjugate its irrational side through reason and moving away from belief in God or any other divine being. Science had become God, as the twentieth century adage proclaimed. Twentieth century man turned to science to cure all the ills of the world, eager to believe that it could remedy what faith could not. Science fiction in the early twentieth century was possessed of an excess of optimism fueled by this belief. Then the bomb dropped, literally, first on Hiroshima and then on Nagasaki, and mankind's illusions concerning the redemptive powers of science were ripped to shreds.

Science fiction writers continued to create bright futures for mankind, but now they had seen the dark underside of science and some of their worlds became an escape from the horrors science had wrought instead of a gleeful plunge into the future marvels science would bring. As Asimov, a writer of those aforementioned unabashedly optimistic novels, put it, "Science and technology, which promised an Eden, turned out to be capable of delivering Hell as well" (*Asimov on SF* 161).

People's belief in science, a phrase rich in irony in light of the tension between rational science and irrational belief, became provisional. Solutions believed to be possible in the present shifted forward to an unspecified time in the future, and not everyone was confident that the answers would be provided by science. Disillusionment caused some to decide that the world could not be changed, regardless of the means employed. Others, perhaps those more cognizant of the archetypal foundations of the human mind, reminded themselves that all human endeavor has both a light and a dark side, and science is not an exception. Those are the individuals whom Kreuziger appears to be targeting in his book and to whom he feels science fiction is targeted. These are the people who have hope, the people who can see that the world has flaws and still believe it is possible to transcend those flaws.

> [S]cience fiction is written for "believers." Its language, its fantasy, its laws of time and space, of robots and aliens, and its conventions of time travel, hyper space, parsecs, alternate worlds and telepathy, are for the initiated, for those believers who have made the leap of faith (or not made the leap of un-faith) [15].

"Not made the leap of un-faith" — with this marvelous phrase the author has changed the rules. Hope is not necessarily about saying "yes"; it can also be about refusing to say "no." Just because one has not declared his belief in God does not mean that he must by default agree with Nietzche that God is dead. The readers of science fiction (and fantasy) deal in possibility. They can see the horrors of the world around them — abuse, neglect, starvation, war, pollution, resource exhaustion, illness, ignorance, hatred — but they refuse to accept that the world *must* be that way, and they turn to literature that affirms that the world can be better. Ursula LeGuin emphasizes that the roles of the fantasist and scientist are similar in this regard.

> Fantasists, whether they use the ancient archetypes of myth and legend or the younger ones of science and technology, may be talking as seriously as any sociologist — and a good deal more directly — about human life as it is lived, as it might be lived, and as it ought to be lived. For after all, the great scientists have said and as all children

know, it is above all by the imagination that we achieve perception, and compassion, and hope [*Language* 53].

In Clarke's Rama series, denizens of the Earth travel into space to explore a huge, revolving metallic cylinder traversing our Solar system. Investigation reveals that the cylinder is an artificial habitat created by alien beings. A series of events occurs which results in several of the explorers staying behind in the cylinder after the others have left. Their presence prevents the destruction of the cylinder by Earth's paranoid political powers, who are positive that the aliens' plan must include some form of violence directed at Earth. Several books later in the series, the aliens' actual plan is revealed: to collect members of each sentient life-form in this and other universes and bring them together to offer them the opportunity to learn from and about each other in an effort to ensure galactic peace in the future.

Those beings who prove to be too xenophobic for the venture remain in artificial environments akin to their home worlds; those open to the challenge are gradually introduced to the vast community of the stars. In other words, those who are able to adapt mentally and physically to the new way of seeing the universe, who refuse to make the leap of un-faith, survive and help create a unified universe based on a concept akin to I.D.I.C. (Infinite Diversity in Infinite Combination), an idea taught in another science fiction world, Vulcan, the homeworld of Star Trek's Mr. Spock.

Admittedly, Clarke is one of the old school of science fiction writers. He also has degrees in physics and mathematics, worked in the field of radar during World War II, and won "the Marconi Award in 1982 for his contributions to communications technology," contributions that include the communication satellite (Liukkonen, par. 1–3). He is a "hard" scientist, yet his writing focuses not on a scientific ordering as salvation of the universe, but on a spiritual ordering. In his short story, "The Nine Billion Names of God," a group of Tibetan monks orders a computer to generate all the possible letter combinations that could be the name of God. The lamas believe that this is mankind's purpose on Earth, a spiritual quest to discover the true name of God. They also believe that when God's true name or names have been revealed the world will end. They have been compiling names in an orderly fashion for three centuries and had planned on working patiently for another 15,000 years on their project, but science has provided a way to accomplish it in 100 days. The scientists who have come to install and maintain the computer equipment scoff at the lamas' beliefs and their project. As they are riding away from the monastery at the end of the story, discussing whether the lamas would be disappointed and angry when their list was finished and the world continued, the scientists look up at the night sky and find out that religion has triumphed over science. "'Look,' whispered Chuck, and George lifted his eyes to heaven. (There is always a last time for everything.) Overhead, without any fuss, the stars were going out" (144).

Despite, or perhaps because of, his scientific background, Clarke has clung firmly to his belief in a benevolent force guiding the universe and in the inherent goodness of mankind, if not individual men, throughout decades of mankind's making a considerable showing of his wickedness. The Rama books were published at intervals beginning in 1973 and ending in the 1990s, and sold well to an audience well aware of the dual nature of scientific "progress." The Rama series even spawned a computer game popular at a time when the buyer's hand could as easily have reached out and picked up a copy of the full-blood version of *Doom*.

Belief in the possibility of a better world is not confined to a time period or a generation, it is a human longing, and there will always be some humans who hear its call. Kreuziger, too, sees reminding people of the higher levels to which the human soul may strive as one of the roles of science fiction, and of religion.

> Yet the fact is that we are, all of us, at various times in our lives, reminded in story and song and fable and sermon and testimony that the most ennobling and uplifting human act is to keep alive the hope in a future world free from war and poverty and disease and hatred and prejudice — even though (and perhaps precisely because) we do not know how to make it come about and have never had any direct personal experience of such a world [97].

This is the appeal of Camelot, the idealized society, the appeal of a better future even as the present looms about one in all its imperfection. The lyrics to "Camelot," the final song in the play based on White's *The Once and Future King*, capture this idea nicely:

> Don't let it be forgot,
> That once there was a spot,
> For one brief shining moment
> That was known as Camelot [Lerner & Lowe].

Hope is about brief shining moments. The desire for a better future draws life from those shimmering glimpses in the present that show we can be more than we have been. The romanticized version of the Arthurian story is the one most people have heard, rather than the story of the sixth century chieftain who may or may not have declared his ties to the old Roman military conquerors and who held back the Saxon invaders for a short time. The literary King Arthur, with his accretive reputation — living in the High Middle Ages in a court filled with knights in shining armor and ladies in distress, using might for right instead of might as right, and sending his knights out to seek the Holy artifact known as the Grail — has much greater psychological appeal. He is the great hero, the light who will triumph over the darkness, the god-like man whom death cannot hold. *That* King Arthur holds out a shining future and we can chose to ignore that the truth he offers is of the psyche, not an empirical truth.

Margaret Schlauch, in her book *English Medieval Literature and its Social Foundations*, argues that in the Arthurian tales in particular ". . . the knightly class found the mirror in which it liked to believe its best traits were reflected..." (184). She admits that the romances often show the worst traits of knighthood as well, but adds that these elements tended to be downplayed because the purpose of the literature was not to depict the world as it was but "to ennoble human conduct" by telling a tale "in an enchanted world where everyday reckonings do not have to be made" (191). The writers of romance were expected to create works that allowed "[e]scape from reality or an idealisation [sic] of it..." (191).

Modern man has not lost the ability to dream of a brighter, better world. In the words of a twentieth century believer, Dr. Martin Luther King, Jr., who did not live to see whether his words came true, "I have a dream that my four little children will one day live in a nation where they will not be judged by the color of their skin, but by the content of their character"* (*Bartlett's* 909). "I have a dream," but in order to make that, or any other, dream become a reality in the future, Kreuziger reminds us, we must be conscious of the choices we make in the present (157). By laying out before us the worlds we may be creating for ourselves, science fiction helps make us aware of the possible consequences of our actions and inactions. Making those worlds come alive before us in print lets us judge whether or not they are worlds we wish our world to become. If the world is one we reject, perhaps one set in post-nuclear war chaos like *Canticle for Leibowitz* by Walter M. Miller, Jr., we can

*From Dr. King's 1964 Nobel Peace Prize acceptance speech.

make choices now to prevent it; for example, we can curtail the use of nuclear weapons and/or energy. If the world is one we would like to see become a reality, such as the tranquil world of inter-lifeform peace of the Rama series, we can either foster the things that will bring the world about or suppress the things that would prevent it, continuing space exploration on one hand and, on the other, learning to accept that different does not mean dangerous.

We may not be able to do this by ourselves. We have had nearly 3,000 years as a species intelligent enough to transcribe our thoughts and feelings into a permanent written record and in all those years we have not learned to get along. Perhaps projecting futures based on the world as it is will not be sufficient. Perhaps something more drastic is called for. Science can take us to the limits of the humanly possible, but how do we take the leap beyond that? How do we break free of our human limitations? Kreuziger posits a world that arises from a radical disjunction — events, characters, places, knowledge unknown and, at present, unknowable to us — that will alter our present drastically and therefore our way of creating the future (Chapter 4, 84–109). He is referring specifically to the intervention of a divine being or an alien being that will lift humankind beyond "the limits of human enterprise and knowledge — limits which can never be breached, no matter what the human effort through natural intelligence or with the aid of machines..." (159). Perhaps then we will no longer be bound by the physical laws we believe space and time impose on us, and we will be able to interact with the universe in an entirely new way.

At this time, even our most brilliant scientists can proffer only partial theories to explain the universe, the general theories of relativity and quantum mechanics. Alas, as theoretical physicist Stephen Hawking points out in *A Brief History of Time*, "these two theories are known to be inconsistent with each other — they cannot both be correct" (12). Many scientists would like to believe, says Professor Hawking, that "[t]here really is a complete unified theory, which we will discover if we are smart enough" (166). A unified theory would answer the fundamental questions of man, which he sought to answer first through religion and philosophy and then through science, and which Hawkings reiterates at the beginning of the concluding chapter of his book. "What is the nature of the universe? What is our place in it and where did it and we come from? Why is it the way it is?" (171). But that unified theory would also "presumably determine our actions. And so the theory itself would determine the outcome of our search for it!" (12). This is the limit set upon human knowledge.

This is the juncture at which Kreuziger argues there is a need for the intervention of a divine being to aid humans in making the leap to a transcendent view of the universe. Hawking does not go so far, and maintains the belief that humans can reach this knowledge on their own, but his comment on what it would mean if we were able to reach a unified theory of the universe suggests that he also sees it as signaling a step beyond the bounds of what had previously been seen as the limitations of man:

> Then shall we all, philosophers, scientists, and just ordinary people, be able to take part in the discussion of the question of why it is that we and the universe exist. If we find the answer to that, it would be the ultimate triumph of human reason—for then we would know the mind of God" [175].

Religion is a natural human impulse; it is a form of societal codification. Mankind *wants* to order his universe, *wants* to believe in something, *wants* rules to exist. It is built into our psychological foundations. Anthony Stevens devotes a sizable portion of one chapter in *Archetype: A Natural History of the Self* to just this concept. Significantly, this assertion is to be found in the chapter entitled, "Shadow: the Archetypal Enemy." It is in the absence of rules and clearly defined social strata that the dark side of mankind, the shadow or barbarian as Stevens calls it, assumes the upper hand. As Stevens explains the situation,

> All societies codify themselves; their success and continuity depends on the readiness of new members to learn the code. The alternative is social anarchy and a collective incapacity for competition or defence. If societies fail to codify themselves efficiently, therefore, or lose faith in their doctrines, they are gravely at risk [220].

When the choice between what is ethically or socially acceptable and what is not is unambiguous, individuals are able to make decisions with a clear understanding of the consequences to follow. If you forget to make an offering to the god or goddess of fertility, you will not be surprised when your crops fail. If you drive 90 miles per hour through a small town, the police officer pulling you over and handing you a ticket will be expected. When there are no rules and everything is random, then there is no reason to adhere to a particular form of behavior because there will be no correlation between what you do and what happens. This is the realm of the Shadow: "The barbarian is one whose ethical complex has failed to mature: he has not 'learned the rules' (because his 'culture,' if he may be said to possess one, has few rules to learn) and, as a consequence, moral distinctions do not concern him" (221).

Such a state of moral ambiguity and confusion reigns in the Western World at the start of the twenty-first century. Having eschewed religion in favor of science, much of society finds itself without an anchor, without a sense of a motive force in the universe that legitimizes our existence as something other than a collection of animate cells. Yet, this state of uncertainty makes man uncomfortable, and he will not allow it to continue unchecked. Man needs to have faith in something; "However scientifically sophisticated they become, men will go on creating myths and religions because it is in the nature of their whole approach to reality to do so" (Stevens 223). The something could as easily be science as religion if that science addresses the fundamental needs that man's mythologizing tendencies seek to fulfill. "There is no fundamental incompatibility between the religio-mythological approach and the scientific approach: both are means of apprehending the *Umwelt* [world around one]" (223).

Romance literature is one means of providing mythologies for society, and the works under consideration present a range of systems by which the world may be ordered. In the medieval romance, the preexistent hierarchy of the Catholic Church is adopted and adapted. Other hierarchies, of vassalage and courtly behavior, supplement this structure. In science fiction, the organizing technique is usually scientific. The world follows set physical laws, all of which can be explained logically if one's level of knowledge is sufficient. In fantasy, the social fabric is frequently woven upon magic with a thread of medieval manners intertwined. Each of these approaches is aiming at the same goal, to provide some rationale for the world, a reason that makes it worthwhile to get up each morning and strive toward that better future. People want to believe there is a purpose to existence; they *need* to believe it. If the society around them fails to provide an explanation or an ordering principal, those people most in need of one will either invent their own or turn to the ones others have invented, such as the explanations found in works of medieval romance, science fiction, and fantasy.

15

Hope Springs Eternal*

It is the nature of romance literature to present a hope-filled view of the world. As Frye argues regarding the function of romance literature in *The Secular Scripture*:

> to recreate the past and bring it into the present is only half the operation. The other half consists of bringing something into the present which is potential or possible, and in a sense belongs to the future. This recreation of the possible or future or ideal constitutes the wish-fulfillment element in romance[...] [179].

In its desire to present a future, romance provides hope.

Hope is the belief that life can be better. In order for that improvement to come about, life must continue. Any work that predicts a future for humankind, no matter how bleak that future may be, is providing a degree of hope because the very existence of a future means that mankind has the chance to change itself. Romance literature, however, goes beyond promising a future; it promises a brighter future. "Romance has its own conception of an ideal society, but that society is in a higher world than that of ordinary experience" (150).

Medieval romance offered the hope that man could become more civilized, that he could somehow live up to the ideals of chivalry presented in the tales of knights and maidens. Schlauch contends that the medieval Queen Eleanor encouraged the writing and dissemination of

*Alexander Pope, *An Essay on Man*, I. 95.

romances for exactly this reason, "to elevate uncouth Western manners to the standards of Eastern European courtesy and public decorum" (117). Frye takes a similar stance: "The dragon-killing and giant-quelling of chivalric romance suggests a civilizing force gradually increasing its control of a turbulent natural order" (*Secular* 173). As modern man is aware, more "civilized" is not always an improvement in the case of humans; the important point each author is making is that mankind is trying to reach a level of behavior and existence that it believes is higher and nobler than the one at which it currently exists.

As Neumann points out, part of the hero's role is "shaping and transforming the archetypal contents of his age" (377). In so doing, he "brings the new and shatters the fabric of old values" successfully overcoming "the whole weight of tradition and the power of the collective, [which] ever strives to obstruct the birth of the new" (377). To this end, the knight rides off to do battle, to prove not only that he is the best of the men of his generation, but that he can be more than the best and set a new standard for men to follow.

It is easy to fall into the error of romanticizing the Middle Ages. A number of modern writers have been guilty of just such romanticization, as Schlauch notes in the foreword to her book.

> certain individual writers, alarmed by the crises and dangers of our own times, have created for themselves an idealised concept of medieval orderliness and have turned to it as a refuge. Using the greatest master-pieces only as a foundation for their cult, they have glorified the medieval way of life as offering a plan of escape from present anxieties [xv].

These modern writers are not doing anything new; they are simply doing in our time what the medieval authors did in their own time. If the world of the medieval romance had been the actual world of the medieval writer, it would not have been necessary to write the romance. If you are living in a world filled with honor and bravery, you do not have to invent one. If your world supports growth, knowledge, peace, and benevolent governance, you can enjoy them firsthand rather than vicariously through literature.

As this study has tried to show, in times of distress and danger, people create positive, hope-inspiring images based on a variety of archetypes. The function of these images, as Schlauch observes, is to make a difficult time in life or civilization more bearable. It is not necessary to romanticize the medieval lifestyle; in fact, to do so would undermine the argument here presented. The medieval writers *themselves* romanticized their world as a way of coping with it and providing the hope needed to continue striving to create a future. This is especially true of Malory, who was writing at the end of the medieval time period looking back at the "good old days," days which are never, in any era, as good as they seem in memory. Modern authors can easily romanticize the medieval period by looking at its literature in lieu of its history. A similar process is employed when the modern writer sets a fantasy novel in that idealized medieval world or recasts the knight adventurer as a space adventurer and turns his quest outward to the stars.

The very fact that fantasy authors, and at times science fiction authors as well, look to the medieval period for a world that will allow them to express what they are trying to express argues in favor of fantasy and science fiction's ties to the romance mode. Further evidence has been provided here to substantiate that connection. The type of hero each form of literature presents fits the mold of the romance hero originally created by Aristotle and refined by Frye. The hero is a man of his time and beyond it, like his peers and superior to them, a creation of his world and a recreator of that world. He is similar enough to us that readers can relate to him and his actions but different enough from us that the reader is impressed by what he does. He is a figure of action, a taker of chances, a repository of values. He is the one clearing the pathway into the future for us if we have the courage to follow.

He is also capable of change as the time period dictates. In medieval romance, he was always male, usually noble, and nearly always a prime physical specimen. In the medieval world, this was the type of person who could tame his environment, defeat dangers, and mold the upcoming generation. As the world has become less oriented toward physical prowess, however, this literature of hope has expanded to encompass heroes who still fit the basic requirements of being superior to their peers and being role models of a higher level of human evolution but who are female or androgynous or mentally gifted but physically weak or nonhuman or partly human or a variety of other types who are not Conan the Barbarian look-alikes. In one way, this is evidence that the literature is succeeding in sending out its message. More people, and more varied people, are taking up the quest and believing they have a chance to succeed.

The romance mode is also apparent in the overall balance of plot and character and in the type of plot structuring most commonly used.

Action, not introspection, dominates. The reader is not told how to act; he or she is shown. The hero is not proposing a plan for the future; he is carrying it out. If a science fiction writer had a man wake up to discover he had been turned into a giant cockroach, as Kafka has Gregor Samsa do, the story would not focus on the cockroach's loss of humanity, his sense of alienation from his family, the resurgence of gumption in the previously passive family members, and a wasting away into death to get himself out of the way. Instead, the reader might expect to hear the human/cockroach thinking something like, "Wow! I'm a cockroach. No insecticide known to man can kill me, maybe not even nuclear radiation can kill me. I can get into all kinds of places humans don't want me to be, and I can walk on ceilings." Then the cockroach would tumble out of bed, squeeze through one of those impossibly small spaces no one can believe a cockroach can fit through, and set off to save humanity from itself (and maybe make the world a better place for cockroaches of all sizes, too). He would not cower under a sofa fading slowly from humanity to entomicity.

Our buggy hero might meet with adversity, find a mentor who would teach him how to use his new talents, or team up with a helper who would provide aid in a moment of crisis. He would probably win a battle or two against evil, lose a battle here and there and need to regroup, or even have to offer himself as the ultimate sacrifice to be crushed under a giant boot heel so others could live on and carry the hero's work into the future. He might wonder why Fate had turned him into a cockroach and wish he could be human again, but he would not lie down on a dust heap and die. Romance plots may travel through the pits of despair, but they rarely end there. From the pit there is always a way to the surface and daylight again, not necessarily an easy way, but a way. As the familiar structures remind us—after winter, there is always spring, after death, rebirth.

If science fiction and fantasy are to be admitted into the fold of romance literature, then the purpose of that literature should be their purpose as well, and it is. All these forms of literature seek to provide the necessary archetypes to allow humans to regain their psychological equilibrium in times of societal and individual distress. Science fiction and fantasy, like medieval romance, became popular during times of extreme turbulence in their worlds. The history of the entire medieval period reads like a list of crises with barely room to breathe between one and the next. Small wonder people would want a form of literature that would reassure them and hold out hope that somewhere in the future, if they tried hard enough and believed strongly enough in God, the world would improve.

Science fiction, too, is the offshoot of a time of crisis and rapid change. Asimov, in fact, attributes the invention of the form to the pace of change at the end of the nineteenth and beginning of the twentieth centuries. He claims that the rate of scientific change and the concomitant social change had to reach the point where it was observable within a single lifetime before science fiction could be possible because it was only at that point that "The future is then, for the first time, discovered" (*Asimov on SF* 18). Within fifty-eight years, well within the average lifespan, man left first the ground and then the planet as the world progressed from the first airplane flight in 1903 to jet aircraft in 1939 and manned spaceflight in 1961. The rapid pace of technological change was not confined to one area but was culture-wide. While most of the changes may have been positive, the speed at which they were occurring still induced stress in the population, stress which the science fiction novel sought to alleviate by showing the wonderful things science could do for mankind's future.

This is not to ignore the influence of social disruption on the genre. The Golden Age of science fiction is generally considered to be from the 1920s to the 1940s, a period that begins just after World War I, includes the American Depression, and ends after World War II. Clearly, this was a time period during which people in America, and Europe, needed to be reminded that there would be a future and that the future would be worth reaching. The Golden Age, or perhaps more accurately the age of innocence, ended with the dropping of the Atomic bomb. Science fiction could no longer claim that science would make everything better. Instead, it now had to find a way to reassure people that we could survive our own quest for knowledge and our own destructive tendencies.

Fantastic literature has been a part of human existence for centuries, but the genre known commercially as fantasy is generally considered to have begun with Tolkien. When The Lord of the Rings came out in the 1950s, Tolkien repeatedly disavowed any connection between the events in the trilogy and the events of World War II, but the war was fresh in people's minds and it was difficult for many readers to ignore the similarities between the shattered lives of the Hobbits and their own shattered existences. The same social background of war and disaster that spawned a need for science fiction generated a need for fantasy as well.

If science could not solve the problems of the world, perhaps the world needed to return to the basic archetypes and try again and see if a better solution could be found. Perhaps the world could be healed by magic, or a new religion, or some other reminder that man is not a machine. Like Mr. Spock, the half-human, half-Vulcan character in the Star Trek series and films, mankind must acknowledge and accept its irrational side or risk having it break free at an inopportune moment and remind us it is there. Fantasy can help readers achieve this inner harmony between rational and irrational.

For Jung, this compensatory function is the role of art and literature:

> Therein lies the social significance of art: it is constantly at work educating the spirit of the age, conjuring up the forms in which the age is most lacking. The unsatisfied yearning of the artist reaches back to the primordial image in the unconscious which is best fitted to compensate the inadequacy and one-sidedness of the present. The artist seizes on this image, and in raising it from deepest unconsciousness he brings it into relation with conscious values, thereby transforming it until it can be accepted by the minds of his contemporaries according to their powers [*Spirit* 82–3].

As the preceding chapters have shown, romance literature is especially well suited to this role.

In each age, certain archetypes are sought to balance the imbalances in the world. Medieval romance, science fiction, and fantasy turn to many of the same archetypes in response to their worlds, although the images in which the archetypes are cast differ. The Middle Ages did not need science fiction or fantasy because romance literature filled the same psychological need in its audience. In a typical romance, the hero rode off seeking adventure and found it. Because he was usually a superior specimen of knighthood, the hero survived by dint of his own prowess in any straightforward physical combat. If magic was involved, as it often was, the knight might need to seek assistance from a fair damsel, a dwarf, a wizard, a hermit, or some other archetypal helper. He might also turn to God for supernatural aid. If he was a good knight who lived by the codes of chivalry and/or Christianity, he would probably survive and return to tell his tale. His success would encourage a new generation of knights to emulate and outstrip him, and the cycle of bettering mankind through human striving and God's blessings would continue.

The hero's quest provides the structure for most of these tales, old and new. Modern Star Trek audiences eagerly awaiting the next installment of the story of that group of daring souls willing to "boldly go where no man has gone before" could easily recognize the spirit behind the medieval knight's quest. The Starfleet missions of searching out new life forms, opening new worlds to settlement, arbitrating interplanetary disputes, and maintaining safe passage through space are not very far removed from the aims of the knight as he sought new opponents to challenge, dragons to slay, castles to storm or defend, and realms to subdue. The tale of departure, triumph over adversity, and return is as old as human awareness of the daily rising and setting of the sun and provides the same reassurance of a tomorrow to the modern reader as it did to the medieval reader.

Archetypes recur in new garb but their meanings and purposes remain unchanged. The child-hero still rides out to seek a future which his very existence assures us will come. He is no longer Parzival, awe-struck by the gleaming armor of the knights whose like he had never seen, but he might very well be Earthling-bred but Martian-accultured Valentine Michael Smith meeting a woman for the first time or Simon, a young apprentice, watching his teacher turn from a mild, scholarly old man to a wizard powerful enough to hold armed guards and an evil magician at bay while the boy made his escape. The guise has changed but over and over these works cast the young in the hero's role. The young bring new life, new ideas, fewer biases, and more open minds to bear on solving the problems of our world. Often they find innovative solutions to things previously deemed insoluble. In the final book of Asimov's original Foundation trilogy, the centuries-old mystery of where the Second Foundation is based is solved by 14-year-old Arcadia Darell.

The child-hero is often accompanied in the story by the wise old man, who still appears when needed and dispenses wisdom which the hero must be clever enough to use in a way that will help him achieve his goals. The wise old man's presence serves as a reminder that in forging a future mankind cannot disregard the past. Although George Santayana may have overstated the case a bit when he said, "Those who cannot remember the past are condemned to repeat it" (Bartlett's 703), the general premise is sound. Mankind needs to build its future based solidly on the knowledge of the past as well as the creative insights of the present. The wise old man and child-hero embody these two important foundations and the deeper archetypes associated with the freshness of the new and the wisdom of the old. Together they bring us closer to achieving that better world that romance literature assures us is waiting for us if we can just keep trying to reach it.

The images of the mother archetype remind readers that life goes on, and even in times of despair women keep having, raising, loving, and guiding children. The hero has his character molded by the woman who raises him, and then he breaks away to try and find out how he can take the lessons he has learned, apply them to the world, and shape a unique personality for himself. He will combat dragons and monsters, face stronger and cleverer opponents, and present his personality to the world. If he succeeds in his endeavors, he will earn the right to self-hood and a chance to shape future generations. If he fails, new heroes will take his place in the striving and keep the momentum of life surging forward.

At the end of the story, the hero must be transformed. This is an essential feature of the romance and part of its embodiment of hope. All of the hero's experiences, all he has learned from others and about himself, must coalesce into a being superior to the one who set out on the initial journey. In this way, the reader can see that the effort is worth making, that man can better himself and his world. Any one of us, individually, may fail, but ultimately mankind has the means, either alone or with the help of a supernatural agent, whether God or alien, to rise above what he has been and become what he has only dreamed of being. *The Dreams Our Stuff Is Made Of,* the title of Thomas Disch's critical study of science fiction's influence on society, emphasizes this while at the same time linking science fiction once again to the larger category of fantastic writing.

Sometimes giving up may seem the most attractive option. Like Frodo, when the One Ring has been cast back into Mount Doom and the world is falling apart around him, we may want to sit down and say, "'Hopes fail. An end comes. We have only a little time to wait now. We are lost in ruin and downfall, and there is no escape'" (Tolkien, *Return* 281). That is not the message of romance literature, however, and the reader is reminded of that by Sam, Frodo's companion, whose position is that they should try to get away from the destruction to a safer place because, "'I don't want to give up yet. It's not like me, somehow, if you understand'" (281). At Sam's urging, the two move away from the mountain to a hilltop where they are seen, rescued, and live to have further adventures in the Shire. Giving up is not acceptable; giving up is letting despair win, and these works are about hope, not despair.

This is an important reason why people read medieval romance, science fiction, and fantasy — because it offers a light against the darkness. It is literature which assures the reader that, even though the here and now may be spinning wildly out of control, life need not always be that way. Time after time, this literature presents the reader with archetypes essential to heal in times of distress, and more than that, to grow. Images of youth, wisdom, mothers, the quest, rebirth, and transformation provide our psyches with the raw materials we need to bring about our own and our society's maturation and progress. After all, *Le Morte D'Arthur* has held out the promise to us that "King Arthur is not dead, but had by the will of our Lord Jesu into another place; and men say that he shall come again, and he shall win the holy cross" (Caxton 527). In their turn, science fiction and fantasy assure us that there will, in fact, be a world here waiting when Arthur does return.

Bibliography

a Kempis, Thomas. *Of the Imitation of Christ.* New Canaan, CT: Keats Publishing, 1973.

Aldiss, Brian. *Billion Year Spree: The True History of Science Fiction.* New York: Schocken, 1974.

_____. *The Detached Retina: Aspects of SF and Fantasy.* Syracuse, NY: Syracuse University Press, 1995.

Amis, Kingsley. *New Maps of Hell: A Survey of Science Fiction.* London: Victor Gollancz, 1961.

"Amis and Amiloun." Ed. and trans. Edith Rickert. *Early English Romances in Verse: Romances of Friendship.* New York: Cooper Square, 1967. 1–49.

Aristotle. *Aristotle's Theory of Poetry and Fine Art.* Trans. S. H. Butcher. New York: Dover, 1951.

Armstrong, Karen. *A History of God: The 4000-Year Quest of Judaism, Christianity and Islam.* New York: Knopf, 1994.

Arnitt, Lucy, ed. *Where No Man Has Gone Before: Women and Science Fiction.* New York: Routledge, 1991.

Asimov, Isaac. *Asimov on Science Fiction.* Garden City, NY: Doubleday, 1981.

_____. *Foundation.* 1951; rpt. New York: Avon, 1966.

_____. *Foundation and Empire.* 1952: rpt. New York: Avon, 1966.

_____. *Second Foundation.* 1953; rpt. New York: Avon, 1964.

Bagwell, Timothy J. "Science Fiction and the Semiotics of Realism." *Intersections: Fantasy and Science Fiction.* Eds. George E. Slusser & Eric S. Rabkin. Carbondale, IL: Southern Illinois University Press, 1987. 36–47.

Bainbridge, William Sims. *Dimensions of Science Fiction.* Cambridge, MA: Harvard University Press, 1986.

Barr, Marlene. *Feminist Fabulation: Space/Postmodern Fiction.* Iowa City: University of Iowa Press, 1992.

Barron, Neil. *Anatomy of Wonder: Science Fiction.* New York: Bowker, 1976.

Barron, W. R. J. *English Medieval Romance.* New York: Longman, 1987.

Bartlett, John. *Bartlett's Familiar Quotations.* Ed. Emily Morison Beck. 15th ed. Boston: Little, Brown, 1980.

Beale, Lewis. "Intellectual Science Fiction Is Hollywood's Orphan." *The New York Times* 15 July 2001. Online. Available: <http://www.nytimes.com/2001/07/08/arts/08BEAL.html>. 15 July 2001.

Bédier, Joseph. *The Romance of Tristan and Iseult.* Trans. Hilaire Belloc. Completed by Paul Rosenfeld. New York: Pantheon, 1945.

Benford, Gregory, and David Brin. *Heart of the Comet.* New York: Bantam, 1986.

Berger, Peter. *The Sacred Canopy: Elements of a Sociological Theory of Religion.* Garden City, NY: Doubleday, 1967.

Bradbury, Ray. *Fahrenheit 451.* New York: Ballantine, 1953.

Bradley, Marion Zimmer. *City of Sorcery.* New York: DAW, 1984.

_____. *The Mists of Avalon.* New York: Knopf, 1982.

Brewer, Derek S. "The Lord of the Rings as Romance." *J. R. R. Tolkien, Scholar and Storyteller: Essays in Memoriam.* Eds. Mary Salu and Robert T. Farrell. Ithaca, NY: Cornell University Press, 1979. 249–264.

Brooks, Terry. *The Elfstones of Shannara.* New York: Ballantine, 1984.

Butler, Octavia E. *Dawn.* New York: Warner, 1987.

Cantor, Norman E. *The Civilization of the Middle Ages.* New York: HarperCollins, 1993.

Card, Orson Scott. *Ender's Game.* New York: Tor, 1985.

Carpenter, Humphrey. *Tolkien: A Biography.* New York: Ballantine, 1978.

Clareson, Thomas D. "The Emergence of the Scientific Romance, 1870–1926." *Anatomy of Wonder: Science Fiction.* Ed. Neil Barron. New York: Bowker, 1976. 33–50.

_____. *SF: The Other Side of Realism: Essays on Modern Fantasy and Science Fiction.* Bowling Green, OH: Bowling Green University Press, 1971.

_____. *Understanding Contemporary American Science Fiction: The Formative Period (1926–1970).* Columbia: University of South Carolina Press, 1990.

Clarke, Arthur C. *The City and the Stars.* New York: Signet, 1957.

_____. *Earthlight.* New York: Ballantine, 1955.

_____. "The Nine Billion Names of God." *Other Worlds, Other Gods.* Ed. Mayo Mohs. 1953; rpt. New York: Avon, 1971. 137–144.

_____. *Profiles of the Future: An Inquiry into the Limits of the Possible.* London: Pan, 1964.

_____. *Rendezvous with Rama.* New York: Bantam, 1973.

_____. *3001: The Final Odyssey.* New York: Ballantine, 1998.

Clarke, Arthur C., and Gentry, Lee. *Garden of Rama.* New York: Bantam, 1991.

_____, and _____. *Rama Revealed.* New York: Bantam, 1995.

_____, and _____. *Rama II.* New York: Bantam, 1989.

Cohen, Edmund D. *C. G. Jung and the Scientific Attitude.* New York: Philosophical Library, 1975.

Coyle, William, ed. "Introduction: The Nature of Fantasy." *Aspects of Fantasy: Selected Essays from the Second International Conference on the Fantastic in Literature and Film.* Westport, CT: Greenwood, 1986. 1–3.

da Palestrina, Giovanni Pierluigi. "The Strife Is O'er, the Battle Done." 1591. *The Hymnbook.* New York: Presbyterian Church in the United States, 1955.

del Rey, Lester. "Helen O'Loy." *The Science Fiction Hall of Fame.* Vol. I. Ed. Robert Silverberg. New York: Avon, 1971. 62–73.

Delaney, Samuel. "The Gestation of Genres: Literature, Fiction, Romance, Science

Fiction, Fantasy...." *Intersections: Fantasy and Science Fiction.* Eds. George E. Slusser and Eric S. Rabkin. Carbondale: Southern Illinois University Press, 1987. 63–73.

Disch, Thomas M. *The Dreams Our Stuff Is Made Of: How Science Fiction Conquered the World.* New York: The Free Press, 1998.

_____. "The Embarrassments of Science Fiction." *Science Fiction at Large.* Ed. Peter Nicholls. New York: Harper & Row, 1976. 141–155.

E.T.: The Extra-Terrestrial. Dir. Steven Spielberg. Amblin Entertainment. 1982.

Elgin, Suzette. *The Judas Rose.* New York: DAW, 1994.

_____. *Native Tongue.* New York: DAW, 1984.

The Empire Strikes Back. Dir. George Lucas. 20th Century–Fox, 1980.

Fredricks, Casey. *The Future of Eternity: Mythologies of Science Fiction and Fantasy.* Bloomington: Indiana University Press, 1982.

Frye, Northrop. *Anatomy of Criticism: Four Essays.* Princeton: Princeton University Press, 1971.

_____. *The Secular Scripture: A Study of the Structure of Romance.* Cambridge, MA: Harvard University Press, 1976.

Geoffrey of Monmouth. *The History of the Kings of Britain.* Ed. and intro. Lewis Thorpe. New York: Penguin, 1966.

Gibbs, A. C., ed. & intro. *Middle English Romances.* York Medieval Texts Series. Gen eds. Elizabeth Salter and Derek Pearsall. Evanston, IL: Northwestern University Press, 1966.

Gibson, William. *Neuromancer.* New York: Ace, 1984.

Gies, Frances, and Joseph. *Marriage and Family in the Middle Ages.* New York: Harper & Row, 1989.

Godwin, Tom. "The Cold Equations." *The Science Fiction Hall of Fame.* Vol. I. Ed. Robert Silverberg. New York: Avon, 1971. 543–569.

Green, Simon R. *Beyond the Blue Moon.* New York: Roc, 2000.

Gunn, James. "The Worldview of Science Fiction." *Extrapolation* Summer 1995 (36): 91–95. Online. Expanded Academic ASAP. Article # A18700321. Available: <http://web4.infotrac.galegroup> 20 Feb. 2001.

Guy of Warwick. Trans. Caroline Clive, 1821. Ed. William B. Todd. Austin: University of Texas Press, 1968.

Hadewijch of Brabant. "Union with God." *Visions and Longings: Medieval Woman Mystics.* Ed. Monica Furlong. Boston: Shambala, 1996. 109.

Hansen, Arlen. "The Meeting of Parallel Lines: Science, Fiction, and Science Fiction." *Bridges to Fantasy.* Eds. George E. Slusser, Eric S. Rabkin and Robert Scholes. Carbondale: Southern Illinois University Press, 1982. 51–8.

Hawking, Stephen W. *A Brief History of Time: From the Big Bang to Black Holes.* New York: Bantam, 1988.

Heinlein, Robert. "Science Fiction: Its Nature, Faults and Virtues." *The Science Fiction Novel: Imagination and Social Criticism.* Intro. and ed. Brian Davenport. Chicago: Advent, 1959. 14–48.

_____. *Stranger in a Strange Land.* 1961; rpt. New York: Berkley, 1968.

Henderson, Joseph L. "Ancient Myths and Modern Man." *Man and His Symbols.* Ed. Carl G. Jung. New York: Dell, 1964. 95–156.

Herbert, Frank. *Dune.* New York: Berkley, 1965.

_____. "Some Arthur, Some Tolkien." *The New York Times Book Review* April 10, 1977: 15, 25. Online. Available: Literature Resource Center/Terry Brooks/Literary Criticism. <http://galenet.galegroup.com>. August 16, 2005.

"HIV/AIDS Facts." *Black Coalition on AIDS.* 2001. Online. Available: <www.bcoa. org>. July 26, 2005.

Hollister, C. Warren. *Medieval Europe: A Short History.* 3rd ed. New York: Wiley, 1974.

Holy Bible. King James Version. Camden, NJ: Thomas Nelson, 1970.

Huizinga, J. *The Waning of the Middle Ages.* Garden City, NY: Doubleday, 1956.

Hume, Kathryn. "Medieval Romance and Science Fiction: The Anatomy of a Resemblance." *Journal of Popular Culture* 16.1 (1982): 15–26.

Hunt, Robert. "Visionary States and the Search for Transcendence in Science Fiction." *Bridges to Science Fiction.* Eds. George E. Slusser, George R. Guffey, and Mark Rose. Carbondale: Southern Illinois University Press, 1980. 64–77.

Jacobi, Jolande. *Complex/Archetypes/Symbol in the Psychology of C. G. Jung.* Trans. Ralph Manhiem. Foreword C. G. Jung. New York: Pantheon, 1959.

Jordan, Robert. *The Dragon Reborn.* New York: Tor, 1991.

_____. *The Eye of the World.* New York: Tor, 1990.

_____. *Winter's Heart.* New York: Tor, 2000.

Jung, Carl G. *The Archetypes and the Collective Unconscious.* 2nd. ed. Trans. R. F. C. Hull. Princeton: Princeton University Press, 1969.

_____. *Flying Saucers: A Modern Myth of Things Seen in the Skies.* Trans. R.F.C. Hall. New York: Harcourt, Brace, 1959.

_____. *Modern Man in Search of a Soul.* New York: Harcourt, Brace & World, 1933.

_____. "On the Relation of Analytic Psychology to Poetry." *The Spirit in Man, Art, and Literature.* Trans. R. F. C. Hull. Princeton: Princeton University Press, 1966. 65–83.

Kafka, Franz. "The Metamorphosis." *The Norton Anthology of World Masterpieces.* 4th ed. Vol. 2. New York: Norton, 1979. 1518–58.

Kay, Guy Gavriel. *The Darkest Road.* New York: ROC, 1992.

_____. *The Summer Tree.* New York: ROC, 1992.

_____. *The Wandering Fire.* New York: ROC, 1992.

Kosko, Bart. "The Future of God (Is There a Need for Fantasy?)." *Free Inquiry* Summer 1995: 43–4. Online. Expanded Academic ASAP. Article # A17098043. Available: <http://web4.infotrac.galegroup> 11 Jan. 2001.

Kreuziger, Fredrick A. *The Religion of Science Fiction.* Bowling Green, OH: Bowling Green State University Popular Press, 1986.

Kroeber, Karl. *Romantic Fantasy and Science Fiction.* New Haven: Yale University Press, 1988.

LeGuin, Ursula. *The Language of the Night: Essays on Fantasy and Science Fiction.* New York: HarperCollins, 1989.

_____. *The Left Hand of Darkness.* New York: Ace, 1969.

_____. *Rocannon's World.* New York: Ace, 1966.

Lem, Stanislaw. *Microworlds: 5 Writings on Science Fiction and Fantasy.* Trans. and ed. Franz Rottensteiner. San Diego: HBJ, 1984.

Lerner, Alan Jay, and Fredrick Loewe. "Camelot." *Camelot.* Columbia, 1973.

Levin, Harry. "Science and Fiction." *Bridges to Science Fiction.* Eds. George E. Slusser, George R. Guffey, and Mark Rose. Carbondale: Southern Illinois University Press, 1980. 3–21.

Liukkonen, Petri. "Arthur Charles Clarke (1917-)." *Books and Writers.* Ed. Ari Pesonen. 2000. Online. Available: <http://www.kirjasto.sci.fi/aclarke.htm>. 19 January 2002.

Locke, John. "An Essay Concerning Human Understanding." *Classics of Western*

Philosophy. Ed. Steven M. Cahn. 3rd. ed. Indianapolis: Hackett Publishing, 1977. 617–712.

Loomis, Roger Sherman. *The Grail: From Celtic Myth to Christian Symbol.* New York: Columbia University Press, 1963.

Lorrah, Jean. *Star Trek 38: The IDIC Epidemic.* New York: Pocket, 1988.

Malory, Sir Thomas. *Le Morte D'Arthur.* Ed. Caxton. 1485; rpt. New York: Gramercy Books, 1995.

_____. *Malory's Le Morte D'Arthur.* Adpt. Keith Baines. New York: Penguin, 1962.

_____. *The Morte Arthur: Parts Seven and Eight.* Ed., intro. and notes D.S. Brewer. Evanston, IL: Northwestern University Press, 1974.

McCaffrey, Anne, and Elizabeth Scarborough. *Powers That Be.* New York: Ballantine, 1993.

McCrumb, Sharyn. *Bimbos of the Death Sun.* New York: Ballantine, 1997.

Miller, Walter M., Jr. *Canticle for Leibowitz.* 1955; rpt. New York: Bantam, 1961.

Mustard, Helen M., and Charles E. Passage, trans. and intro. *Parzival.* By Wolfram von Eschenbach. New York: Vintage, 1961.

Neumann, Erich. *The Origins and History of Consciousness.* 1954; rpt. Princeton: Princeton University Press, 1970.

Nietzsche, Friedrich. *Thus Spoke Zarathustra: A Book for None and All.* Trans. Walter Kaufmann. New York: Penguin, 1978.

Norton, Andre. *Witch World.* New York: Ace, 1963.

_____. *Year of the Unicorn.* New York: Ace, 1965.

Patrouch, Joe. "Some Thoughts on American SF." *Extrapolation* Spring 1997 38.1: 5–15. Online. Expanded Academic ASAP. Article #A19416373. Available: <http://web4.infotrac.galegroup> 11 Jan. 2001.

Plato. *The Last Days of Socrates.* Trans. and intro. Hugh Tredennick. New York: Penguin, 1969.

_____. "The Republic." In *The Dialogues of Plato.* Trans. Benjamin Jowett. Chicago: Encyclopedia Britannica, 1992. Vol. 4 of The Great Books of the Western World. Ed. Mortimer J. Adler. 295–441.

Pound, Ezra. *The Spirit of Romance.* Norfolk, CT: New Directions, n.d. (emendations dated 1929).

Propp, V. *Morphology of the Folktale.* Trans. Laurence Scott. Rev. and ed. Louis A. Wagner. 2nd ed. Austin: University of Texas Press, 1968.

Rabkin, Eric S. *The Fantastic in Literature.* Princeton: Princeton University Press, 1976.

Return of the Jedi. Dir. George Lucas. 20th Century–Fox, 1983.

Rickert, Edith, ed. and trans. *Early English Romances in Verse: Romances of Friendship.* New York: Cooper Square, 1967.

Roddenberry, Gene. *Star Trek, The Original Series.* NBC, 1966–69.

"Roswall and Lillian." Ed. and trans. Edith Rickert. *Early English Romances in Verse: Romances of Friendship.* New York: Cooper Square, 1967. 117–137.

Russ, Joanna. *The Female Man.* 1975; rpt. Boston: Beacon Press, 1986.

Schlauch, Margaret. *English Medieval Literature and its Social Foundations.* 1956; rpt. London: Oxford University Press, 1967.

Seed, David, ed. *Anticipations: Essays in Early Science Fiction and Its Precursors.* Syracuse, NY: Syracuse University Press, 1995.

"Sir Amadas." Ed. and trans. Edith Rickert. *Early English Romances in Verse: Romances of Friendship.* New York: Cooper Square, 1967. 49–67.

Sir Cleges/Sir Libeaus Desconus. Prose translations by Jessie L. Weston. New York: New Amsterdam, 1902.

Sir Gawain and the Green Knight. Trans. and intro. Brian Stone. 2nd ed. New York: Penguin, 1974.

Sir Gawain and the Green Knight. Eds. J. R. R. Tolkien and E. V. Gordon. 2nd ed. Ed. Norman Davis. Oxford: Clarendon, 1968.

Sir Gawain and the Green Knight~Pearl~Sir Orfeo. Trans. J. R. R. Tolkien. New York: Ballantine, 1975.

Slusser, George E., Colin Greenland, and Eric S. Rabkin, eds. *Storm Warnings: Science Fiction Confronts the Future.* Carbondale: Southern Illinois University Press, 1987.

The Song of Roland. Trans. Dorothy Sayers. New York: Penguin, 1957.

Spencer, Kathleen. "Victorian Urban Gothic: The First Modern Fantastic Literature." *Intersections: Fantasy and Science Fiction.* Eds. George E. Slusser and Eric S. Rabkin. Carbondale: Southern Illinois University Press, 1987. 87–96.

Stapledon, Olaf. *Star Maker.* Harmondsworth, Middlesex: Penguin, 1972.

Star Wars. Dir. George Lucas. 20th Century–Fox, 1977.

Stevens, Anthony. *Archetype: A Natural History of the Self.* London: Routledge, 1982.

Sturgeon, Theodore. "Microcosmic God." *The Science Fiction Hall of Fame.* Vol. I. Ed. Robert Silverberg. New York: Avon, 1971. 115–144.

_____. *More Than Human.* Harmondsworth, Middlesex: Penguin, 1953.

Suvin, Darko. *Metamorphoses of Science Fiction: On the Poetics and History of a Literary Genre.* New Haven: Yale University Press, 1979.

Tepper, Sheri. *The Gate to Women's Country.* New York: Bantam, 1993.

Three Middle English Romances: King Horn, Havelok, Beves of Hampton. Retold by Laura A. Hibbard. London: David Nutt, 1911.

Todorov, Tzvetan. *The Fantastic: A Structural Approach to a Literary Genre.* Trans. Richard Howard. Cleveland: Press of Case Western Reserve University, 1973.

Tolkien, J. R. R. "Beowulf: The Monster and the Critics." *The Monster and the Critics and Other Essays.* Ed. Christopher Tolkien. Boston: Houghton Mifflin, 1984.

_____. "Fantasy." *Fantasists on Fantasy: A Collection of Critical Reflections.* Eds. Robert H. Boyer and Kenneth J. Zahorski. New York: Avon, 1984.

_____. *The Fellowship of the Ring.* New York: Ballantine, 1965.

_____. *The Hobbit.* Rev. ed. New York: Ballantine, 1966.

_____. *The Return of the King.* New York: Ballantine, 1965.

_____. "Tree and Leaf." *The Tolkien Reader.* New York: Ballantine, 1966. 31–99.

_____. *The Two Towers.* New York: Ballantine, 1965.

Tuchman, Barbara. *A Distant Mirror: The Calamitous 14th Century.* New York: Ballantine, 1978.

2001: A Space Odyssey. Dir. Stanley Kubrick. MGM. 1968.

von Franz, Marie-Louise. "The Process of Individuation." *Man and His Symbols.* Ed. Carl G. Jung. New York: Dell, 1964. 157–254.

Weathers, Winston. *The Archetype and the Psyche: Essays in World Literature.* Tulsa, OK: University of Tulsa, 1968.

White, Lynn, Jr. *Medieval Religion and Technology: Collected Essays.* Berkeley: University of California Press, 1978.

White, T. H. *The Once and Future King.* New York: Ace, 1987.

Williams, Tad. *The Dragonbone Chair.* New York: DAW, 1989.

_____. *Otherland: City of Golden Shadow.* New York: DAW, 1996.

Willis, Connie. *Doomsday Book.* New York: Bantam, 1993.

Wolfe, Tom. *Bonfire of the Vanities.* New York: Bantam, 1987.

Zinn, Howard. *The Twentieth Century: A People's History.* New York: HarperCollins, 1998.

Index